NO ONE LEFT TO FIGHT™

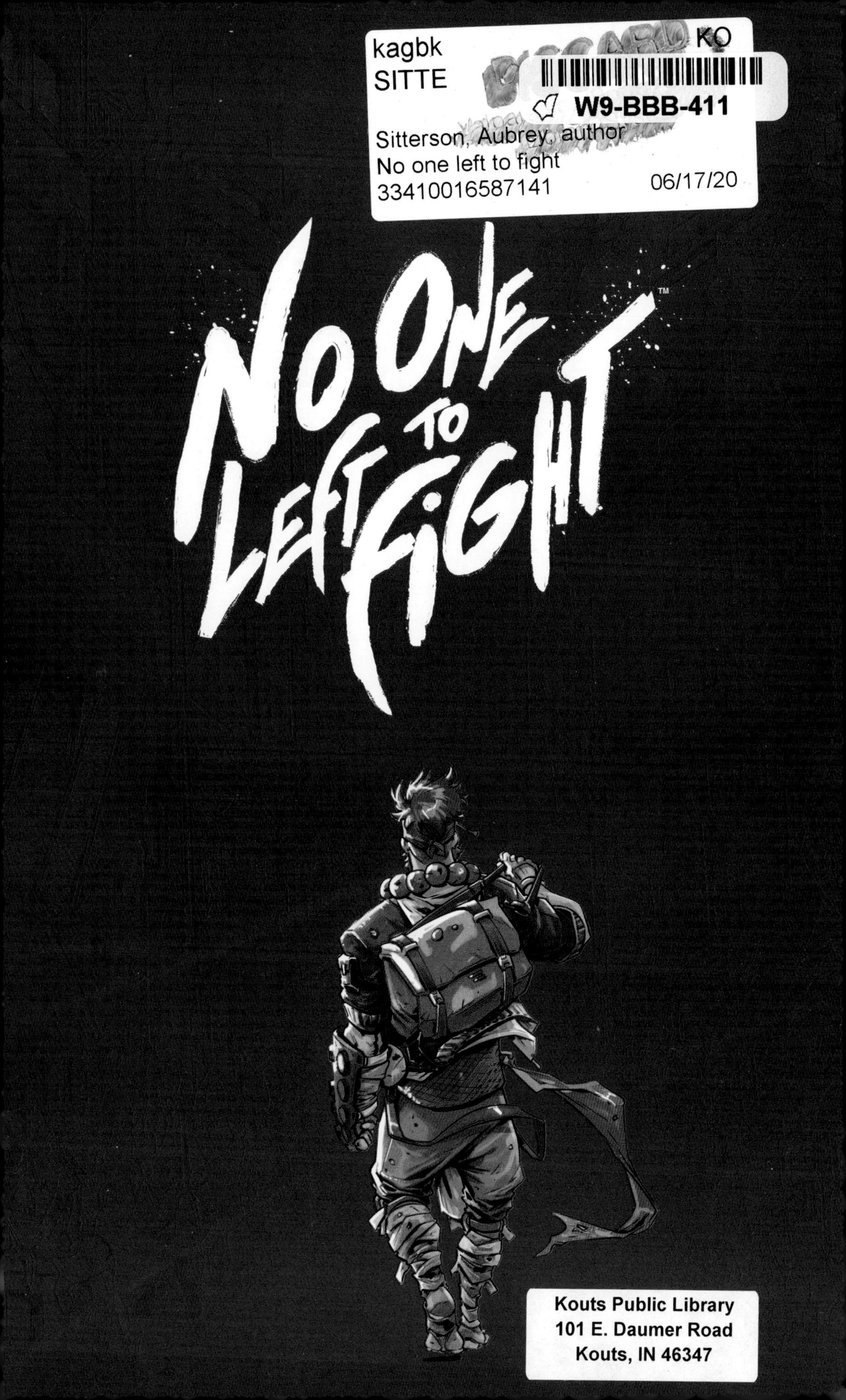

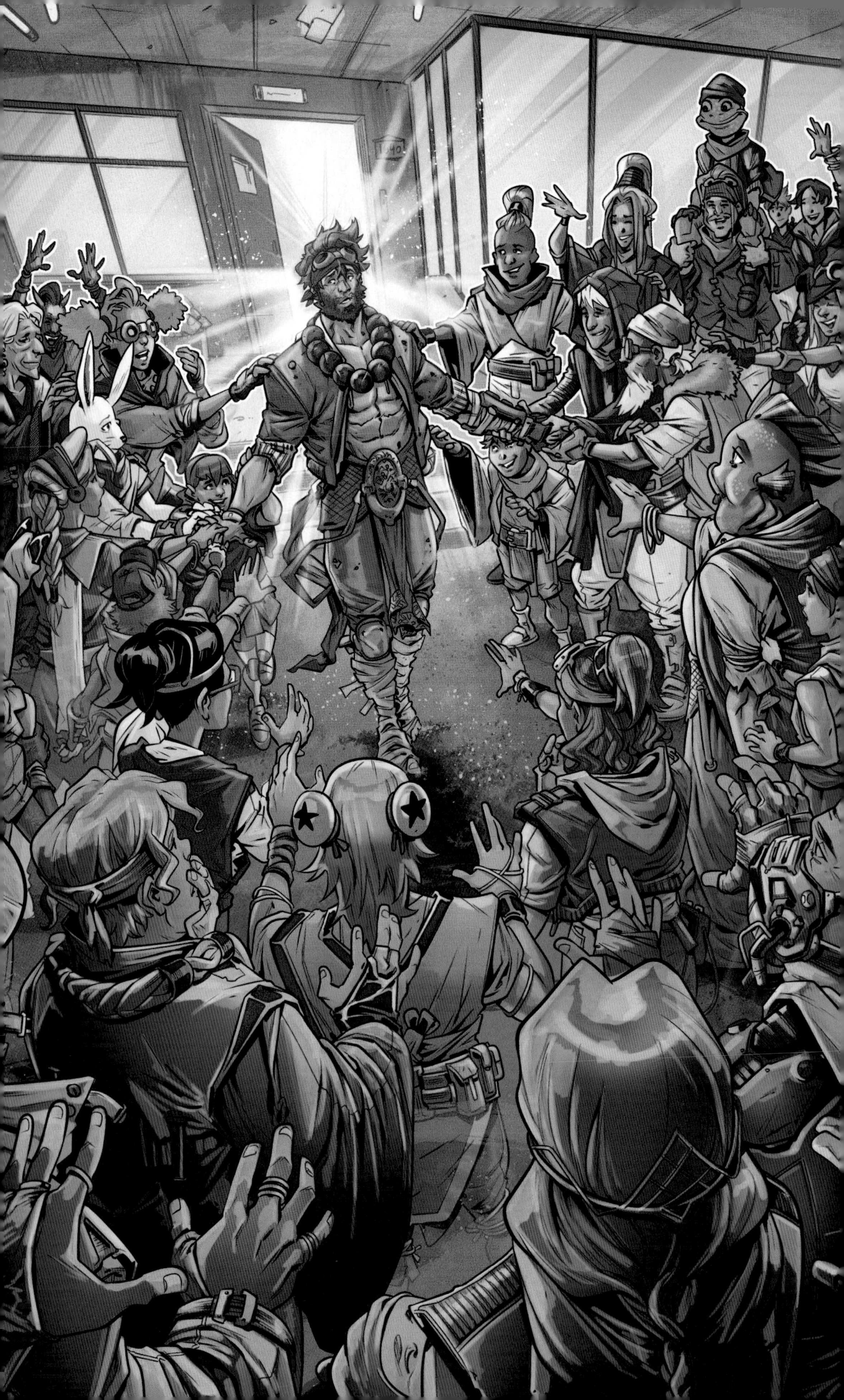

Written by **AUBREY SITTERSON**

Art, Cover, and Chapter Break Art by **FICO OSSIO**

Chapter 3-5 Color Art by **FICO OSSIO** and **RACIEL AVILA**

Letters by **TAYLOR ESPOSITO**

No One Left To Fight Created by
AUBREY SITTERSON and **FICO OSSIO**

DARK HORSE BOOKS

President and Publisher
MIKE RICHARDSON

Editor
BRETT ISRAEL

Collection Designer
SCOTT ERWERT

Digital Art Technician
SAMANTHA HUMMER

NO ONE LEFT TO FIGHT

No One Left To Fight™ © Aubrey Sitterson and Fico Ossio. All rights reserved. No portion of this publication may be reproduced or transmitted, in any form or by any means, without the express written permission of Dark Horse Comics LLC. Names, characters, places, and incidents featured in this publication either are the product of the author's imagination or are used fictitiously. Any resemblance to actual persons (living or dead), events, institutions, or locales, without satiric intent, is coincidental. Dark Horse Comics® and the Dark Horse logo are trademarks of Dark Horse Comics LLC, registered in various categories and countries. and countries.

Published by Dark Horse Books / A division of Dark Horse Comics LLC
10956 SE Main Street / Milwaukie, OR 97222

First edition: March 2020
ISBN 978-1-50671-304-5

10 9 8 7 6 5 4 3 2 1
Printed in China

Comic Shop Locator Service: comicshoplocator.com

This volume collects and reprints the comic book series No One Left To Fight *#1–#5.*

Library of Congress Cataloging-in-Publication Data

Names: Sitterson, Aubrey, author. | Ossio, Fico, artist. | Avila, Raciel, colourist. | Esposito, Taylor, letterer.
Title: No one left to fight / script by Aubrey Sitterson ; art, cover, and chapter break art by Fico Ossio ; color art by Fico Ossio and Raciel Avila ; letters by Taylor Esposito.
Description: First edition. | Milwaukie, OR : Dark Horse Books, 2020. | "No One Left To Fight created by Aubrey Sitterson and Fico Ossio" | Summary: "They've saved the world countless times, growing up together and growing apart in the process. But now, with adulthood tightening its grip, they're forced to reconcile their regrets and resentments, coming to terms with the lives they've chosen. Inspired by the legendary Dragon Ball, critically-acclaimed creators Aubrey Sitterson (The Comic Book Story of Professional Wrestling, G.I. Joe) & Fico Ossio (Spider-Man, Revolution) invite you on an action-packed journey through their expansive new world. Fans of Hellboy, Umbrella Academy, and Black Hammer won't want to miss this exciting new vision of what genre comics can accomplish."– Provided by publisher.
Identifiers: LCCN 2019044164 (print) | LCCN 2019044165 (ebook) | ISBN 9781506713045 (trade paperback) | ISBN 9781506713137 (ebook)
Subjects: LCSH: Comic books, strips, etc.
Classification: LCC PN6728.N625 S58 2020 (print) | LCC PN6728.N625 (ebook) | DDC 741.5/973–dc23
LC record available at https://lccn.loc.gov/2019044164
LC ebook record available at https://lccn.loc.gov/2019044165

NEIL HANKERSON Executive Vice President • TOM WEDDLE Chief Financial Officer • RANDY STRADLEY Vice President of Publishing • NICK MCWHORTER Chief Business Development Officer • DALE LAFOUNTAIN Chief Information Officer • MATT PARKINSON Vice President of Marketing • CARA NIECE Vice President of Production and Scheduling • MARK BERNARDI Vice President of Book Trade and Digital Sales • KEN LIZZI General Counsel • DAVE MARSHALL Editor in Chief • DAVEY ESTRADA Editorial Director • CHRIS WARNER Senior Books Editor • CARY GRAZZINI Director of Specialty Projects • LIA RIBACCHI Art Director • VANESSA TODD-HOLMES Director of Print Purchasing • MATT DRYER Director of Digital Art and Prepress • MICHAEL GOMBOS Senior Director of Licensed Publications • KARI YADRO Director of Custom Programs • KARI TORSON Director of International Licensing SEAN BRICE Director of Trade Sales

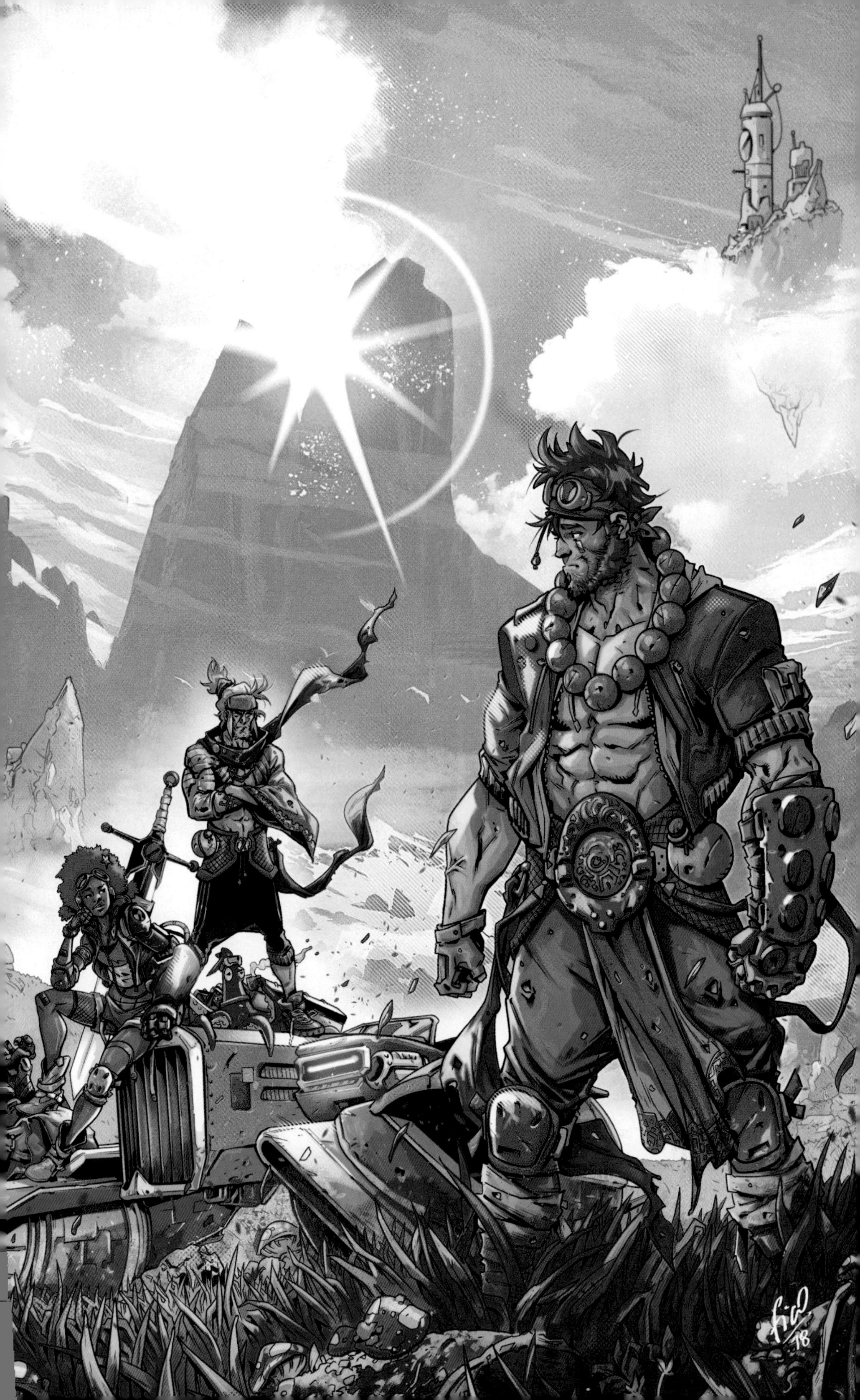

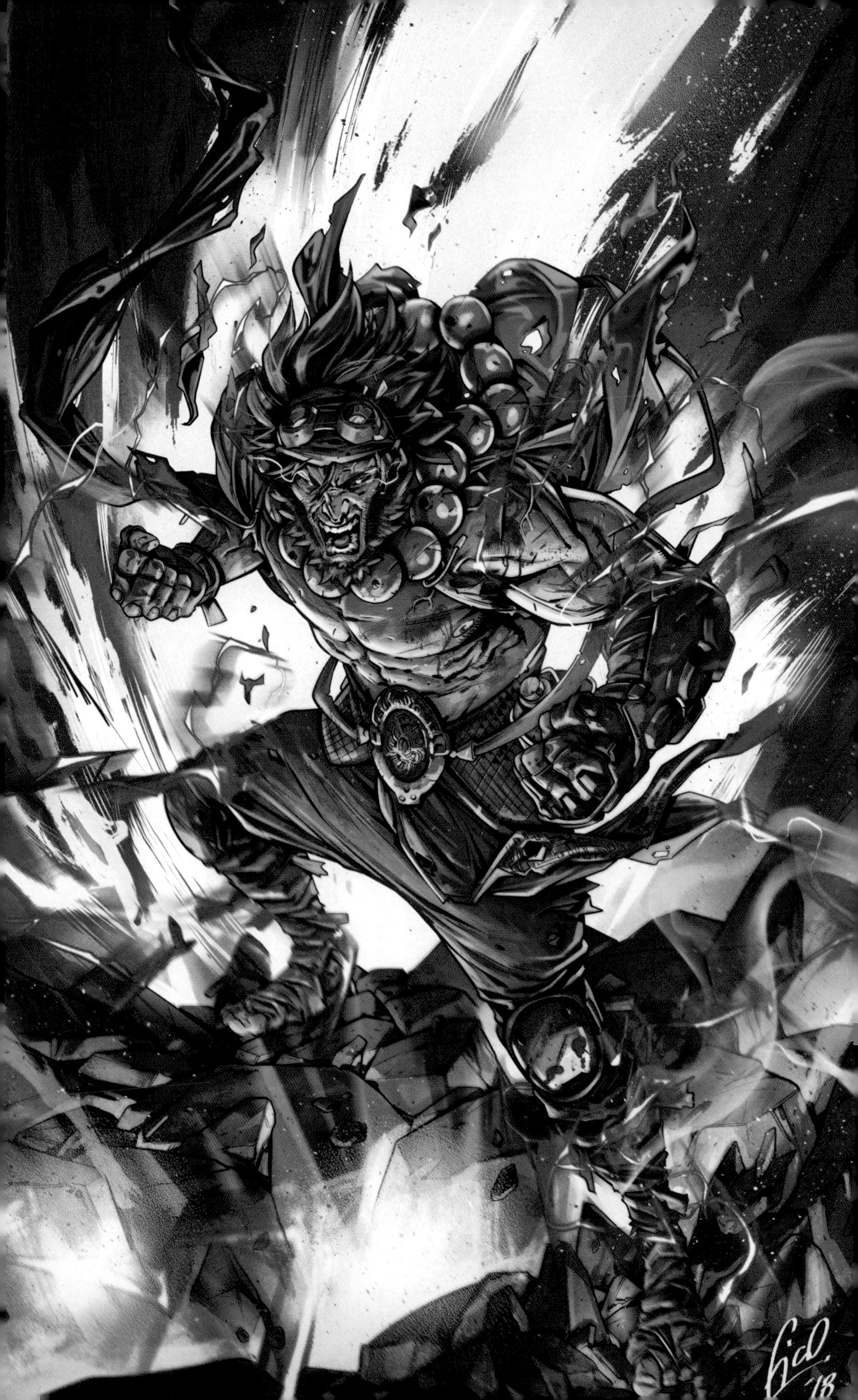

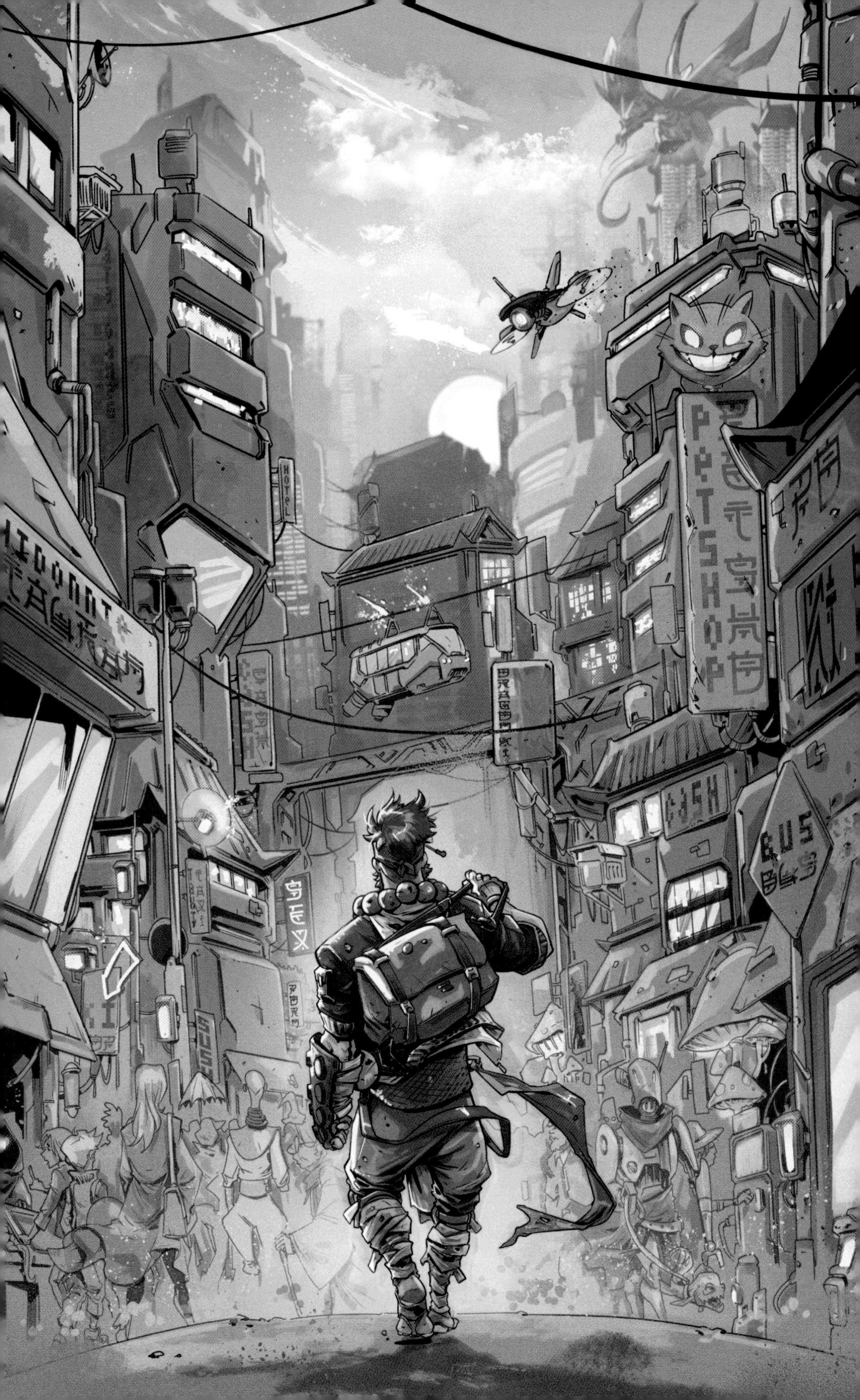
PETSHOP
CASH
BUS

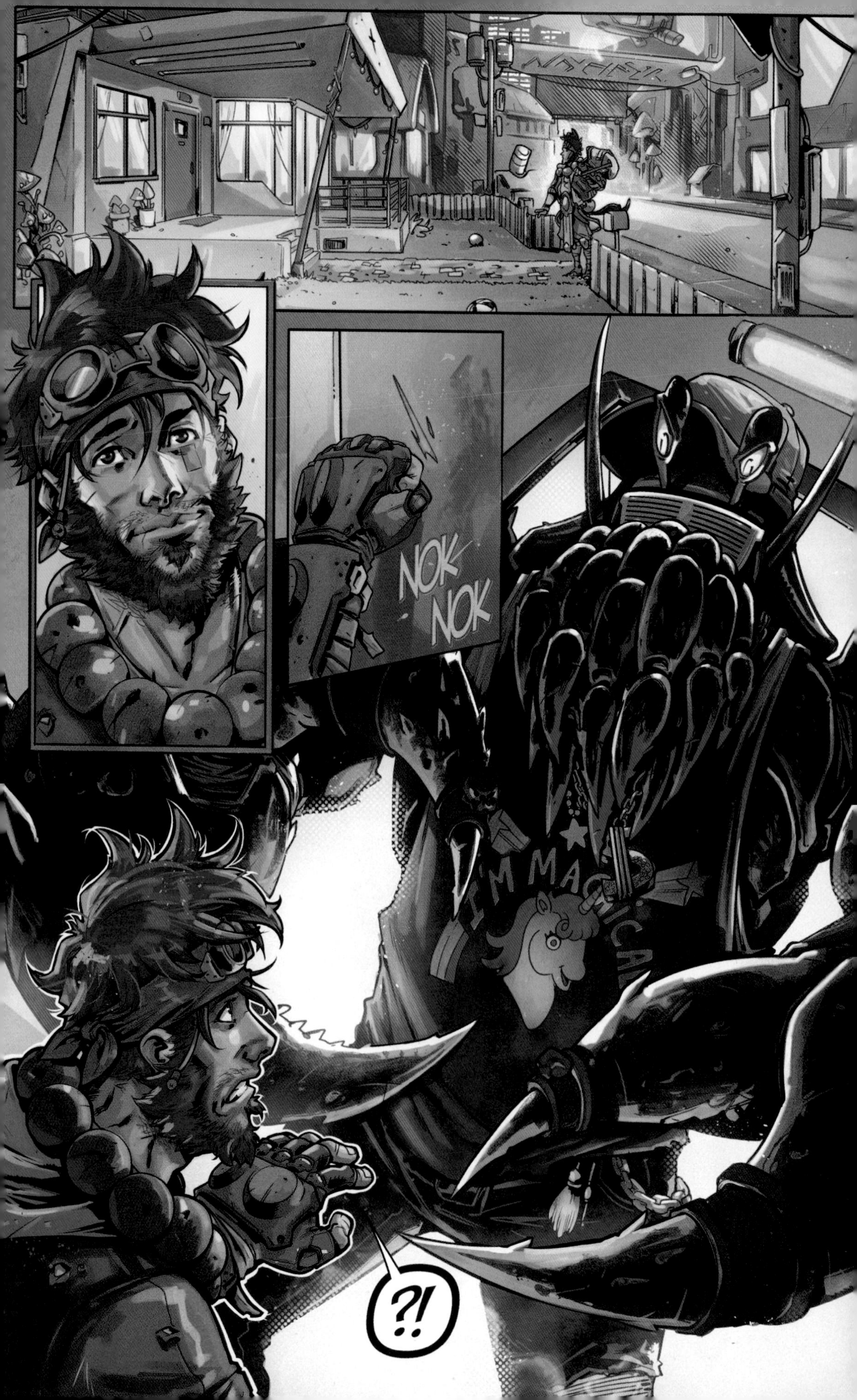
NOK NOK
?!

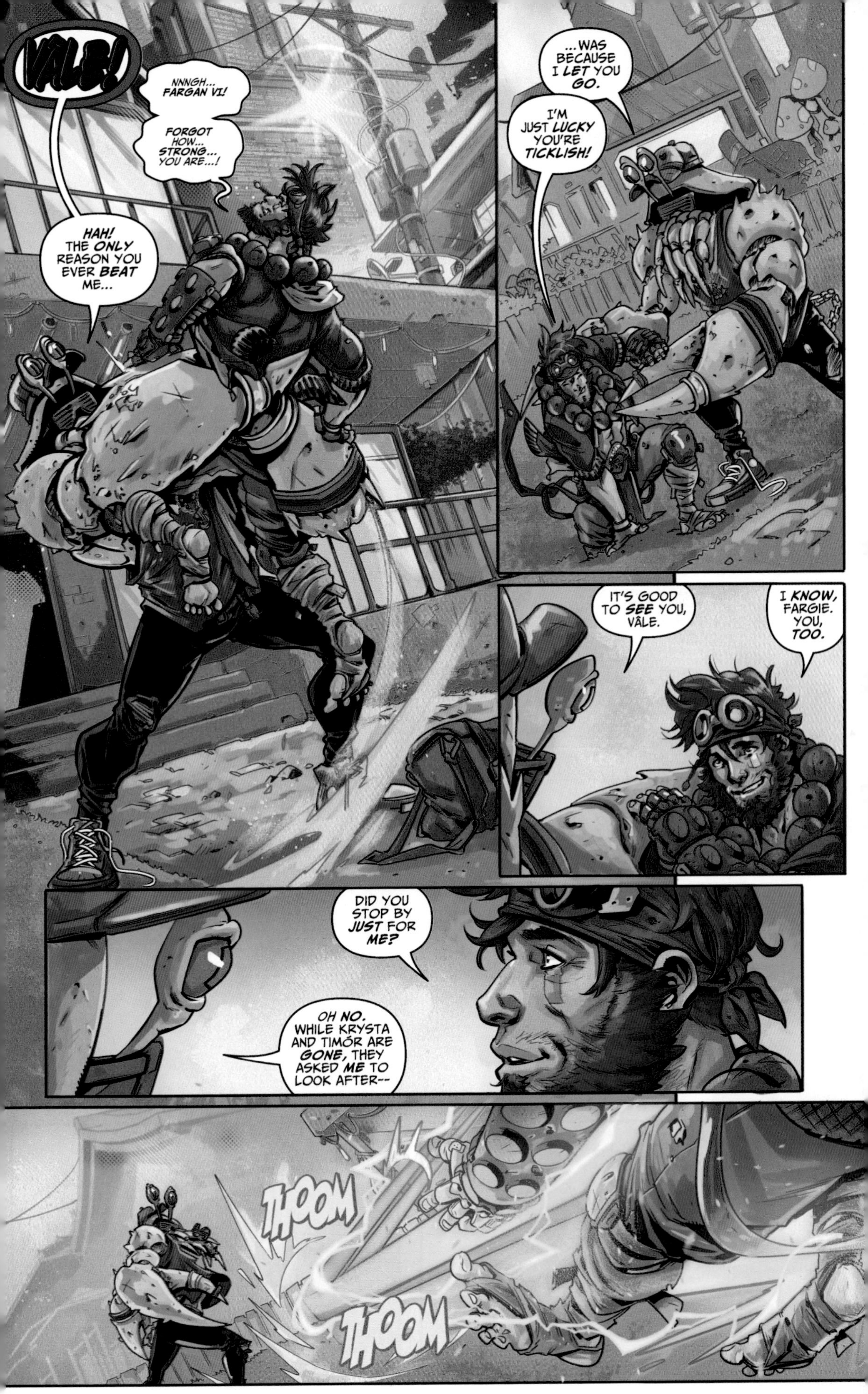
VÂLE!
NNNGH... FARGAN VI!
FORGOT HOW... STRONG... YOU ARE...!
HAH! THE ONLY REASON YOU EVER BEAT ME...
...WAS BECAUSE I LET YOU GO.
I'M JUST LUCKY YOU'RE TICKLISH!
IT'S GOOD TO SEE YOU, VÂLE.
I KNOW, FARGIE. YOU, TOO.
DID YOU STOP BY JUST FOR ME?
OH NO. WHILE KRYSTA AND TIMÓR ARE GONE, THEY ASKED ME TO LOOK AFTER--
THOOM
THOOM

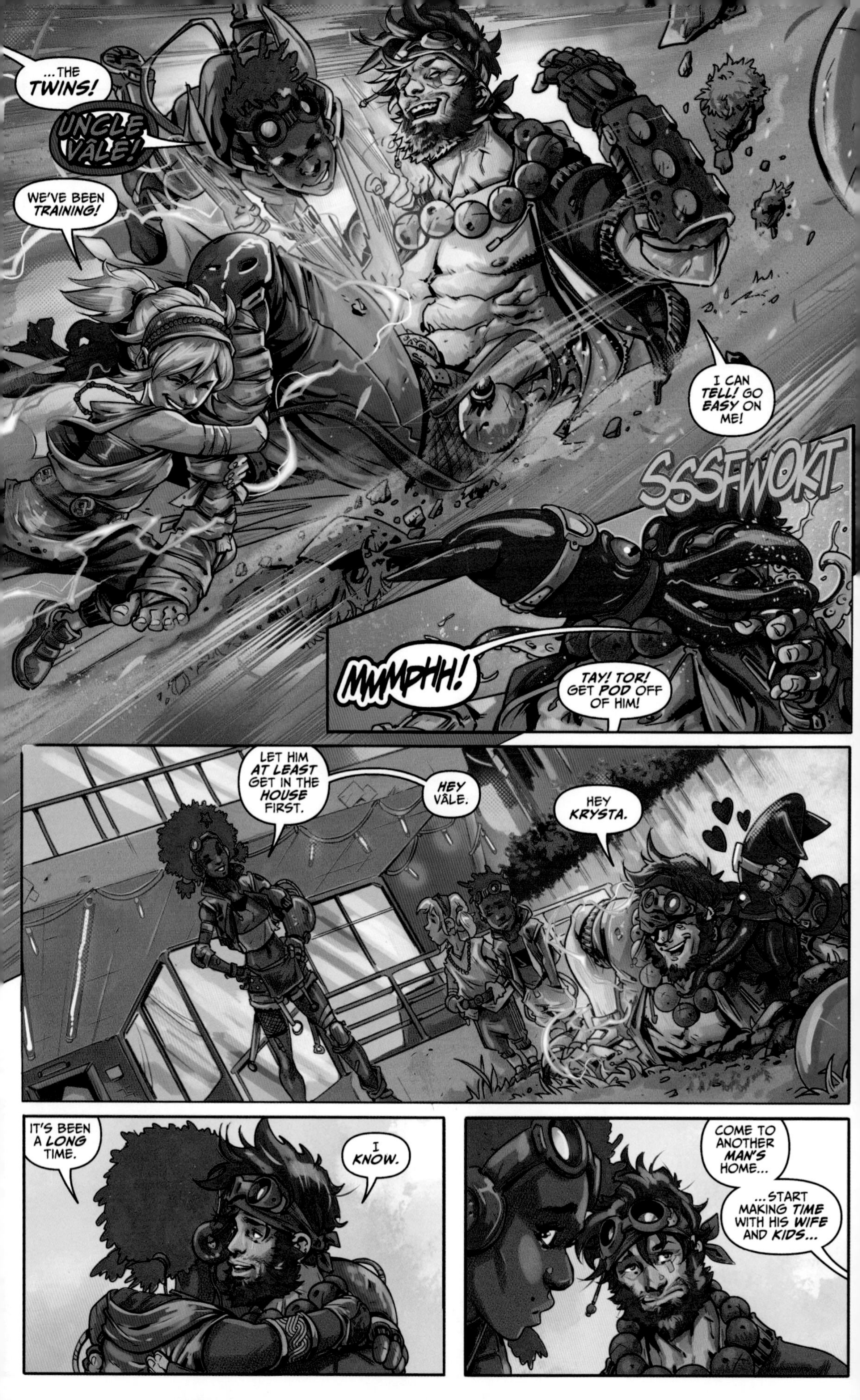
...THE TWINS!
UNCLE VÂLE!
WE'VE BEEN TRAINING!
I CAN TELL! GO EASY ON ME!
SSSFWOKT
MMMPHH!
TAY! TOR! GET POD OFF OF HIM!
LET HIM AT LEAST GET IN THE HOUSE FIRST.
HEY VÂLE.
HEY KRYSTA.
IT'S BEEN A LONG TIME.
I KNOW.
COME TO ANOTHER MAN'S HOME...
...START MAKING TIME WITH HIS WIFE AND KIDS...

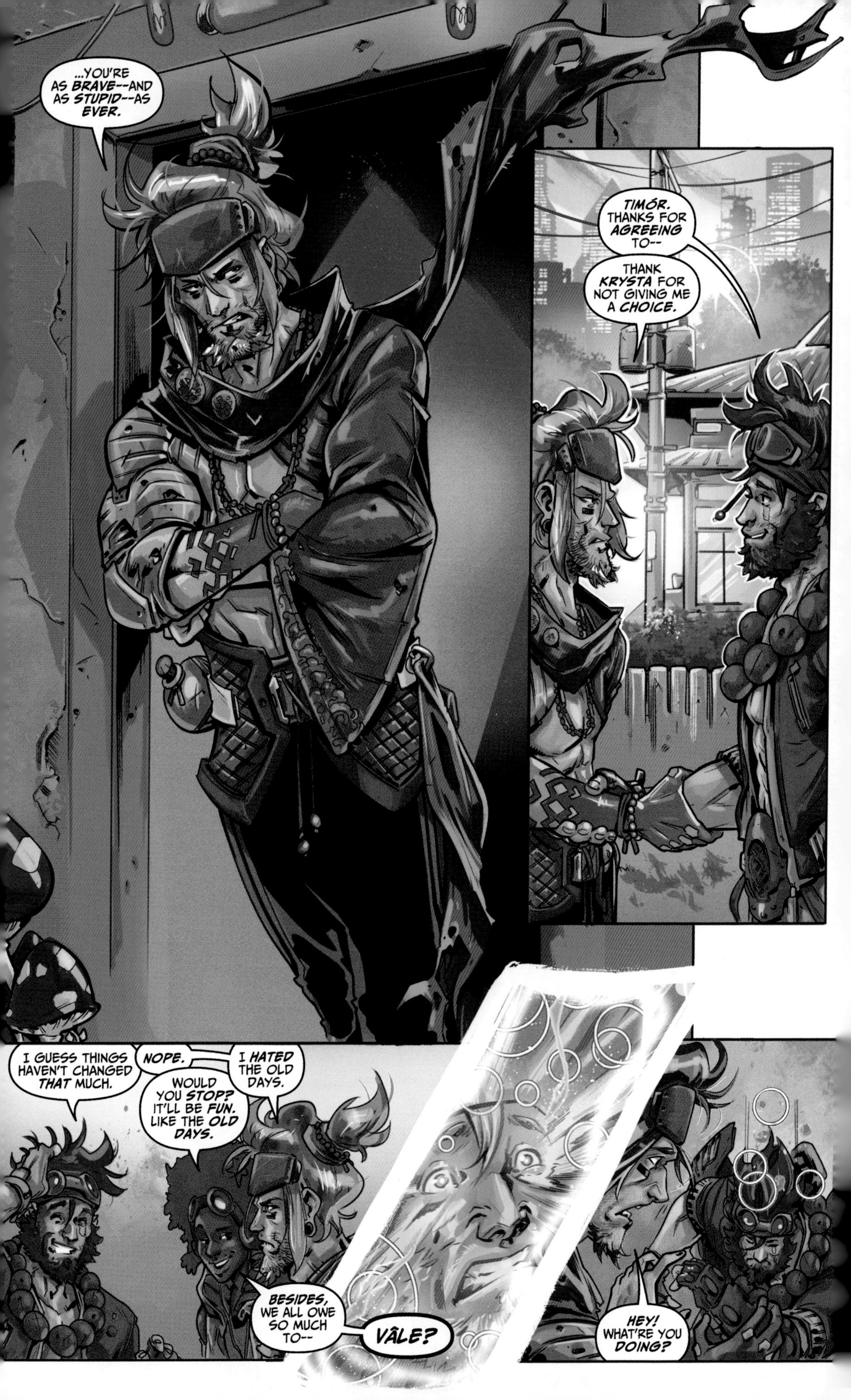
...YOU'RE AS BRAVE--AND AS STUPID--AS EVER.
TIMÓR. THANKS FOR AGREEING TO--
THANK KRYSTA FOR NOT GIVING ME A CHOICE.
I GUESS THINGS HAVEN'T CHANGED THAT MUCH.
NOPE.
I HATED THE OLD DAYS.
WOULD YOU STOP? IT'LL BE FUN. LIKE THE OLD DAYS.
BESIDES, WE ALL OWE SO MUCH TO--
VÂLE?
HEY! WHAT'RE YOU DOING?

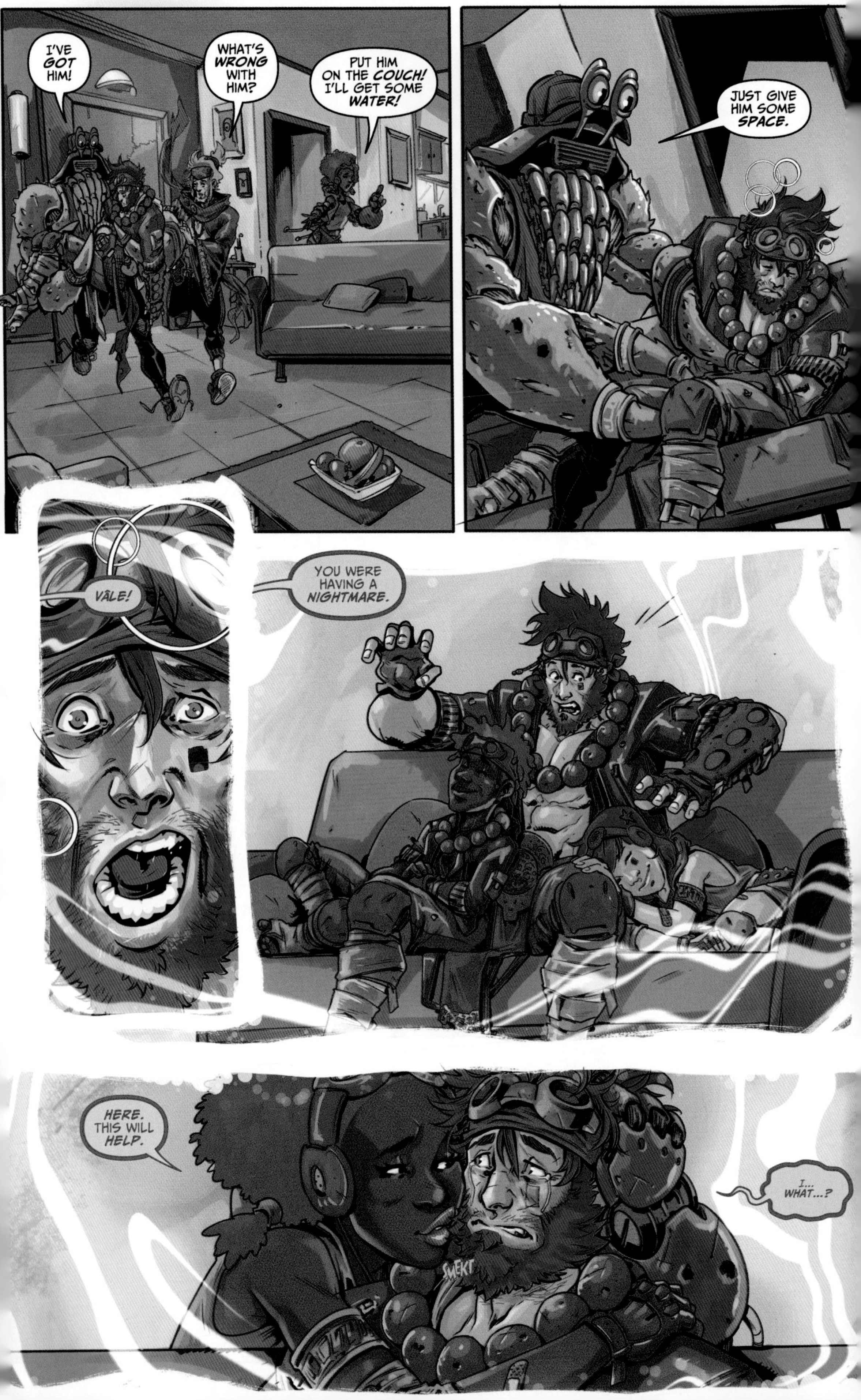
I'VE GOT HIM!
WHAT'S WRONG WITH HIM?
PUT HIM ON THE COUCH! I'LL GET SOME WATER!
JUST GIVE HIM SOME SPACE.
VÂLE!
YOU WERE HAVING A NIGHTMARE.
HERE. THIS WILL HELP.
SMEKT
I... WHAT...?

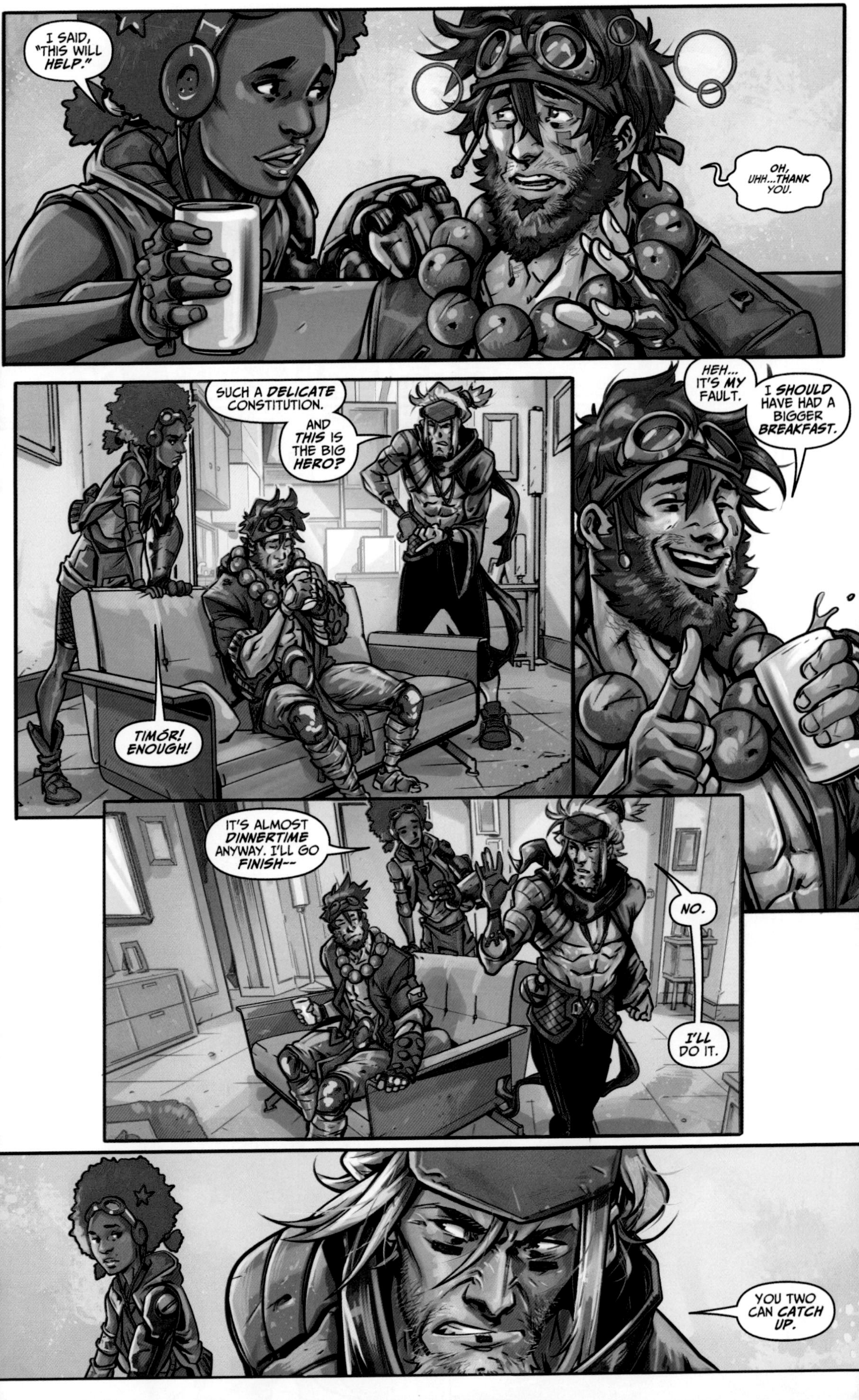
I SAID, "THIS WILL HELP."
OH, UHH...THANK YOU.
SUCH A DELICATE CONSTITUTION.
AND THIS IS THE BIG HERO?
TIMÓR! ENOUGH!
HEH... IT'S MY FAULT.
I SHOULD HAVE HAD A BIGGER BREAKFAST.
IT'S ALMOST DINNERTIME ANYWAY. I'LL GO FINISH--
NO.
I'LL DO IT.
YOU TWO CAN CATCH UP.

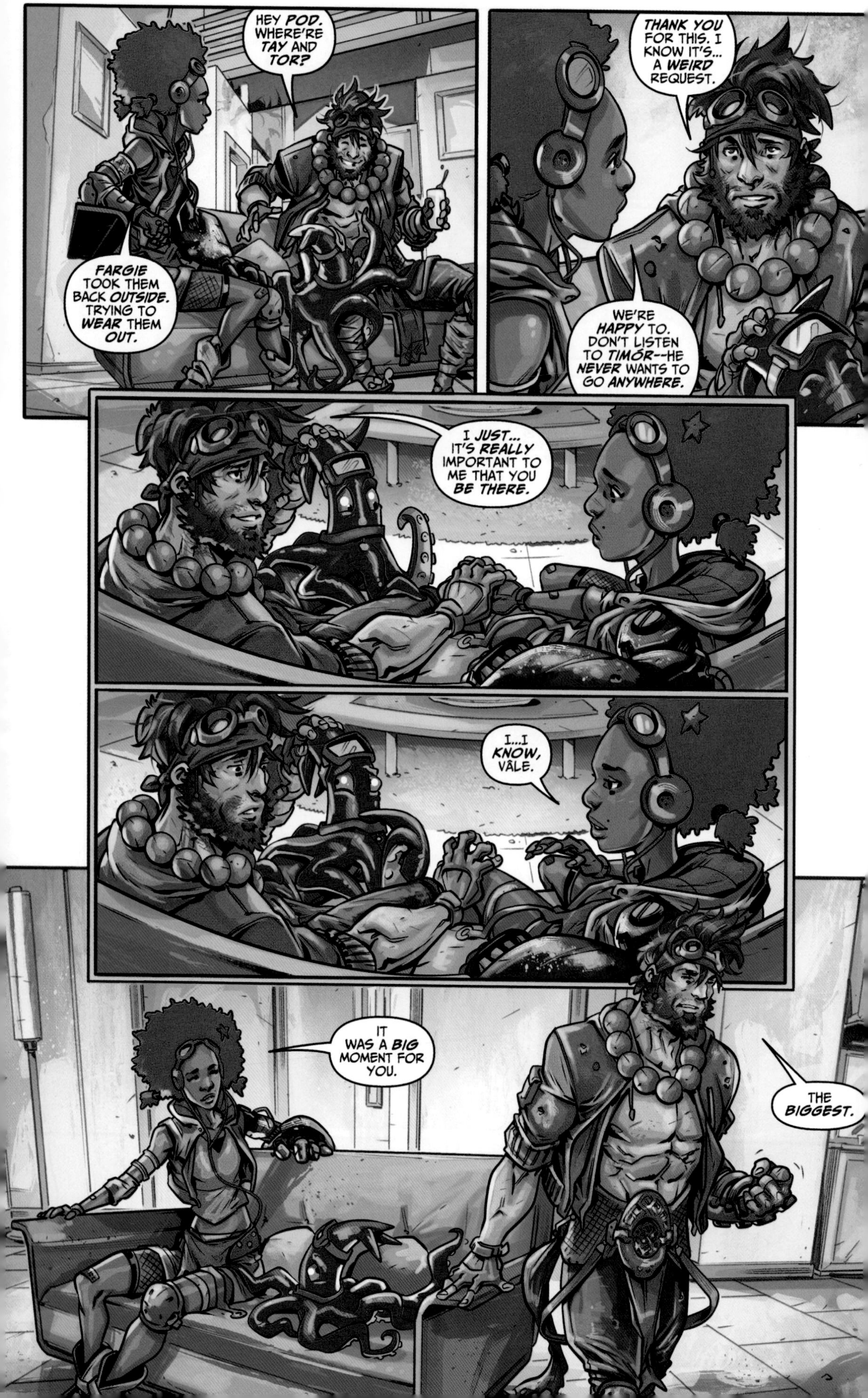

HEY POD. WHERE'RE TAY AND TOR?
FARGIE TOOK THEM BACK OUTSIDE. TRYING TO WEAR THEM OUT.
THANK YOU FOR THIS. I KNOW IT'S... A WEIRD REQUEST.
WE'RE HAPPY TO. DON'T LISTEN TO TIMÓR--HE NEVER WANTS TO GO ANYWHERE.
I JUST... IT'S REALLY IMPORTANT TO ME THAT YOU BE THERE.
I...I KNOW, VÂLE.
IT WAS A BIG MOMENT FOR YOU.
THE BIGGEST.

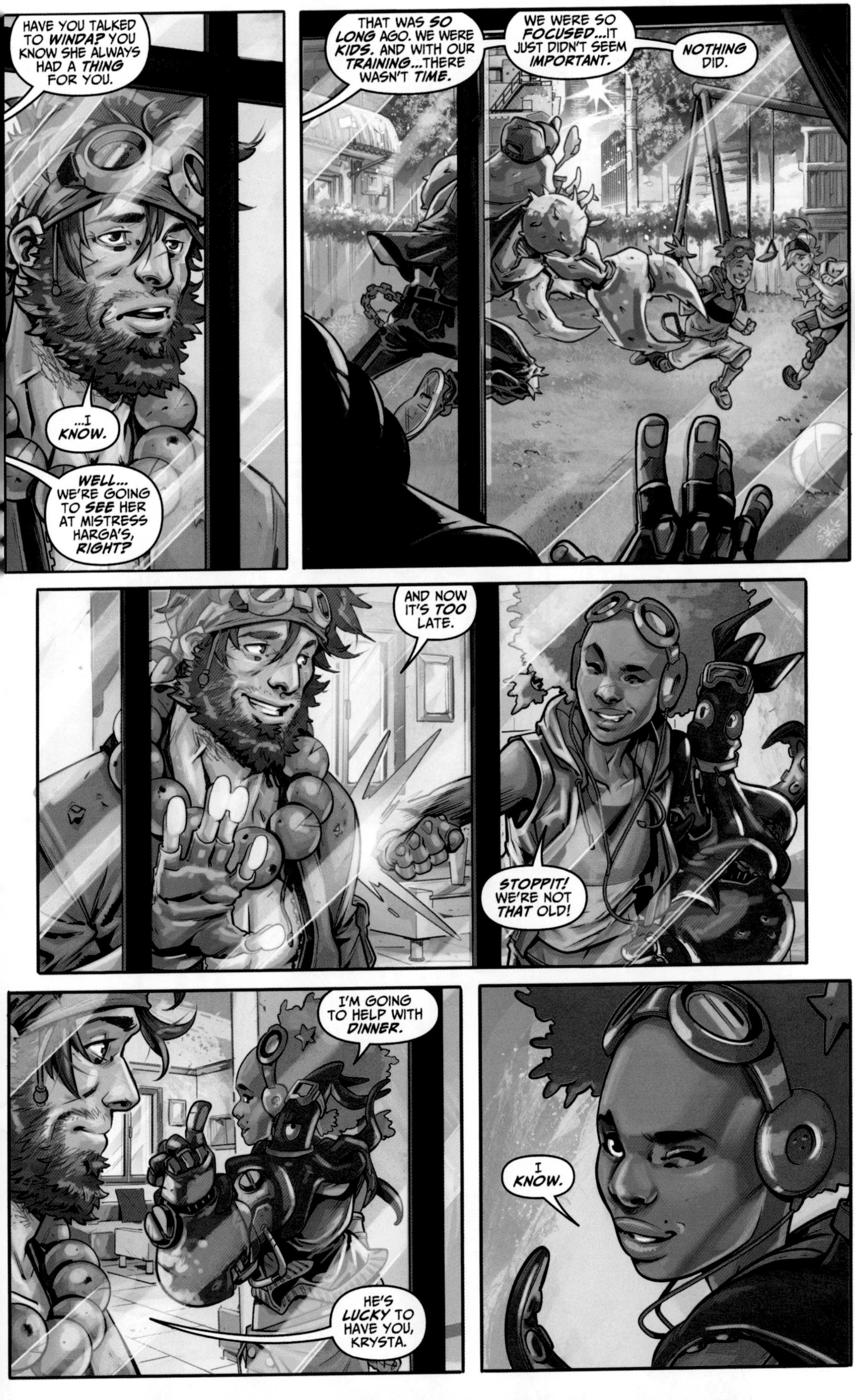
HAVE YOU TALKED TO WINDA? YOU KNOW SHE ALWAYS HAD A THING FOR YOU.
...I KNOW.
WELL... WE'RE GOING TO SEE HER AT MISTRESS HARGA'S, RIGHT?
THAT WAS SO LONG AGO. WE WERE KIDS. AND WITH OUR TRAINING...THERE WASN'T TIME.
WE WERE SO FOCUSED...IT JUST DIDN'T SEEM IMPORTANT.
NOTHING DID.
AND NOW IT'S TOO LATE.
STOPPIT! WE'RE NOT THAT OLD!
I'M GOING TO HELP WITH DINNER.
HE'S LUCKY TO HAVE YOU, KRYSTA.
I KNOW.

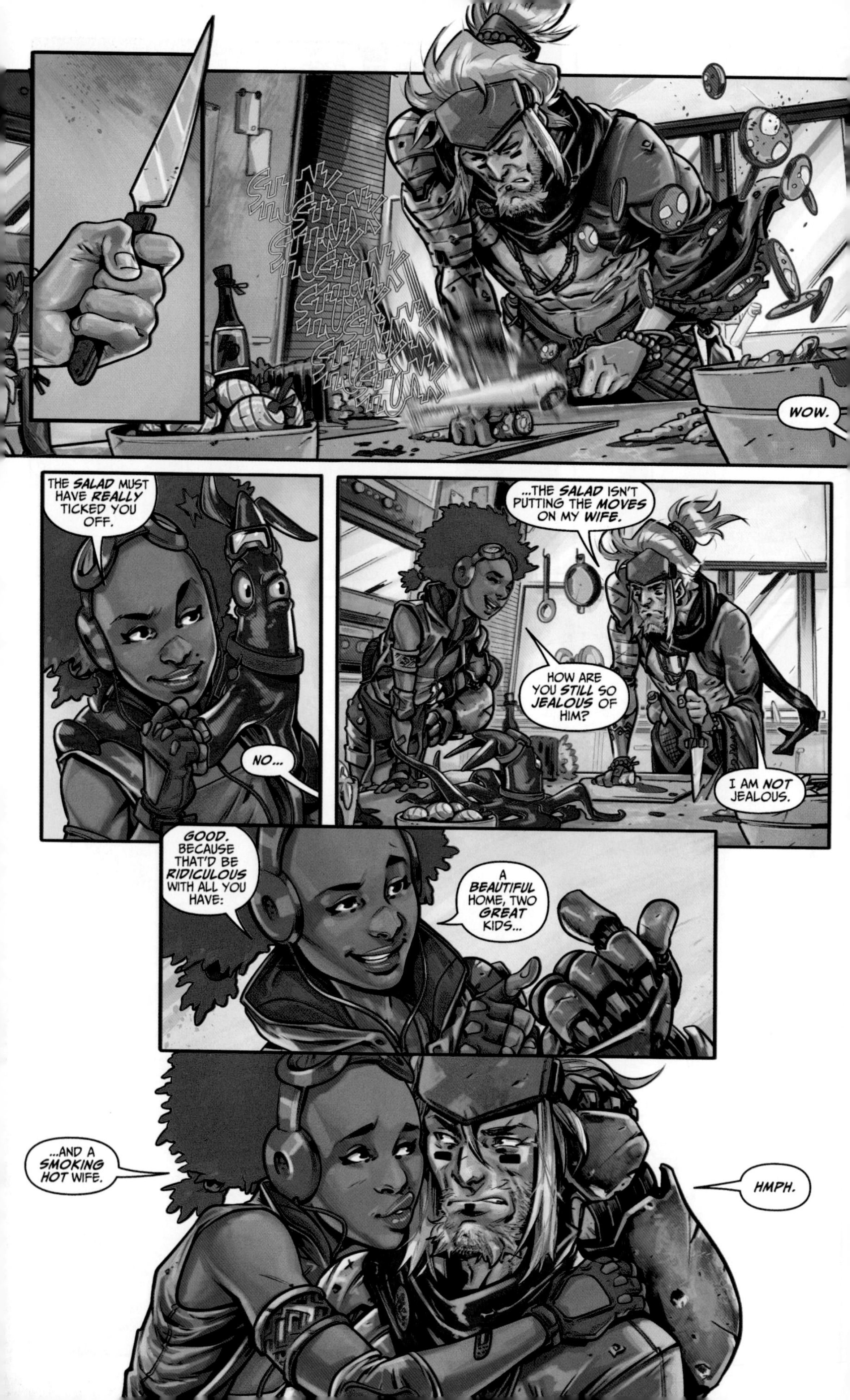
SHUGUNK SHUGUNK SHUGUNK SHUGUNK SHUGUNK
WOW.
THE SALAD MUST HAVE REALLY TICKED YOU OFF.
NO...
...THE SALAD ISN'T PUTTING THE MOVES ON MY WIFE.
HOW ARE YOU STILL SO JEALOUS OF HIM?
I AM NOT JEALOUS.
GOOD. BECAUSE THAT'D BE RIDICULOUS WITH ALL YOU HAVE:
A BEAUTIFUL HOME, TWO GREAT KIDS...
...AND A SMOKING HOT WIFE.
HMPH.

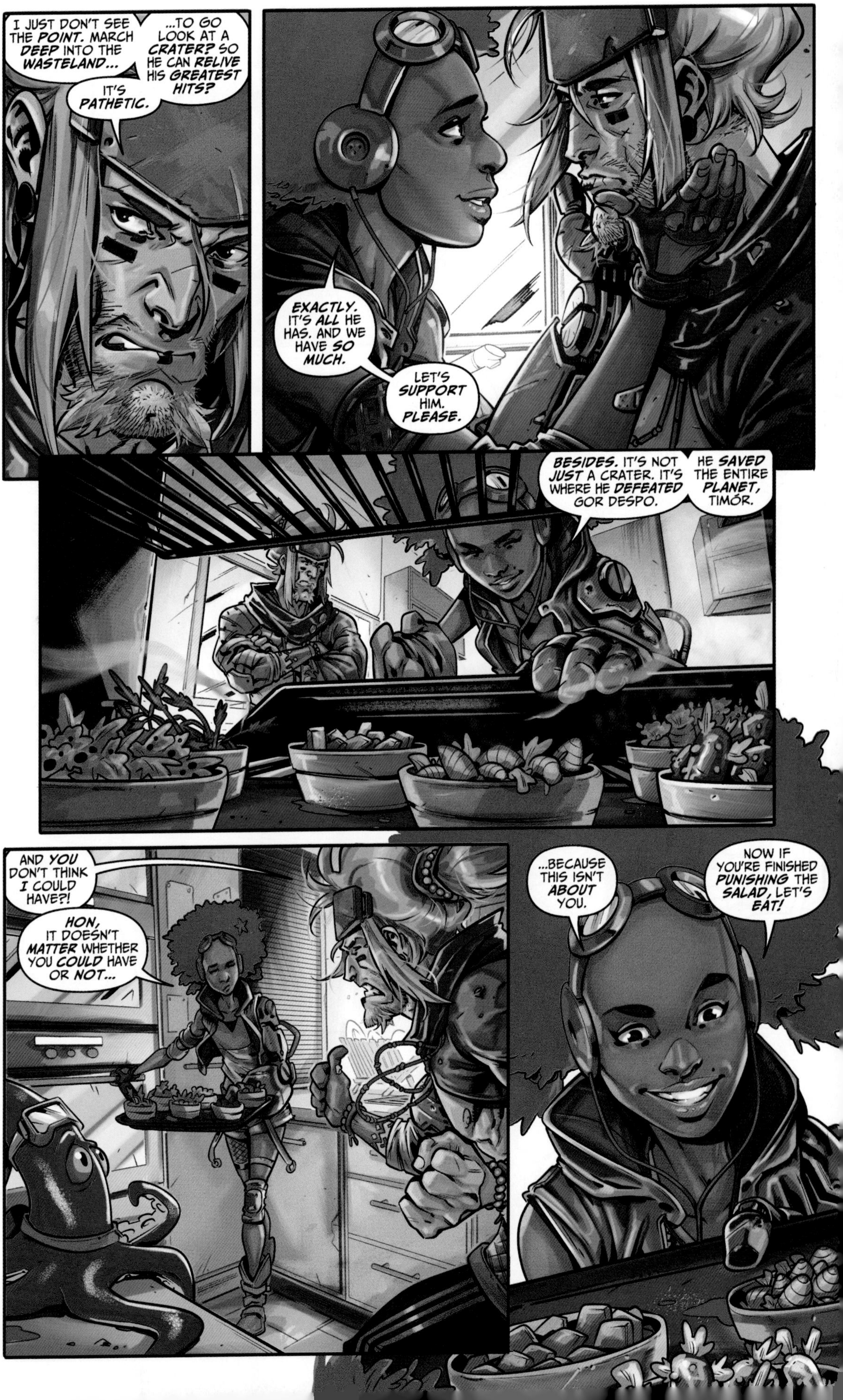
I JUST DON'T SEE THE POINT. MARCH DEEP INTO THE WASTELAND...
...TO GO LOOK AT A CRATER? SO HE CAN RELIVE HIS GREATEST HITS?
IT'S PATHETIC.
EXACTLY. IT'S ALL HE HAS. AND WE HAVE SO MUCH.
LET'S SUPPORT HIM. PLEASE.
BESIDES. IT'S NOT JUST A CRATER. IT'S WHERE HE DEFEATED GOR DESPO.
HE SAVED THE ENTIRE PLANET, TIMÓR.
AND YOU DON'T THINK I COULD HAVE?!
HON, IT DOESN'T MATTER WHETHER YOU COULD HAVE OR NOT...
...BECAUSE THIS ISN'T ABOUT YOU.
NOW IF YOU'RE FINISHED PUNISHING THE SALAD, LET'S EAT!

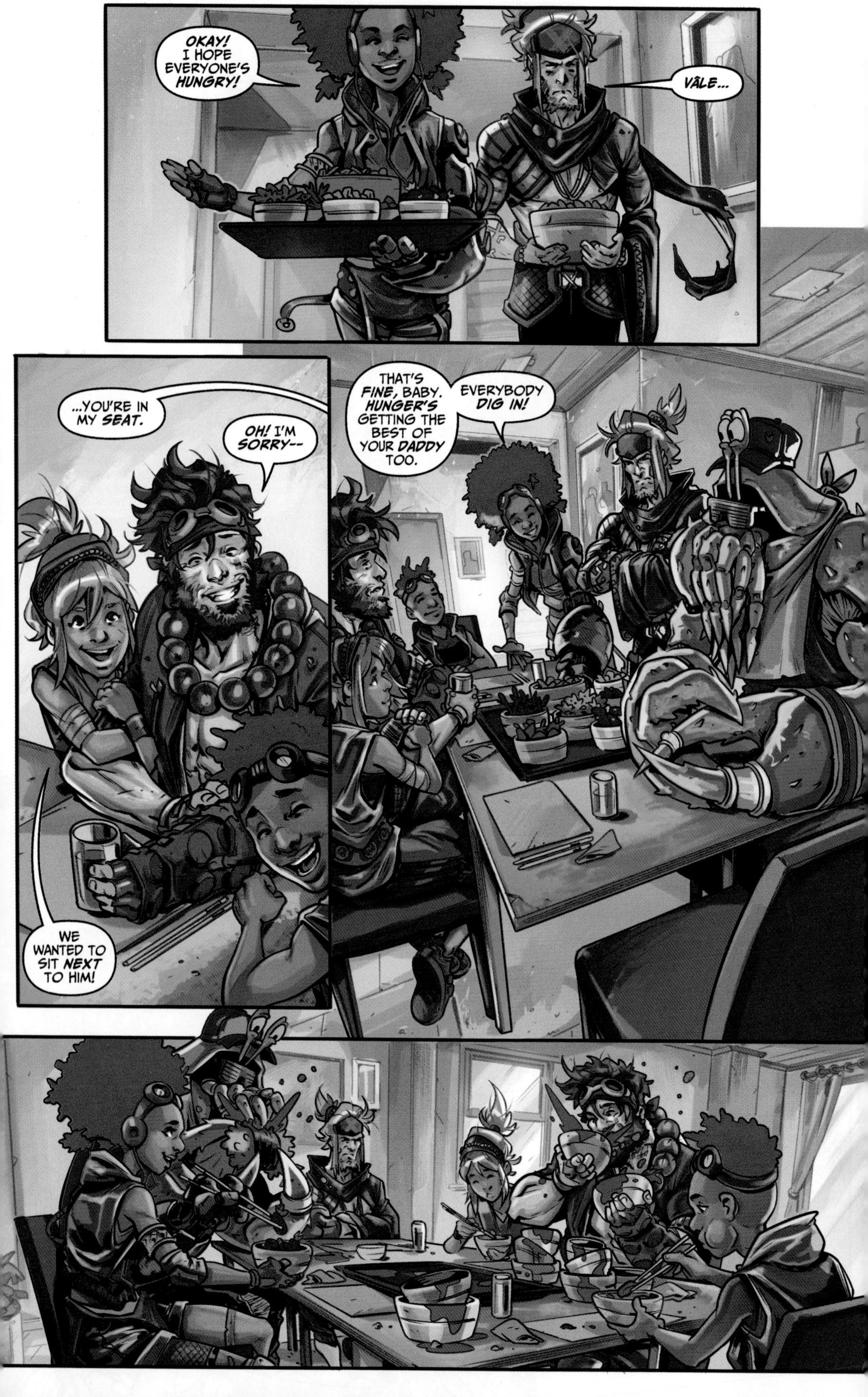
OKAY! I HOPE EVERYONE'S HUNGRY!
VÂLE...
...YOU'RE IN MY SEAT.
OH! I'M SORRY--
WE WANTED TO SIT NEXT TO HIM!
THAT'S FINE, BABY. HUNGER'S GETTING THE BEST OF YOUR DADDY TOO.
EVERYBODY DIG IN!

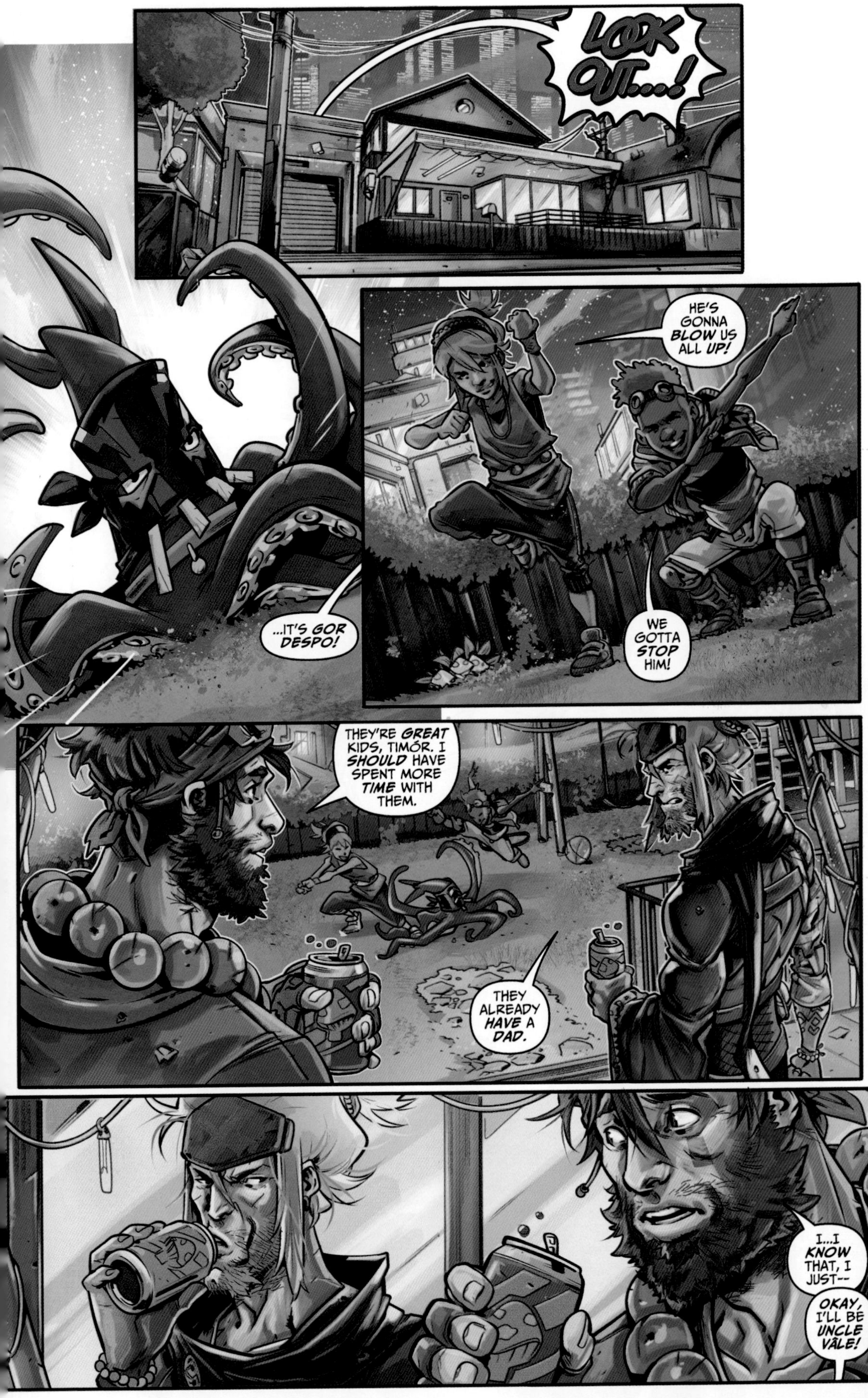
LOOK OUT...!
...IT'S GOR DESPO!
HE'S GONNA BLOW US ALL UP!
WE GOTTA STOP HIM!
THEY'RE GREAT KIDS, TIMÓR. I SHOULD HAVE SPENT MORE TIME WITH THEM.
THEY ALREADY HAVE A DAD.
I...I KNOW THAT, I JUST--
OKAY, I'LL BE UNCLE VÁLE!

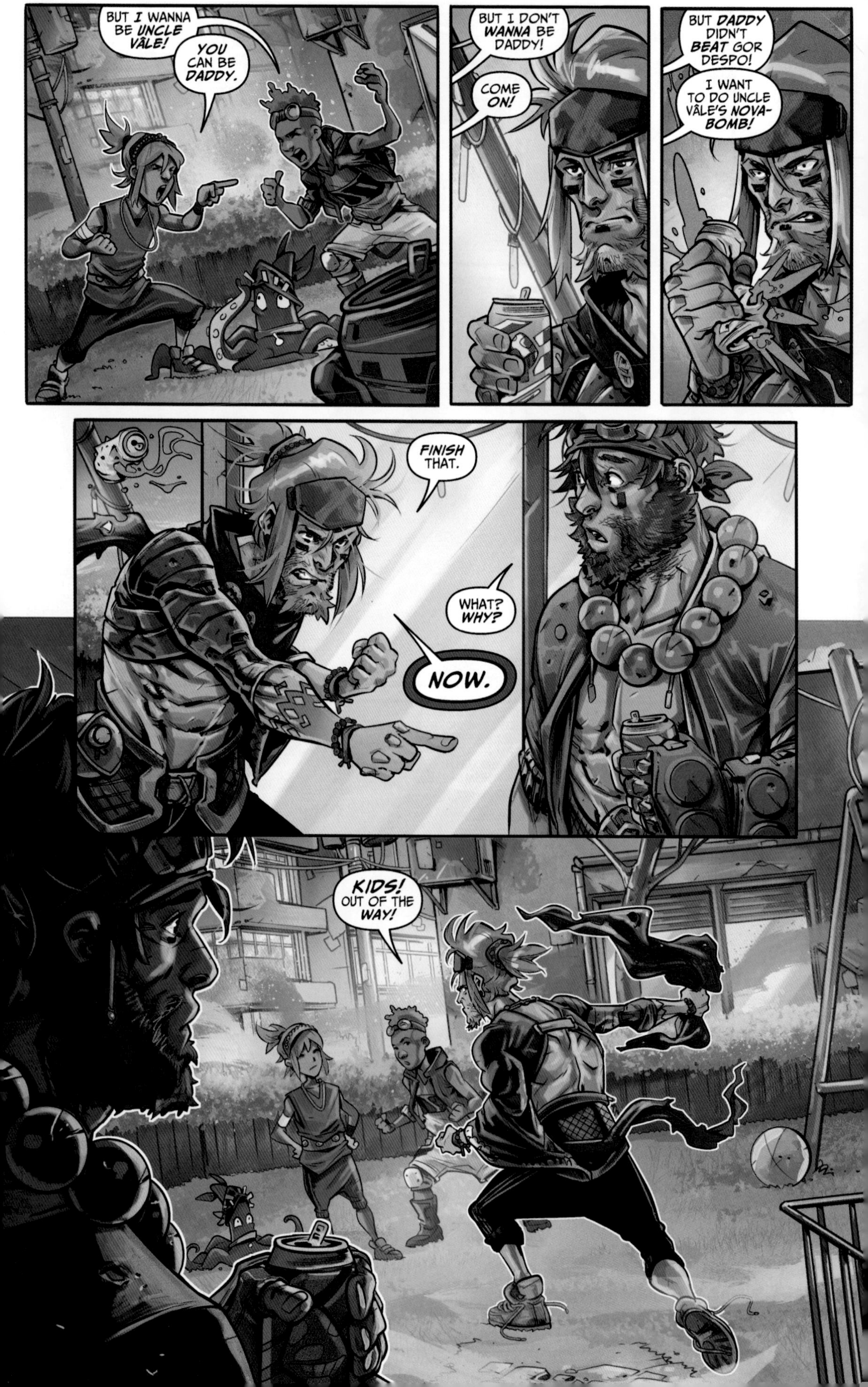
BUT I WANNA BE UNCLE VÂLE!
YOU CAN BE DADDY.
BUT I DON'T WANNA BE DADDY!
COME ON!
BUT DADDY DIDN'T BEAT GOR DESPO!
I WANT TO DO UNCLE VÂLE'S NOVA-BOMB!
FINISH THAT.
WHAT? WHY?
NOW.
KIDS! OUT OF THE WAY!

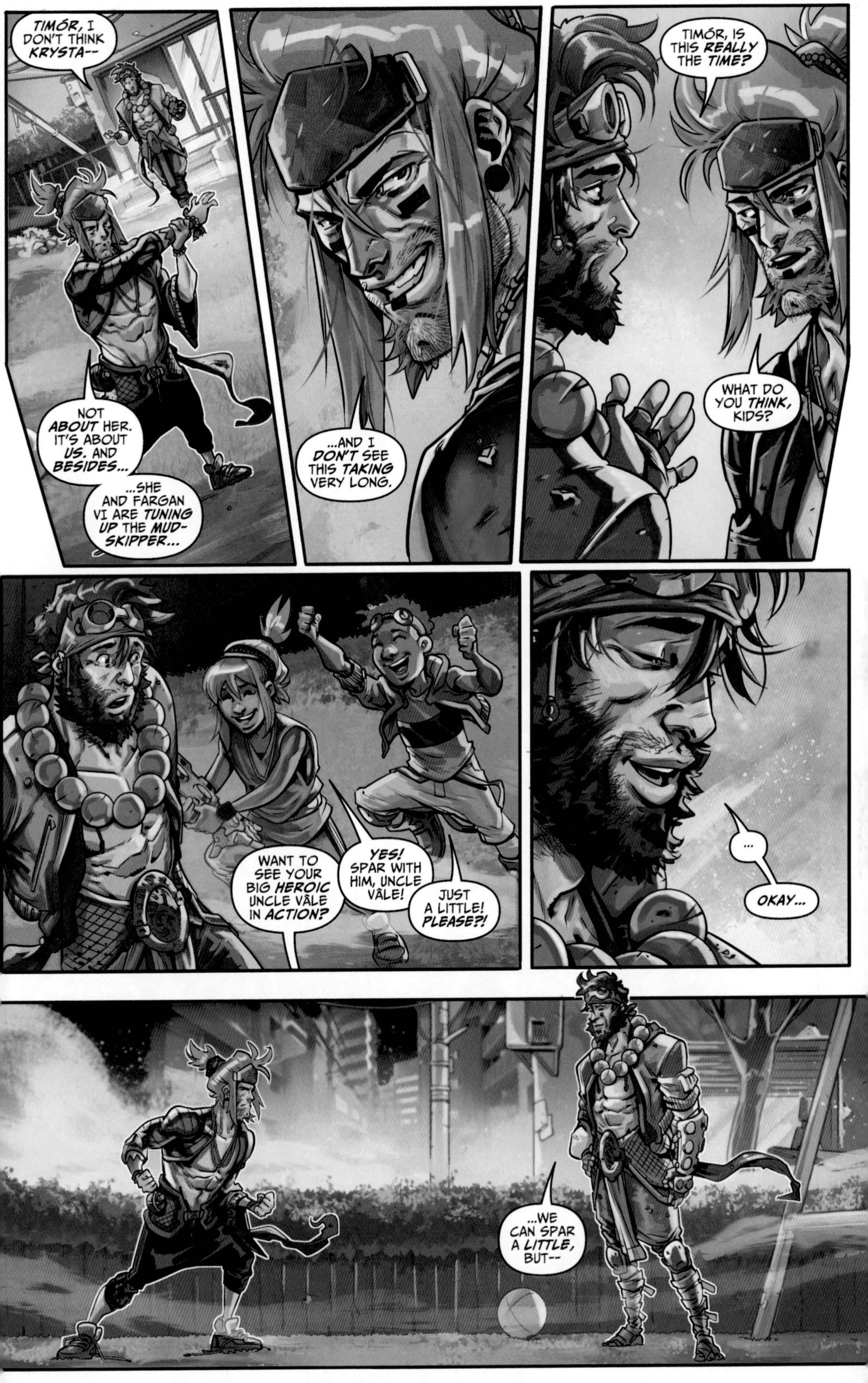
TIMÓR, I DON'T THINK KRYSTA--
NOT ABOUT HER. IT'S ABOUT US. AND BESIDES...
...SHE AND FARGAN VI ARE TUNING UP THE MUD-SKIPPER...
...AND I DON'T SEE THIS TAKING VERY LONG.
TIMÓR, IS THIS REALLY THE TIME?
WHAT DO YOU THINK, KIDS?
WANT TO SEE YOUR BIG HEROIC UNCLE VÂLE IN ACTION?
YES! SPAR WITH HIM, UNCLE VÂLE!
JUST A LITTLE! PLEASE?!
...
OKAY...
...WE CAN SPAR A LITTLE, BUT--

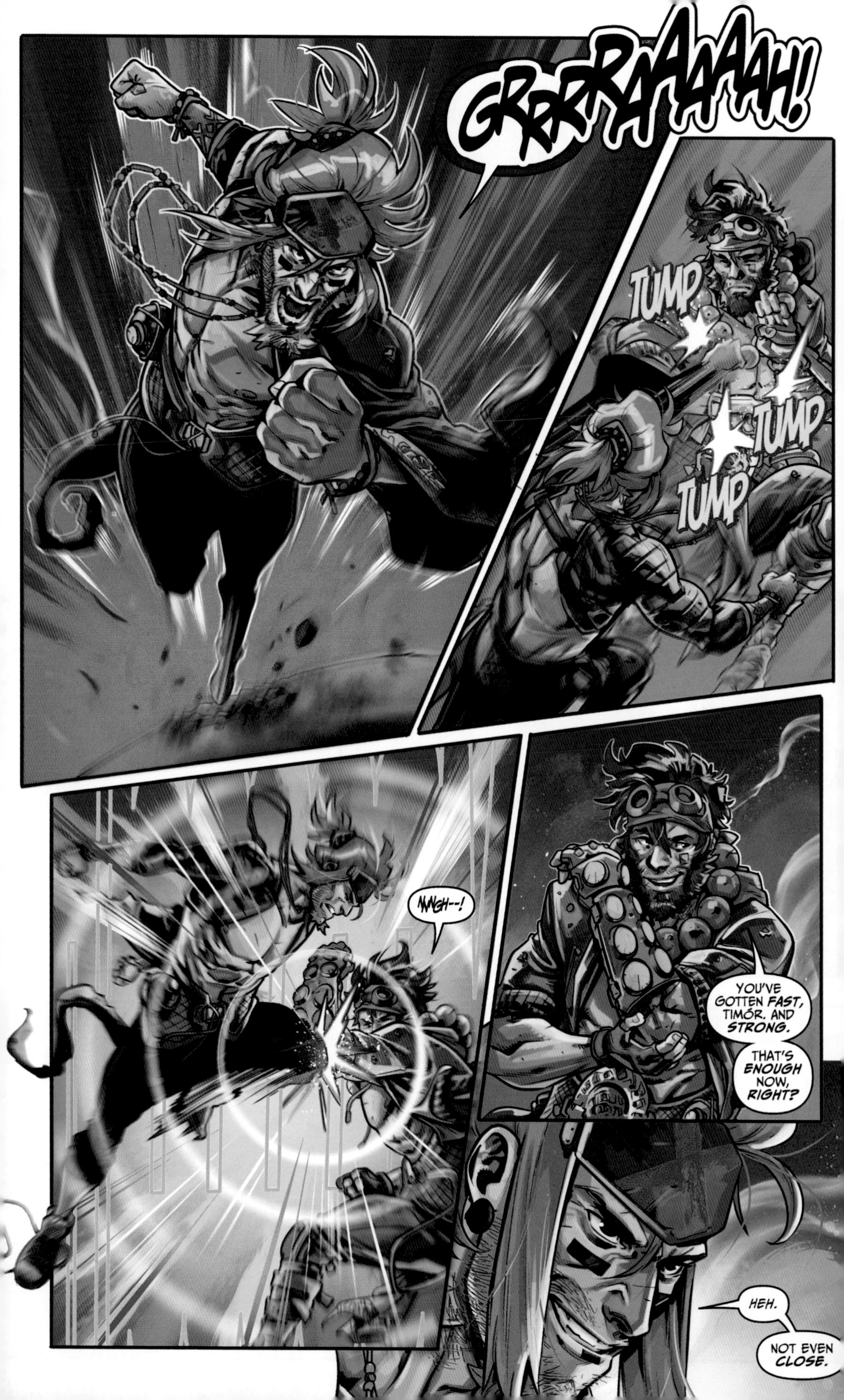
GRRRRAAAAAH!
TUMP
TUMP
TUMP
NNNGH--!
YOU'VE GOTTEN FAST, TIMÓR. AND STRONG.
THAT'S ENOUGH NOW, RIGHT?
HEH.
NOT EVEN CLOSE.

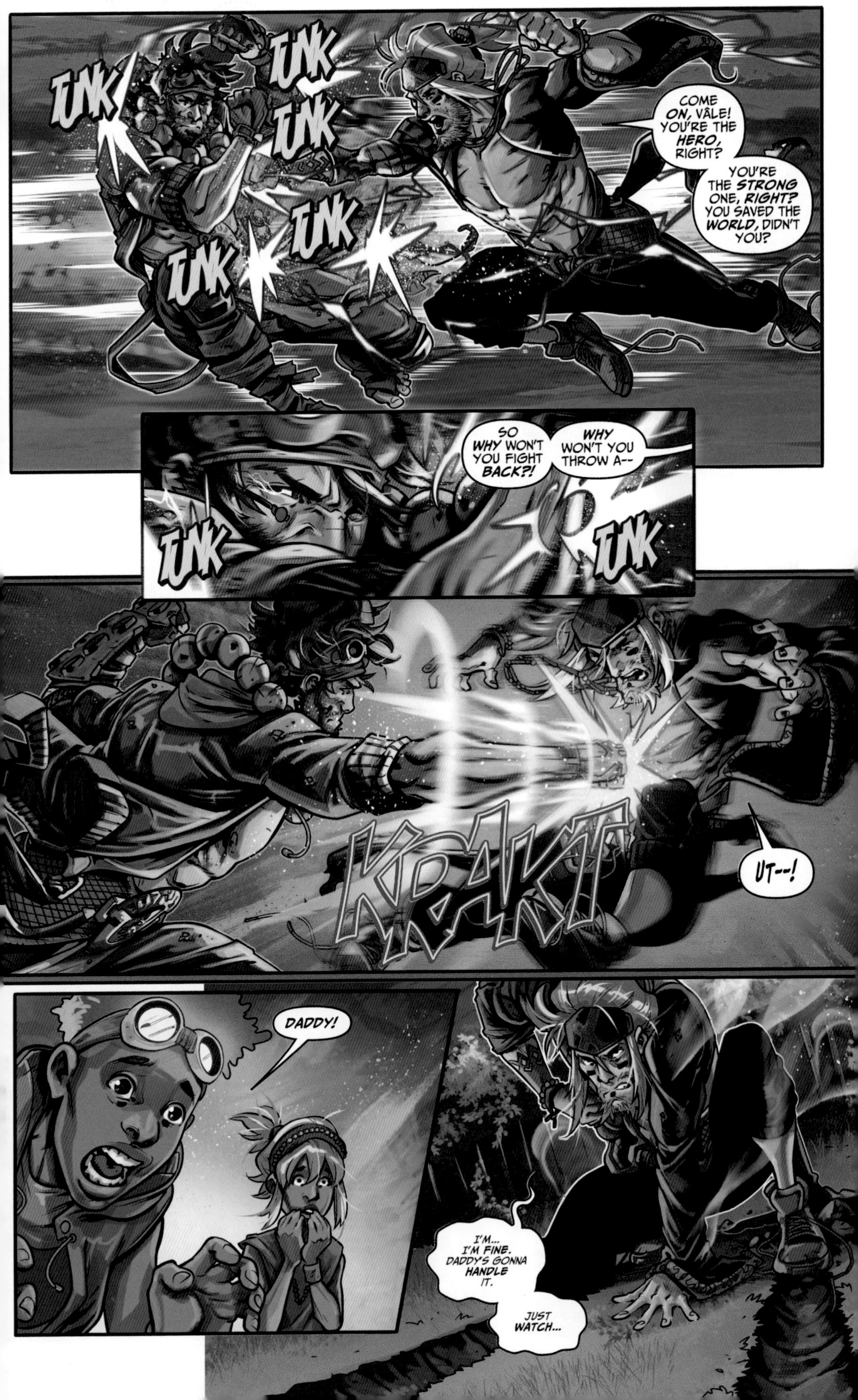
TUNK
TUNK
TUNK
TUNK
TUNK
COME ON, VÂLE! YOU'RE THE HERO, RIGHT?
YOU'RE THE STRONG ONE, RIGHT? YOU SAVED THE WORLD, DIDN'T YOU?
SO WHY WON'T YOU FIGHT BACK?!
WHY WON'T YOU THROW A--
TUNK
TUNK
KRAKT
UT--!
DADDY!
I'M... I'M FINE. DADDY'S GONNA HANDLE IT.
JUST WATCH...

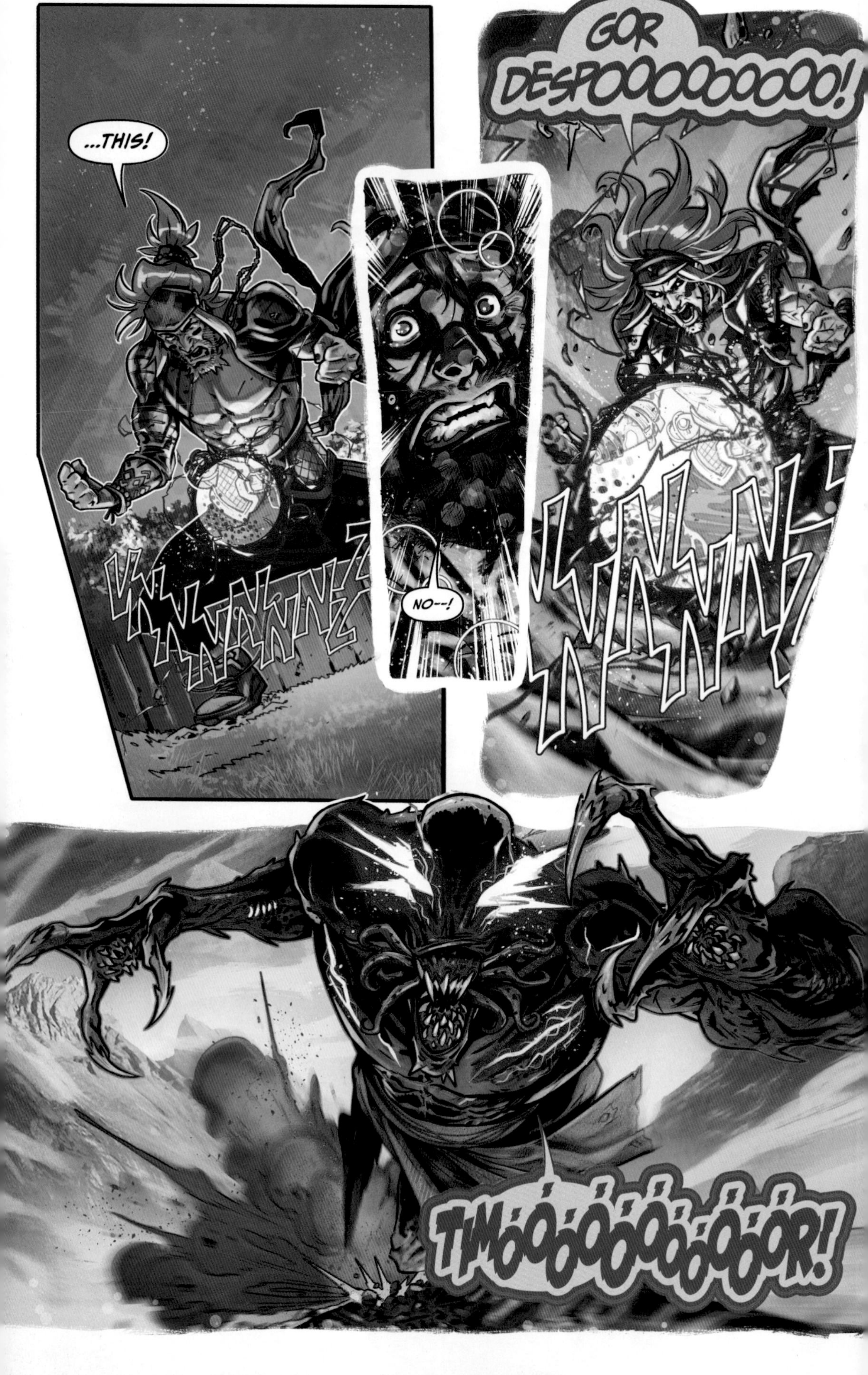
...THIS!
VWNNNNZ
NO--!
GOR DESPOOOOOOOOOO!
VWNNNNZ
TIMOOOOOOOOOR!

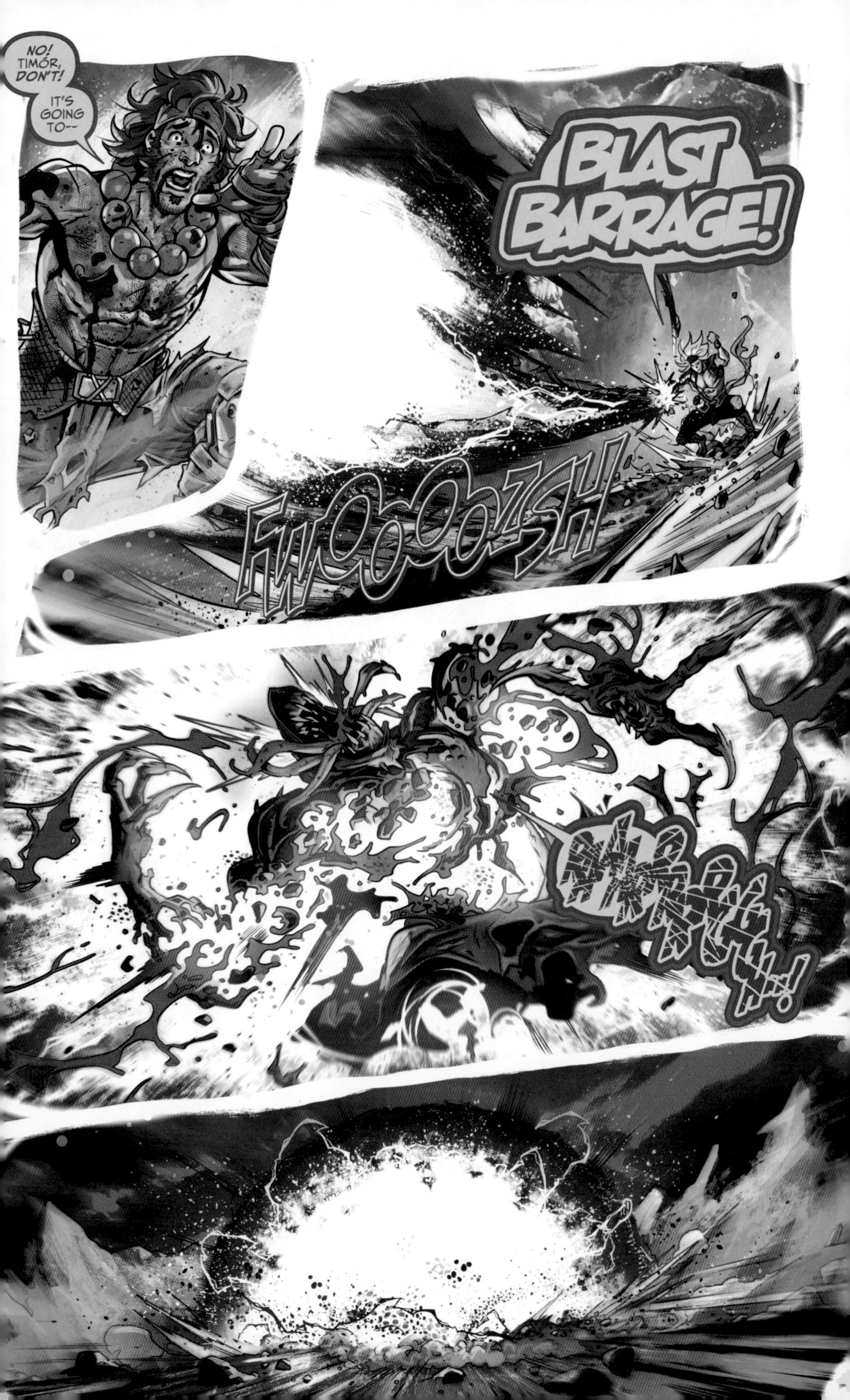
NO! TIMÓR, DON'T!
IT'S GOING TO--
BLAST BARRAGE!

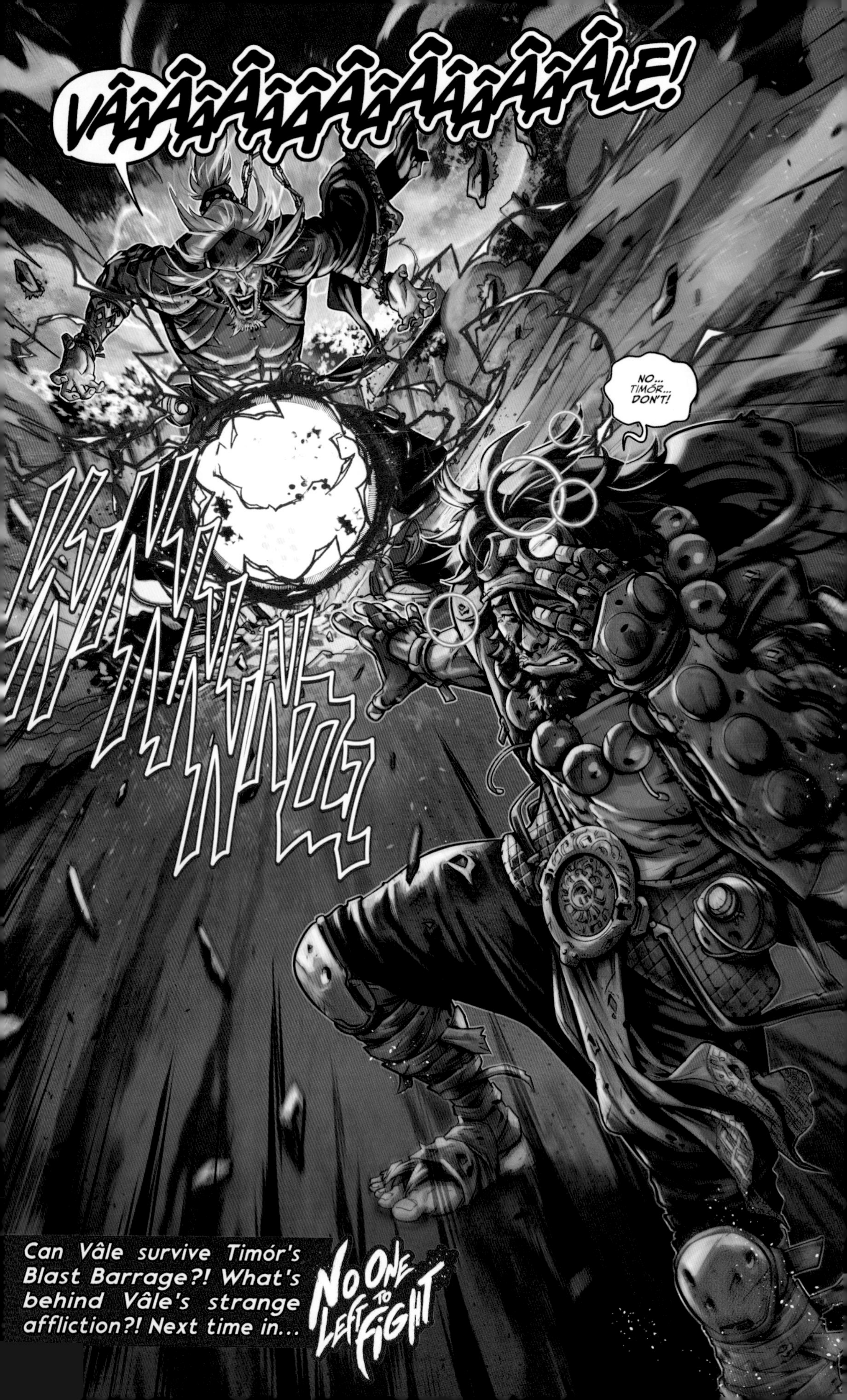
VÂâÂâÂââÂââÂâÂâÂLE!
NO... TIMÓR... DON'T!
Can Vâle survive Timór's Blast Barrage?! What's behind Vâle's strange affliction?! Next time in...
NO ONE LEFT TO FIGHT

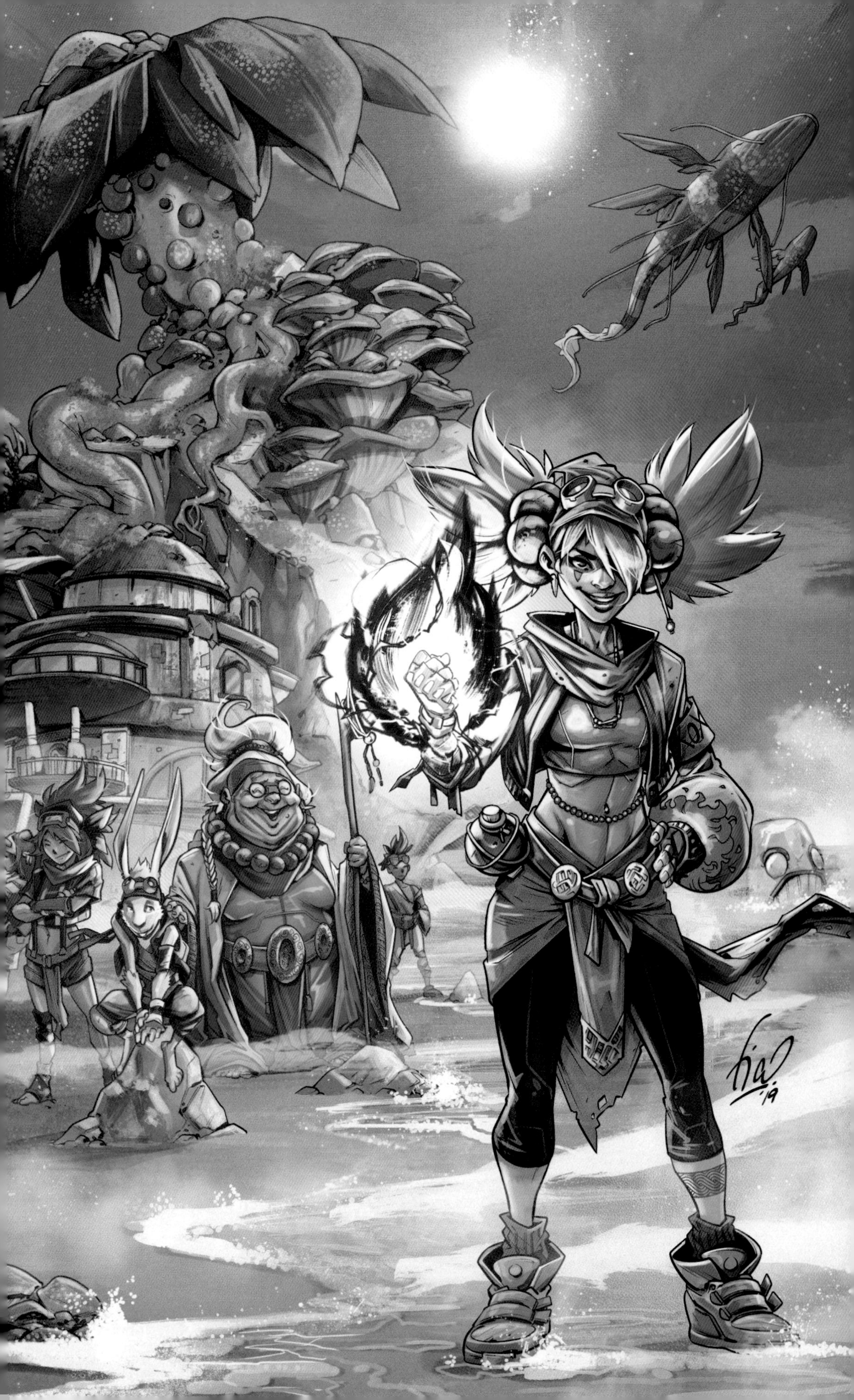

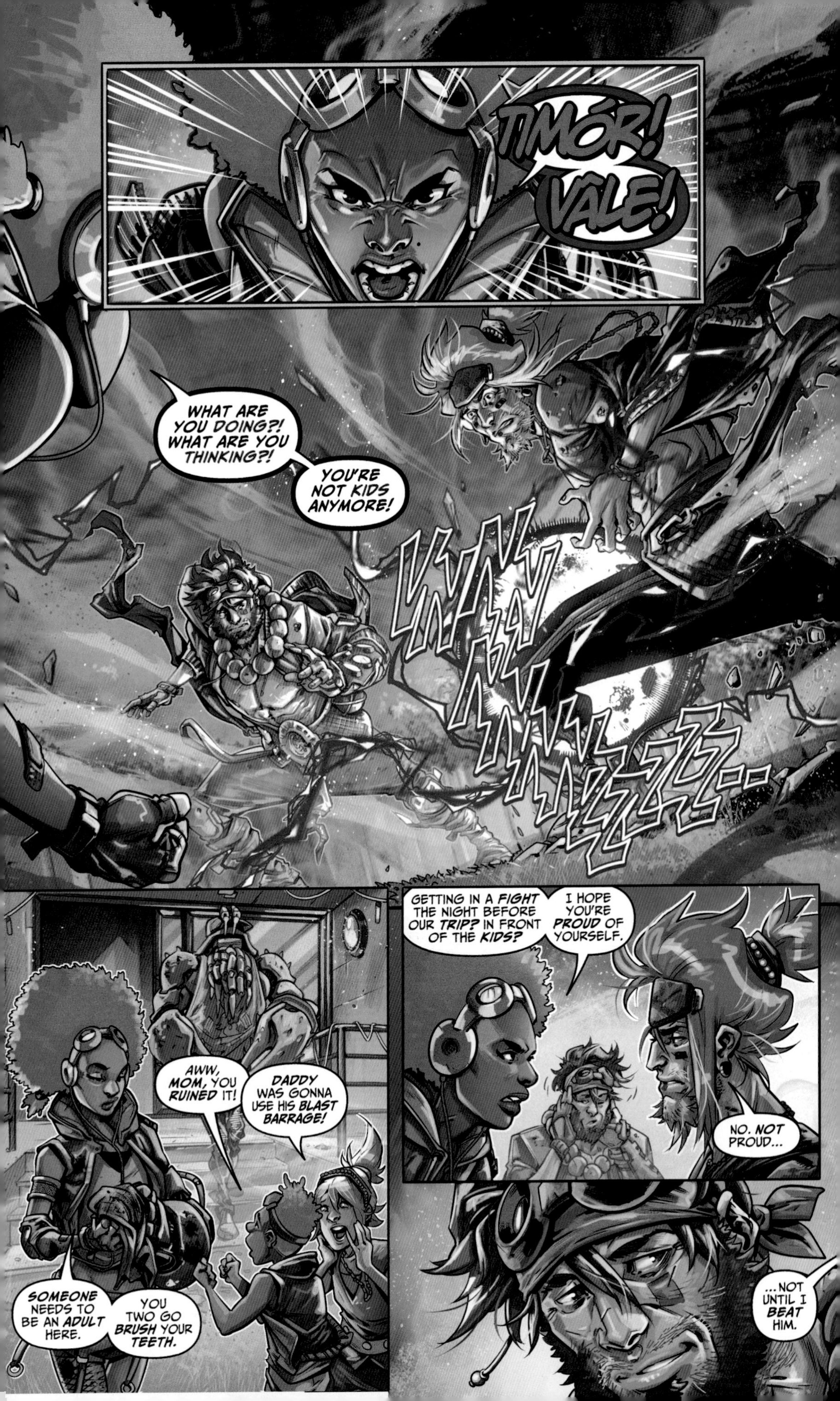
TIMÓR! VÂLE!
WHAT ARE YOU DOING?! WHAT ARE YOU THINKING?!
YOU'RE NOT KIDS ANYMORE!
VVVMMMMZZZZ...
AWW, MOM, YOU RUINED IT!
DADDY WAS GONNA USE HIS BLAST BARRAGE!
SOMEONE NEEDS TO BE AN ADULT HERE.
YOU TWO GO BRUSH YOUR TEETH.
GETTING IN A FIGHT THE NIGHT BEFORE OUR TRIP? IN FRONT OF THE KIDS?
I HOPE YOU'RE PROUD OF YOURSELF.
NO. NOT PROUD...
...NOT UNTIL I BEAT HIM.

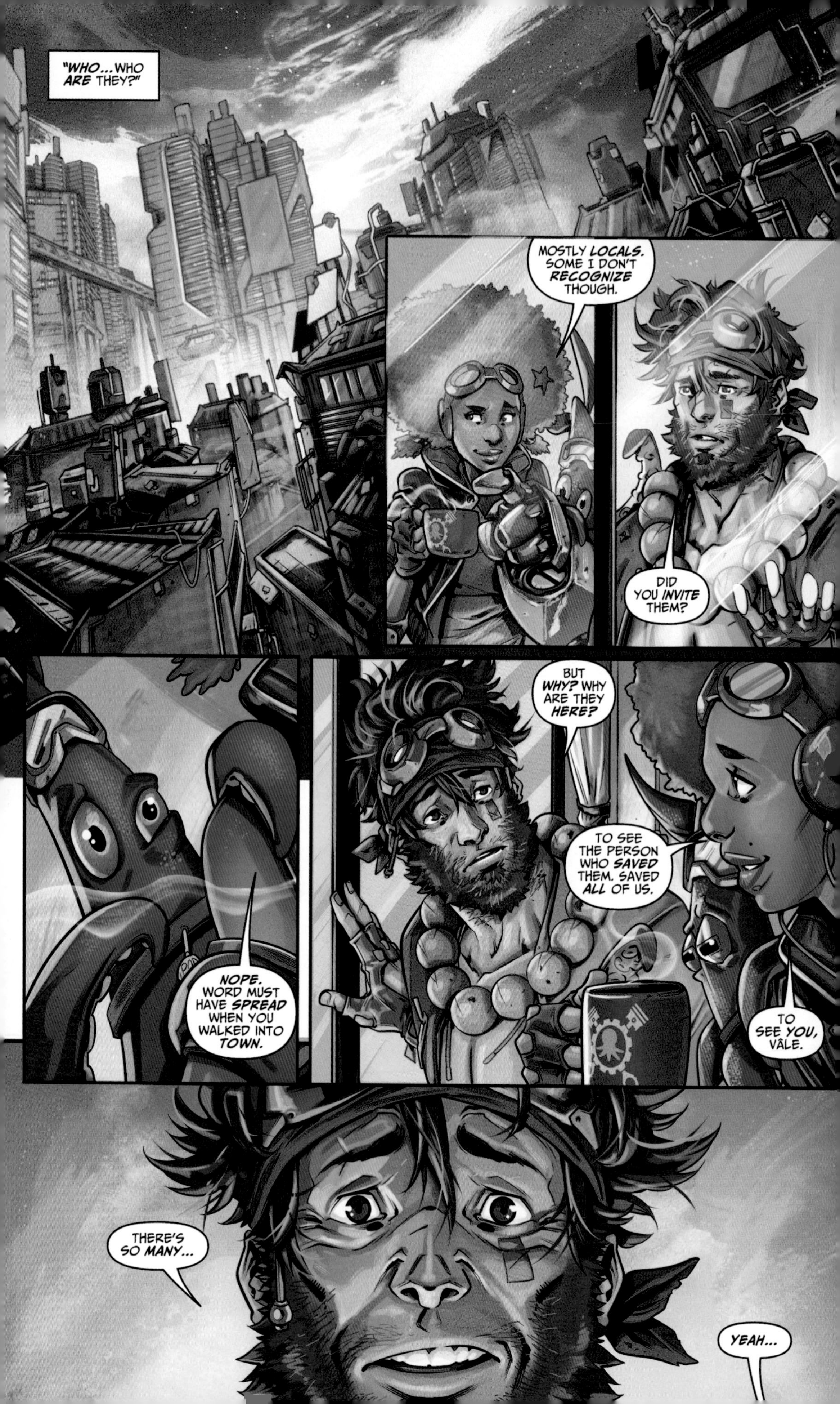
"WHO...WHO ARE THEY?"
MOSTLY LOCALS. SOME I DON'T RECOGNIZE THOUGH.
DID YOU INVITE THEM?
NOPE. WORD MUST HAVE SPREAD WHEN YOU WALKED INTO TOWN.
BUT WHY? WHY ARE THEY HERE?
TO SEE THE PERSON WHO SAVED THEM. SAVED ALL OF US.
TO SEE YOU, VÂLE.
THERE'S SO MANY...
YEAH...

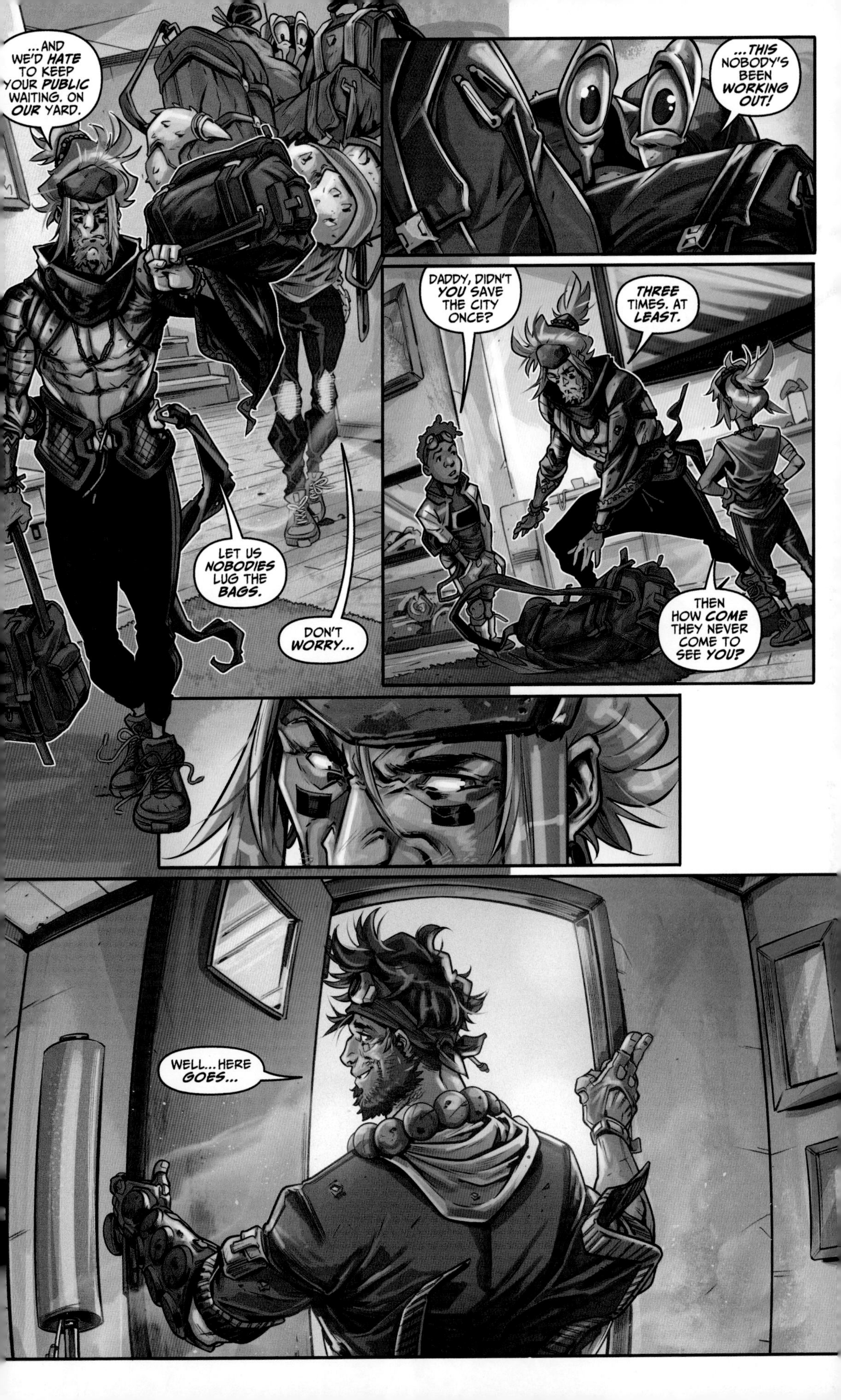
...AND WE'D HATE TO KEEP YOUR PUBLIC WAITING. ON OUR YARD.
...THIS NOBODY'S BEEN WORKING OUT!
LET US NOBODIES LUG THE BAGS.
DON'T WORRY...
DADDY, DIDN'T YOU SAVE THE CITY ONCE?
THREE TIMES. AT LEAST.
THEN HOW COME THEY NEVER COME TO SEE YOU?
WELL...HERE GOES...

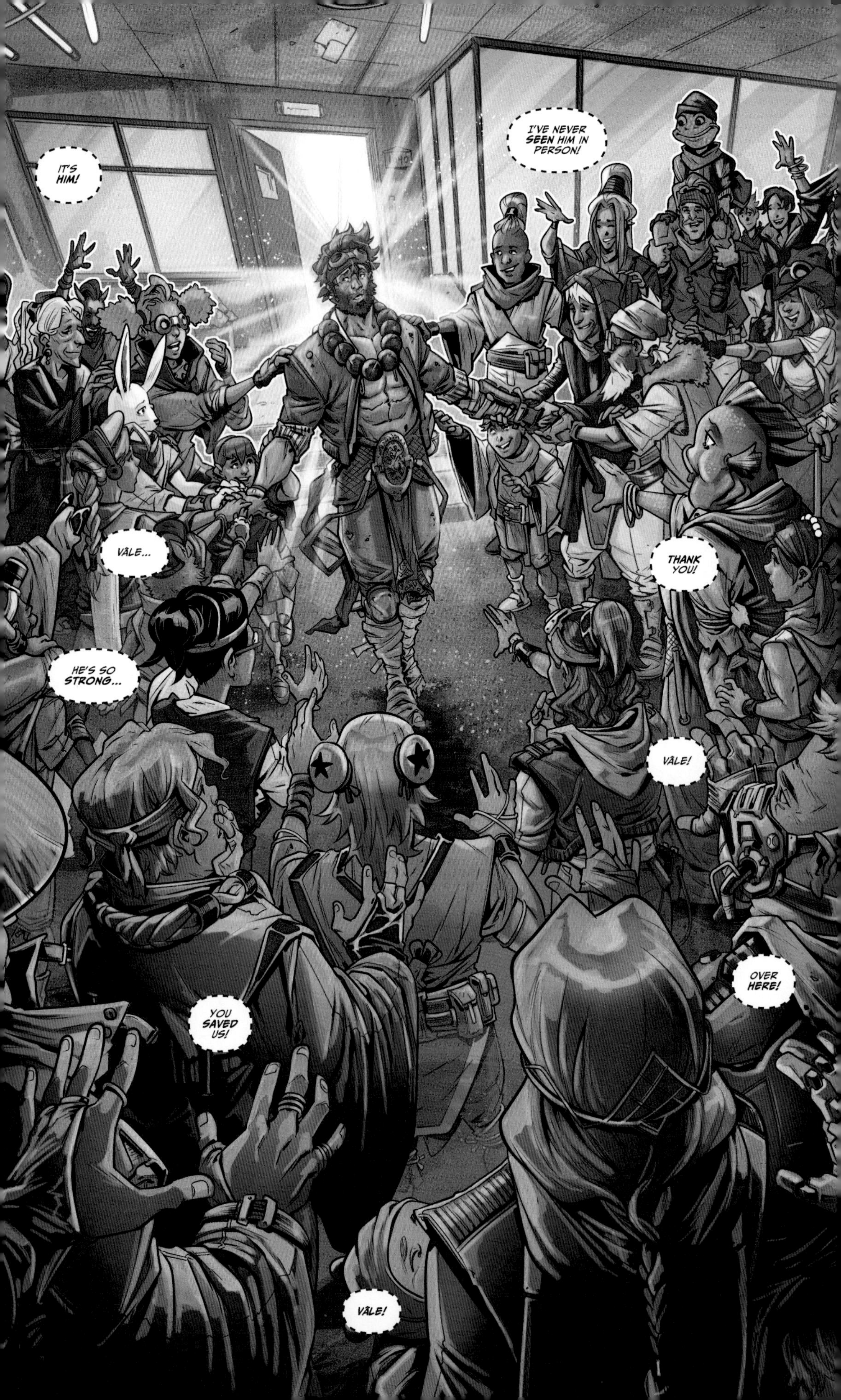
IT'S HIM!
I'VE NEVER SEEN HIM IN PERSON!
VÂLE...
THANK YOU!
HE'S SO STRONG...
VÂLE!
OVER HERE!
YOU SAVED US!
VÂLE!

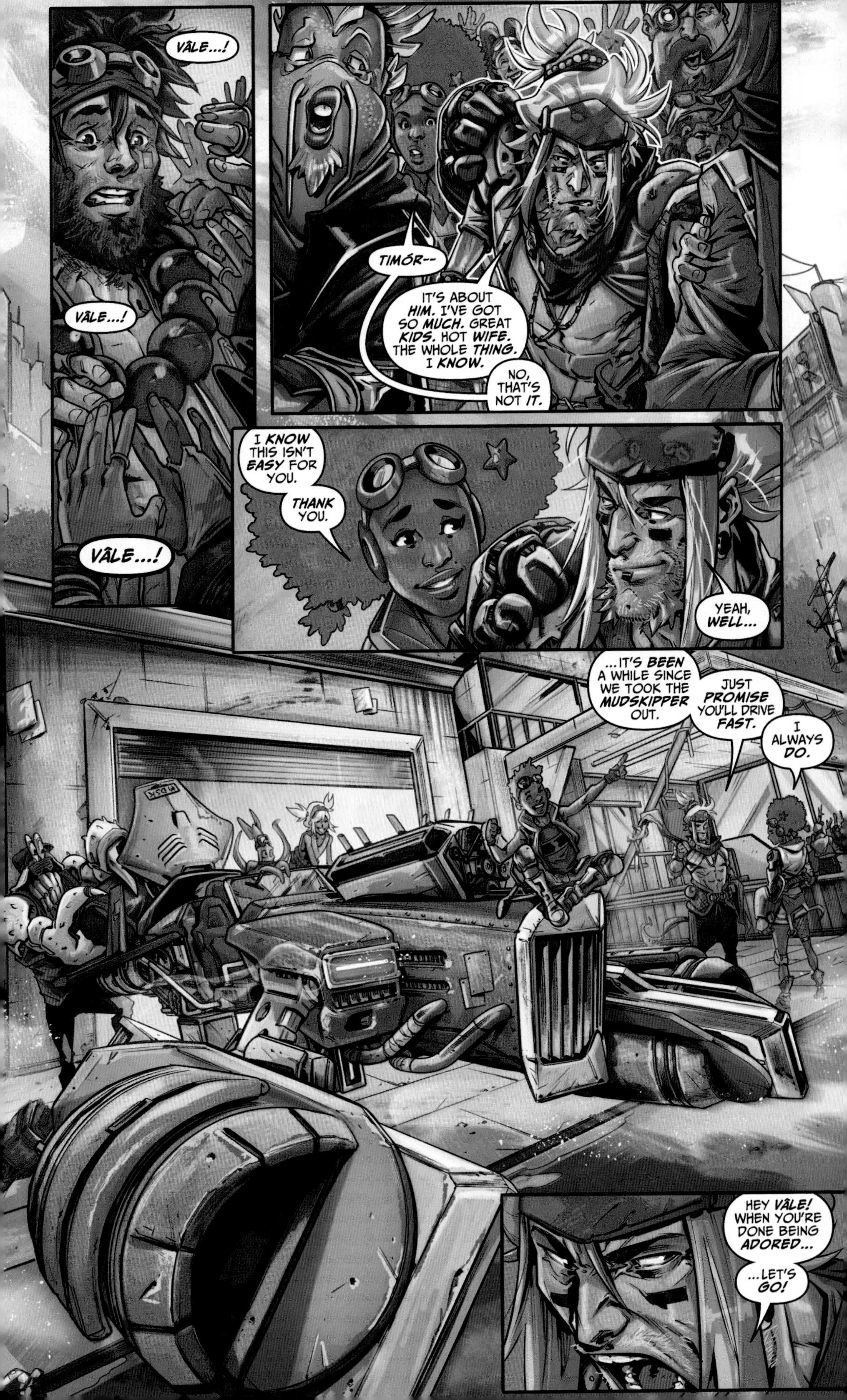
VÂLE...!
VÂLE...!
VÂLE...!
TIMÓR--
IT'S ABOUT HIM. I'VE GOT SO MUCH. GREAT KIDS. HOT WIFE. THE WHOLE THING. I KNOW.
NO, THAT'S NOT IT.
I KNOW THIS ISN'T EASY FOR YOU.
THANK YOU.
YEAH, WELL...
...IT'S BEEN A WHILE SINCE WE TOOK THE MUDSKIPPER OUT.
JUST PROMISE YOU'LL DRIVE FAST.
I ALWAYS DO.
HEY VÂLE! WHEN YOU'RE DONE BEING ADORED...
...LET'S GO!

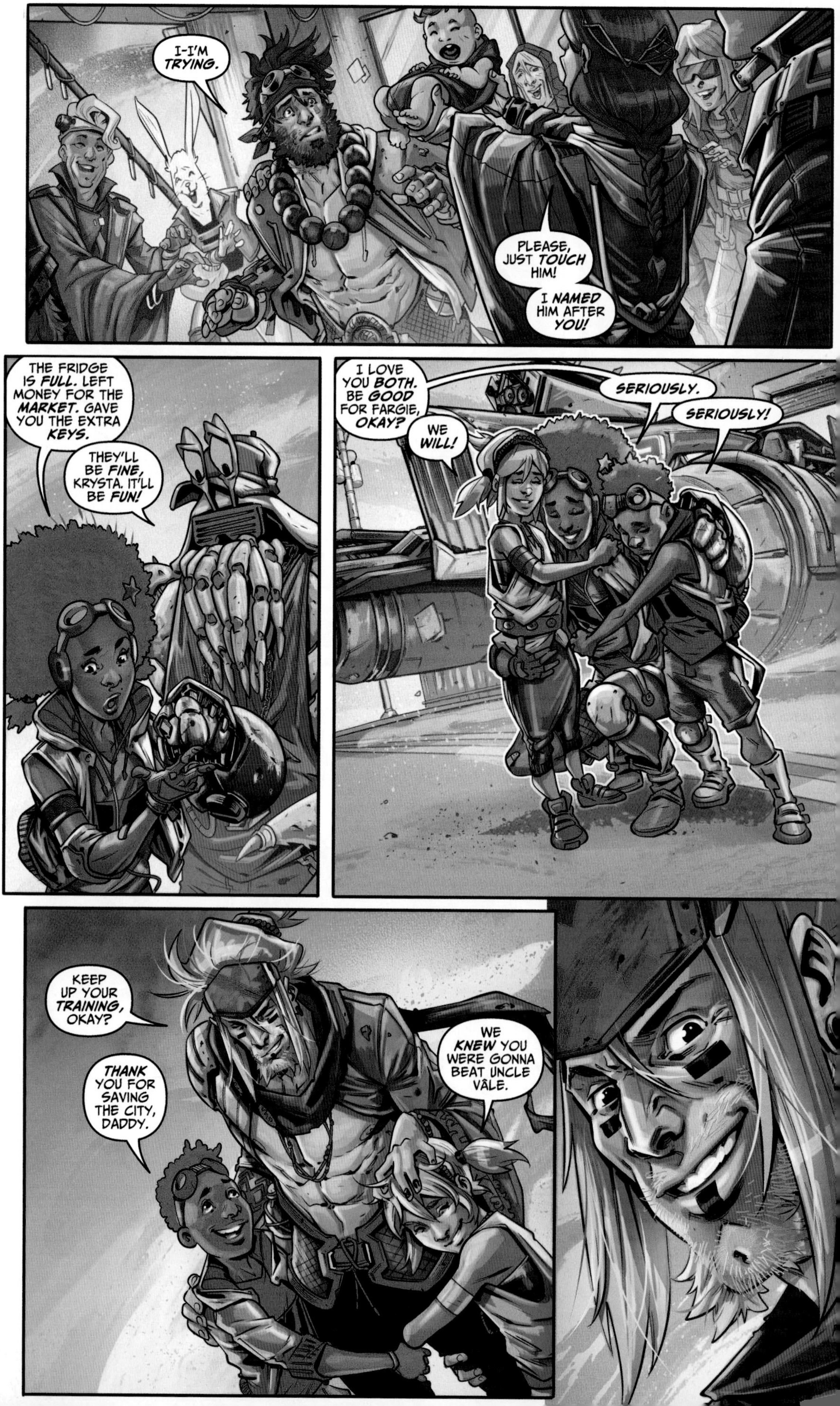
I-I'M *TRYING.*
PLEASE, JUST *TOUCH* HIM!
I *NAMED* HIM AFTER *YOU!*
THE FRIDGE IS *FULL.* LEFT MONEY FOR THE *MARKET.* GAVE YOU THE EXTRA *KEYS.*
THEY'LL BE *FINE,* KRYSTA. IT'LL BE *FUN!*
I LOVE YOU *BOTH.* BE *GOOD* FOR FARGIE, *OKAY?*
WE *WILL!*
SERIOUSLY.
SERIOUSLY!
KEEP UP YOUR *TRAINING,* OKAY?
THANK YOU FOR SAVING THE CITY, DADDY.
WE *KNEW* YOU WERE GONNA BEAT UNCLE VÂLE.

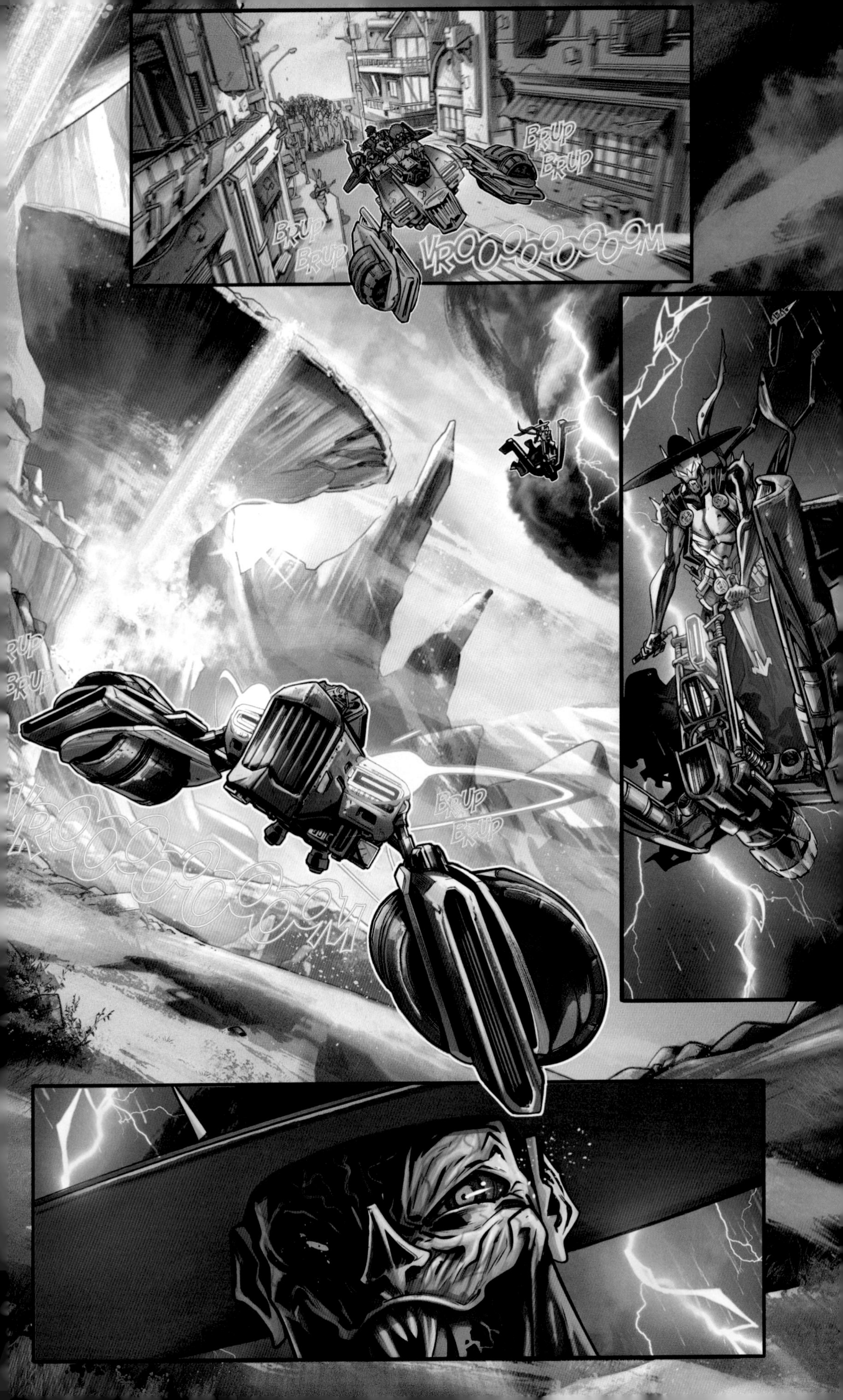
BRUP
BRUP
BRUP
BRUP
VROOOOOOOOOOM
BRUP
BRUP
VROOOOOOOOOOOM
BRUP
BRUP

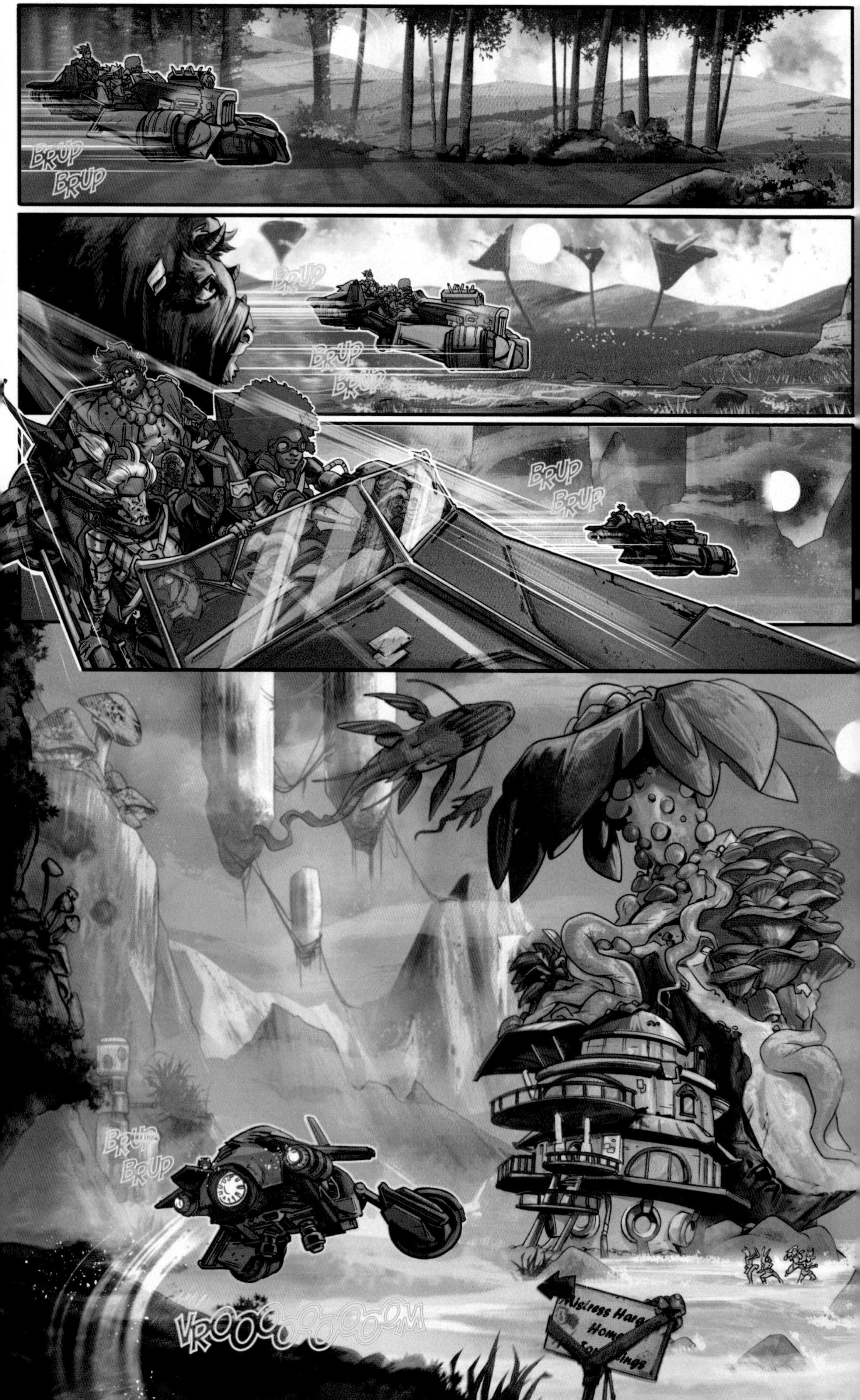

BRUP
BRUP
BRUP
BRUP
BRUP
BRUP
BRUP
BRUP
BRUP
VROOOOOOOOOM

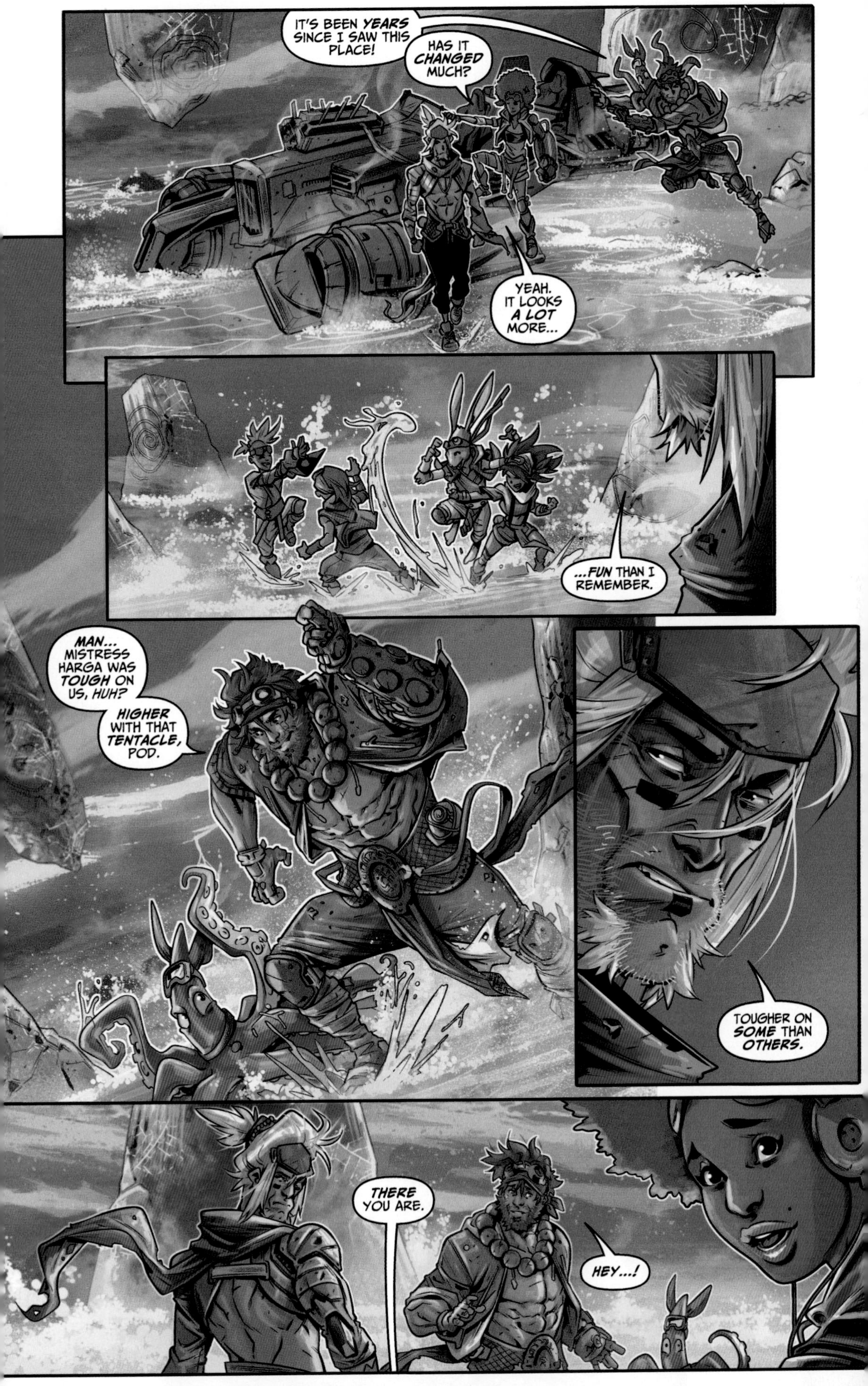
IT'S BEEN YEARS SINCE I SAW THIS PLACE!
HAS IT CHANGED MUCH?
YEAH. IT LOOKS A LOT MORE...
...FUN THAN I REMEMBER.
MAN... MISTRESS HARGA WAS TOUGH ON US, HUH?
HIGHER WITH THAT TENTACLE, POD.
TOUGHER ON SOME THAN OTHERS.
THERE YOU ARE.
HEY...!

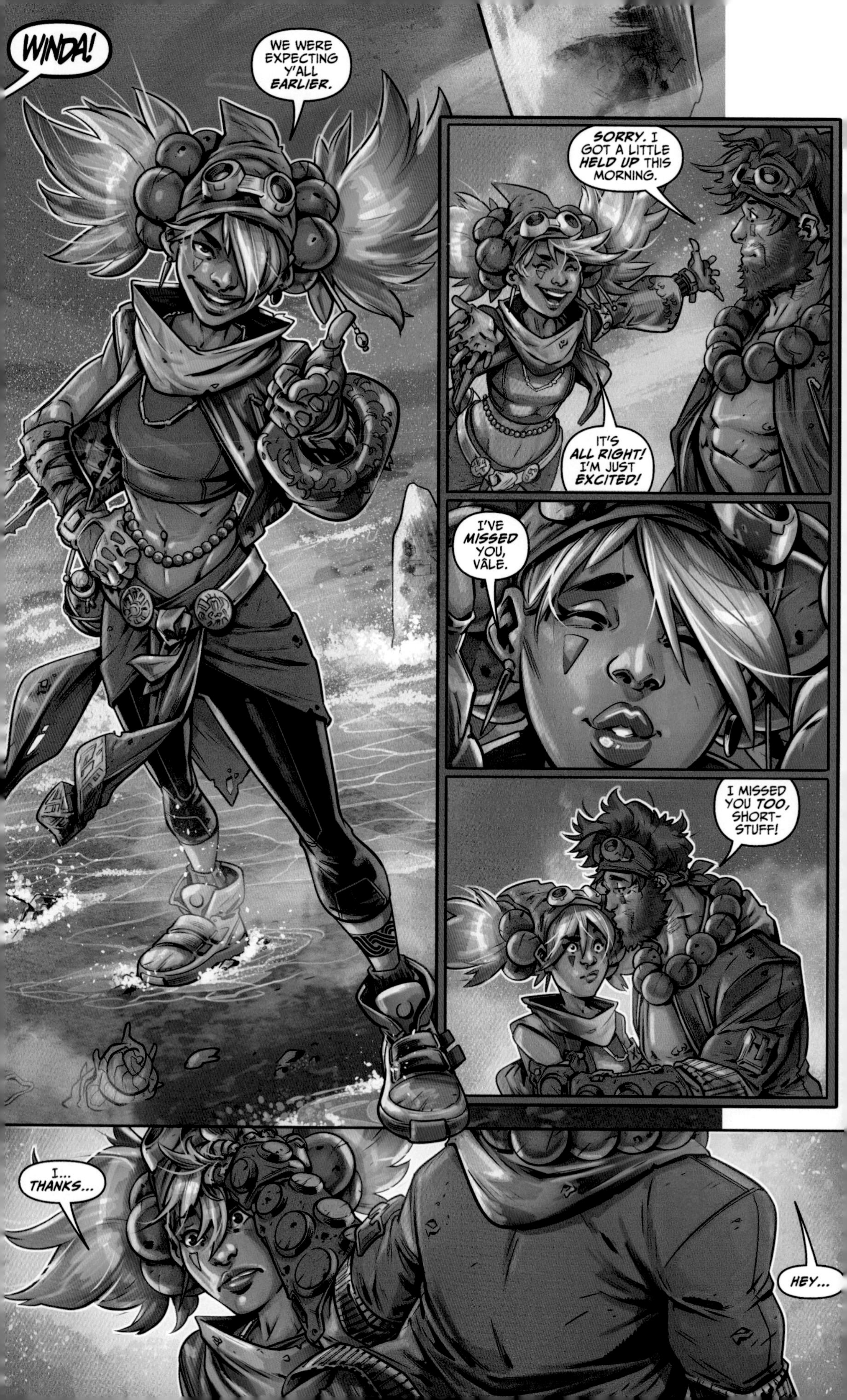
WINDA!
WE WERE EXPECTING Y'ALL EARLIER.
SORRY. I GOT A LITTLE HELD UP THIS MORNING.
IT'S ALL RIGHT! I'M JUST EXCITED!
I'VE MISSED YOU, VÂLE.
I MISSED YOU TOO, SHORT-STUFF!
I... THANKS...
HEY...

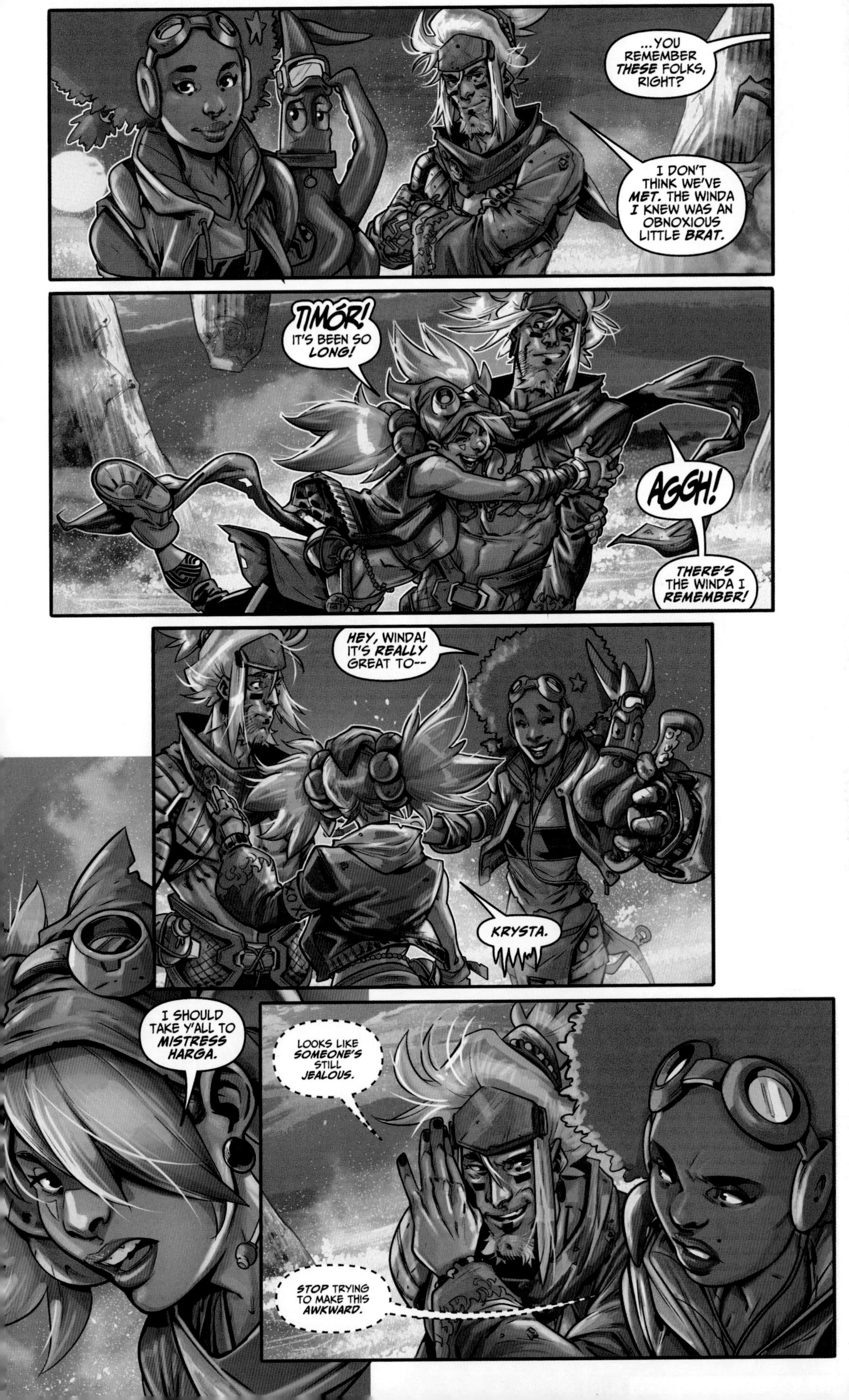

...YOU REMEMBER THESE FOLKS, RIGHT?
I DON'T THINK WE'VE MET. THE WINDA I KNEW WAS AN OBNOXIOUS LITTLE BRAT.
TIMÓR! IT'S BEEN SO LONG!
AGGH!
THERE'S THE WINDA I REMEMBER!
HEY, WINDA! IT'S REALLY GREAT TO--
KRYSTA.
I SHOULD TAKE Y'ALL TO MISTRESS HARGA.
LOOKS LIKE SOMEONE'S STILL JEALOUS.
STOP TRYING TO MAKE THIS AWKWARD.

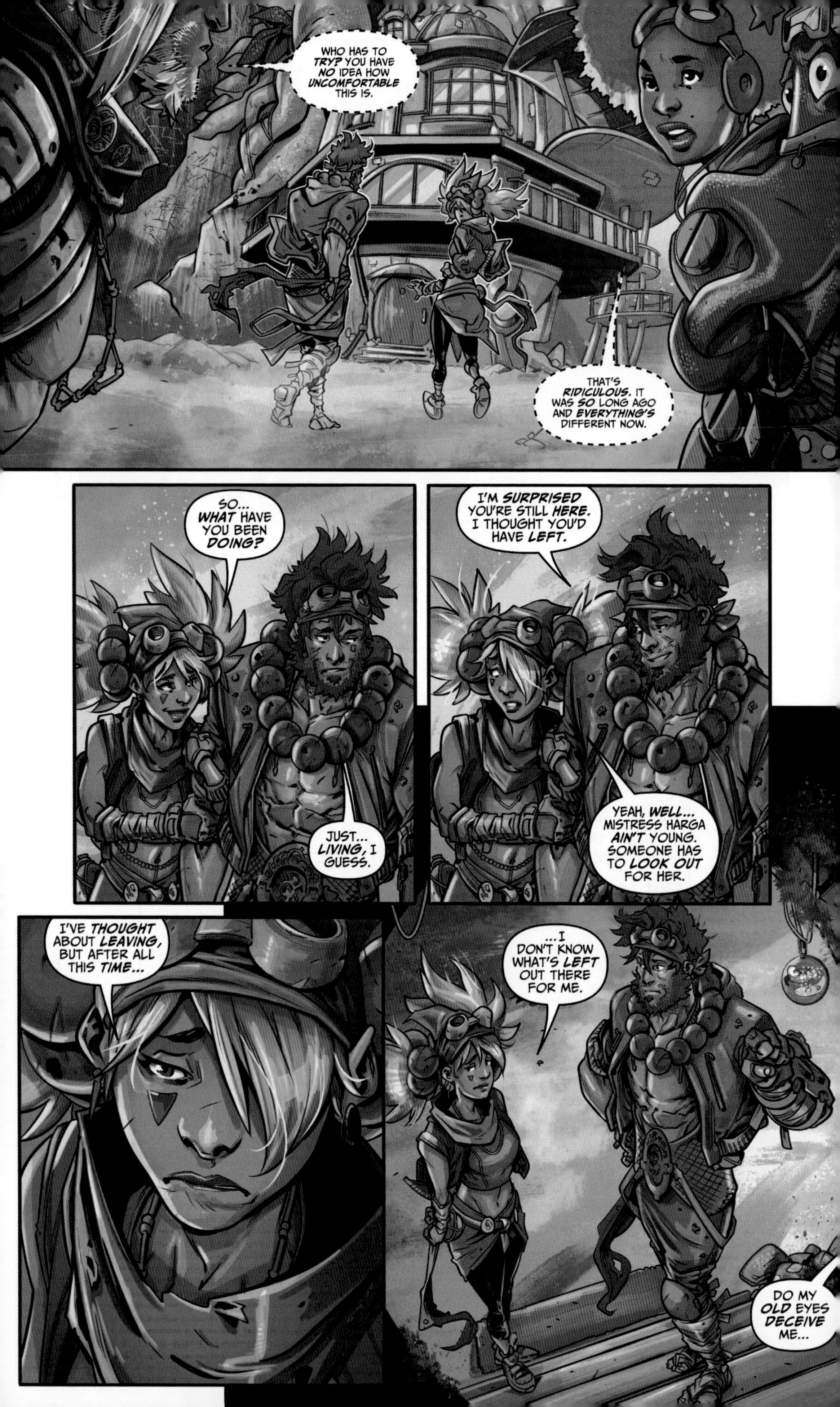
WHO HAS TO TRY? YOU HAVE NO IDEA HOW UNCOMFORTABLE THIS IS.
THAT'S RIDICULOUS. IT WAS SO LONG AGO AND EVERYTHING'S DIFFERENT NOW.
SO... WHAT HAVE YOU BEEN DOING?
JUST... LIVING, I GUESS.
I'M SURPRISED YOU'RE STILL HERE. I THOUGHT YOU'D HAVE LEFT.
YEAH, WELL... MISTRESS HARGA AIN'T YOUNG. SOMEONE HAS TO LOOK OUT FOR HER.
I'VE THOUGHT ABOUT LEAVING, BUT AFTER ALL THIS TIME...
...I DON'T KNOW WHAT'S LEFT OUT THERE FOR ME.
DO MY OLD EYES DECEIVE ME...

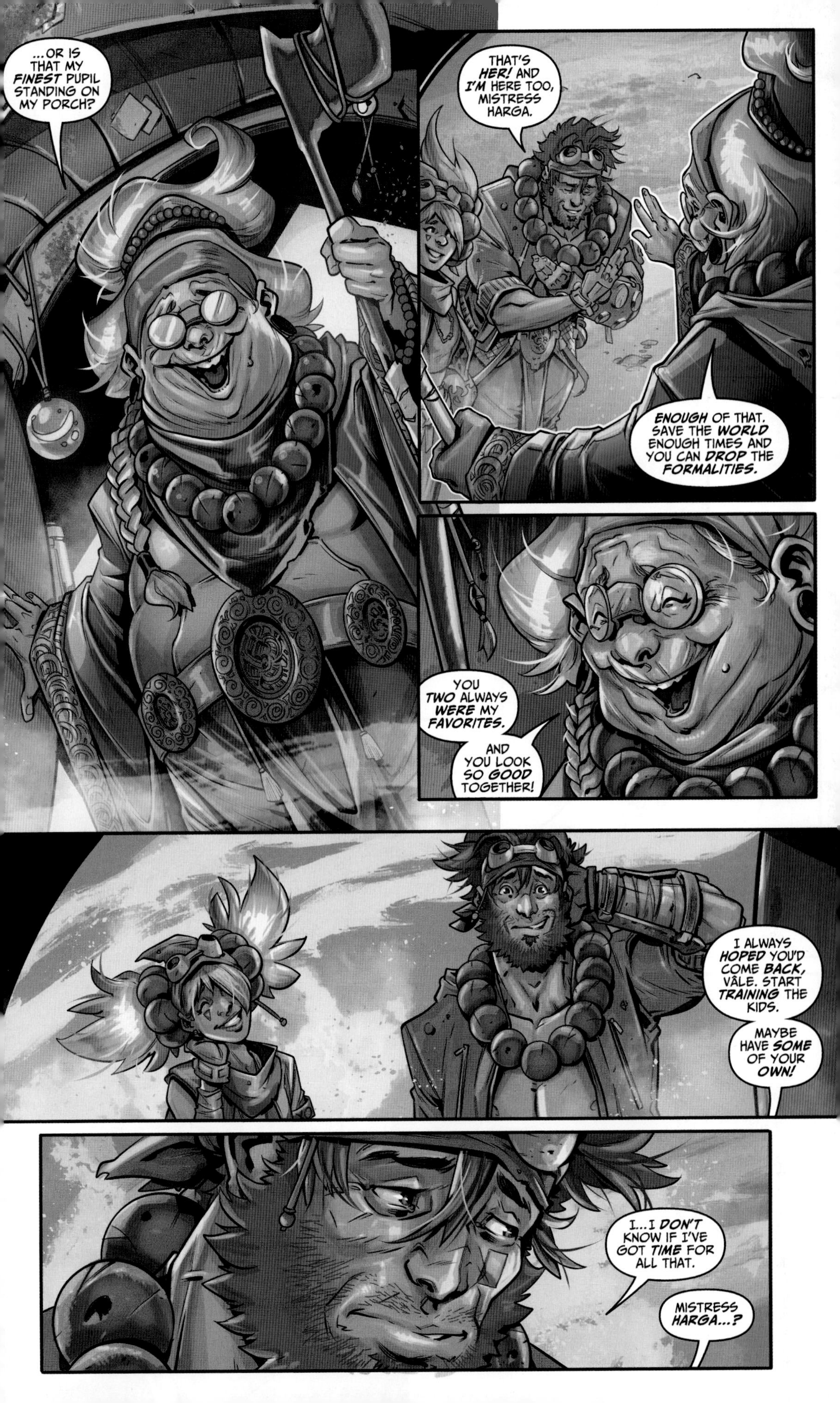
...OR IS THAT MY FINEST PUPIL STANDING ON MY PORCH?
THAT'S HER! AND I'M HERE TOO, MISTRESS HARGA.
ENOUGH OF THAT. SAVE THE WORLD ENOUGH TIMES AND YOU CAN DROP THE FORMALITIES.
YOU TWO ALWAYS WERE MY FAVORITES.
AND YOU LOOK SO GOOD TOGETHER!
I ALWAYS HOPED YOU'D COME BACK, VÂLE. START TRAINING THE KIDS.
MAYBE HAVE SOME OF YOUR OWN!
I...I DON'T KNOW IF I'VE GOT TIME FOR ALL THAT.
MISTRESS HARGA...?

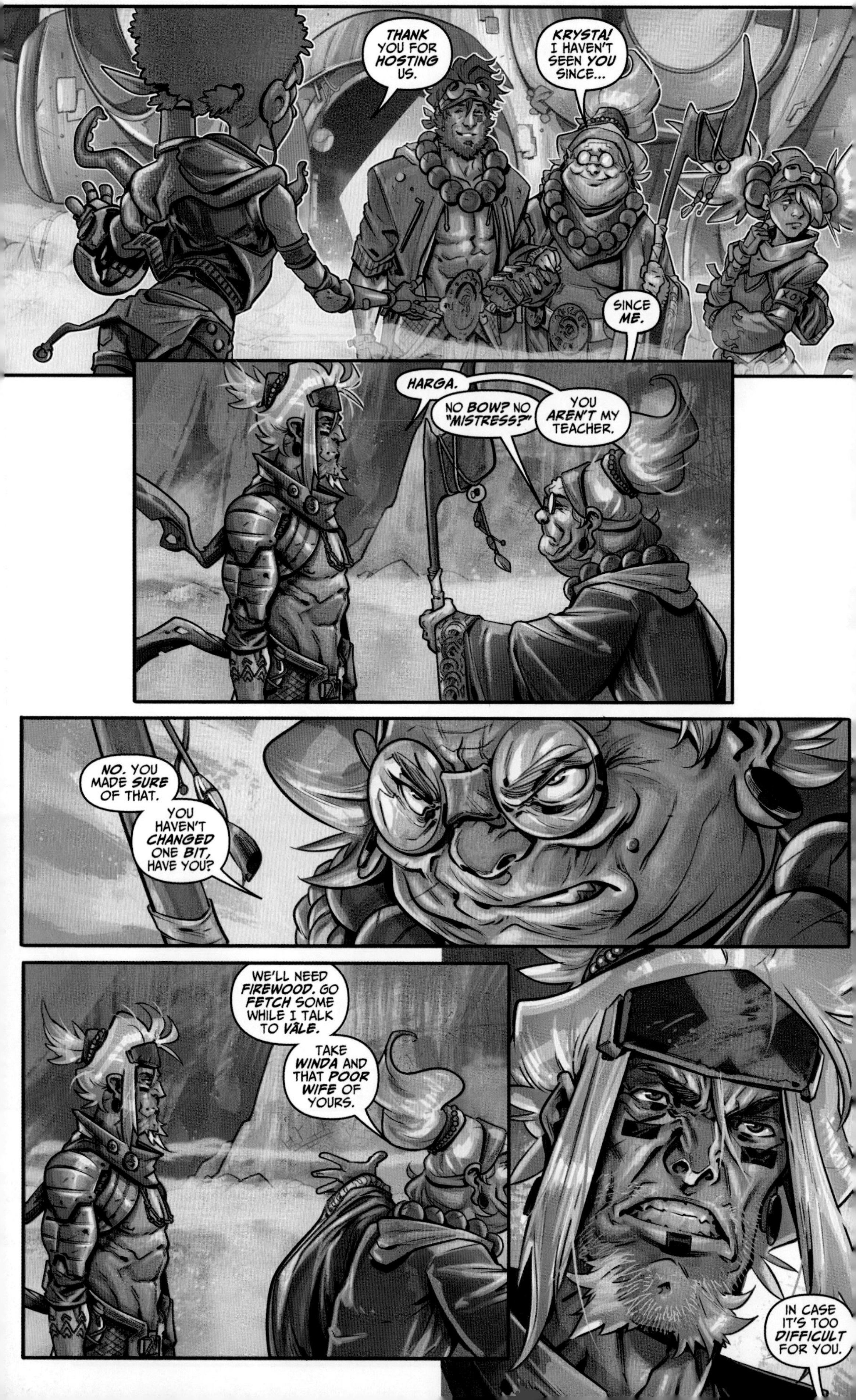

THANK YOU FOR HOSTING US.
KRYSTA! I HAVEN'T SEEN YOU SINCE...
SINCE ME.
HARGA.
NO BOW? NO "MISTRESS?"
YOU AREN'T MY TEACHER.
NO. YOU MADE SURE OF THAT.
YOU HAVEN'T CHANGED ONE BIT, HAVE YOU?
WE'LL NEED FIREWOOD. GO FETCH SOME WHILE I TALK TO VÄLE.
TAKE WINDA AND THAT POOR WIFE OF YOURS.
IN CASE IT'S TOO DIFFICULT FOR YOU.

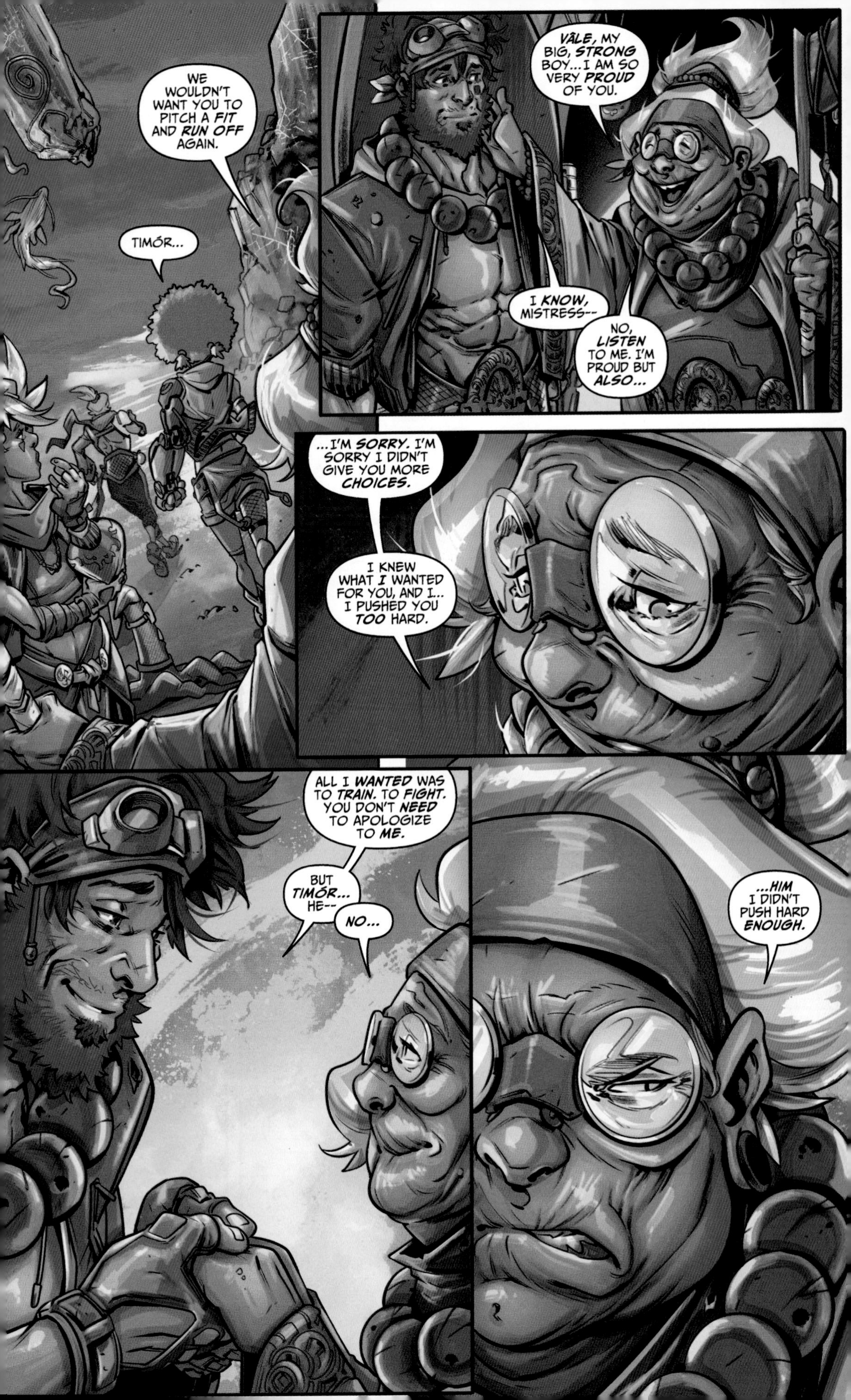
WE WOULDN'T WANT YOU TO PITCH A FIT AND RUN OFF AGAIN.
TIMÓR...
VÂLE, MY BIG, STRONG BOY...I AM SO VERY PROUD OF YOU.
I KNOW, MISTRESS--
NO, LISTEN TO ME. I'M PROUD BUT ALSO...
...I'M SORRY. I'M SORRY I DIDN'T GIVE YOU MORE CHOICES.
I KNEW WHAT I WANTED FOR YOU, AND I... I PUSHED YOU TOO HARD.
ALL I WANTED WAS TO TRAIN. TO FIGHT. YOU DON'T NEED TO APOLOGIZE TO ME.
BUT TIMÓR... HE--
NO...
...HIM I DIDN'T PUSH HARD ENOUGH.

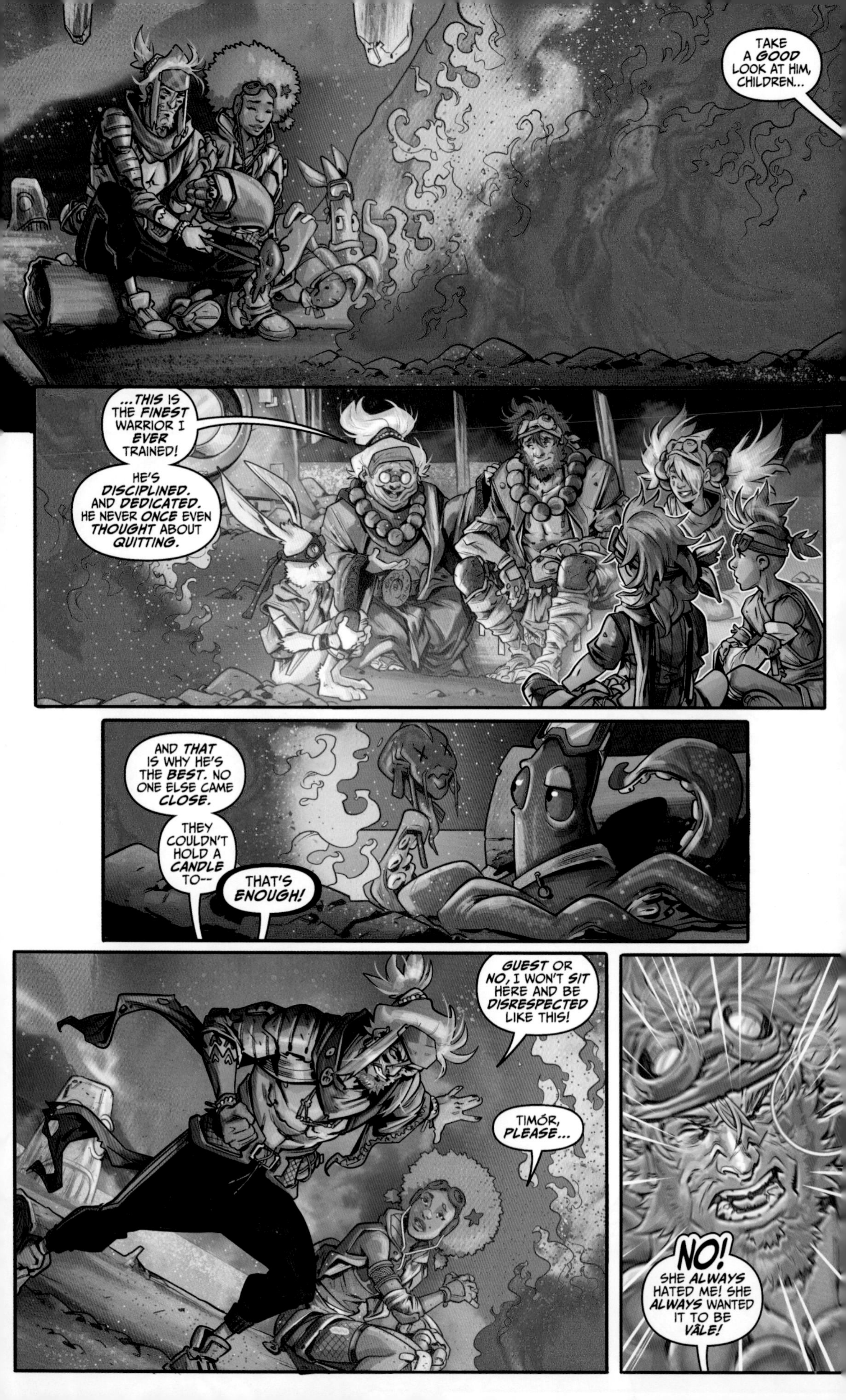
TAKE A GOOD LOOK AT HIM, CHILDREN...
...THIS IS THE FINEST WARRIOR I EVER TRAINED!
HE'S DISCIPLINED. AND DEDICATED. HE NEVER ONCE EVEN THOUGHT ABOUT QUITTING.
AND THAT IS WHY HE'S THE BEST. NO ONE ELSE CAME CLOSE.
THEY COULDN'T HOLD A CANDLE TO--
THAT'S ENOUGH!
GUEST OR NO, I WON'T SIT HERE AND BE DISRESPECTED LIKE THIS!
TIMÓR, PLEASE...
NO!
SHE ALWAYS HATED ME! SHE ALWAYS WANTED IT TO BE VÂLE!

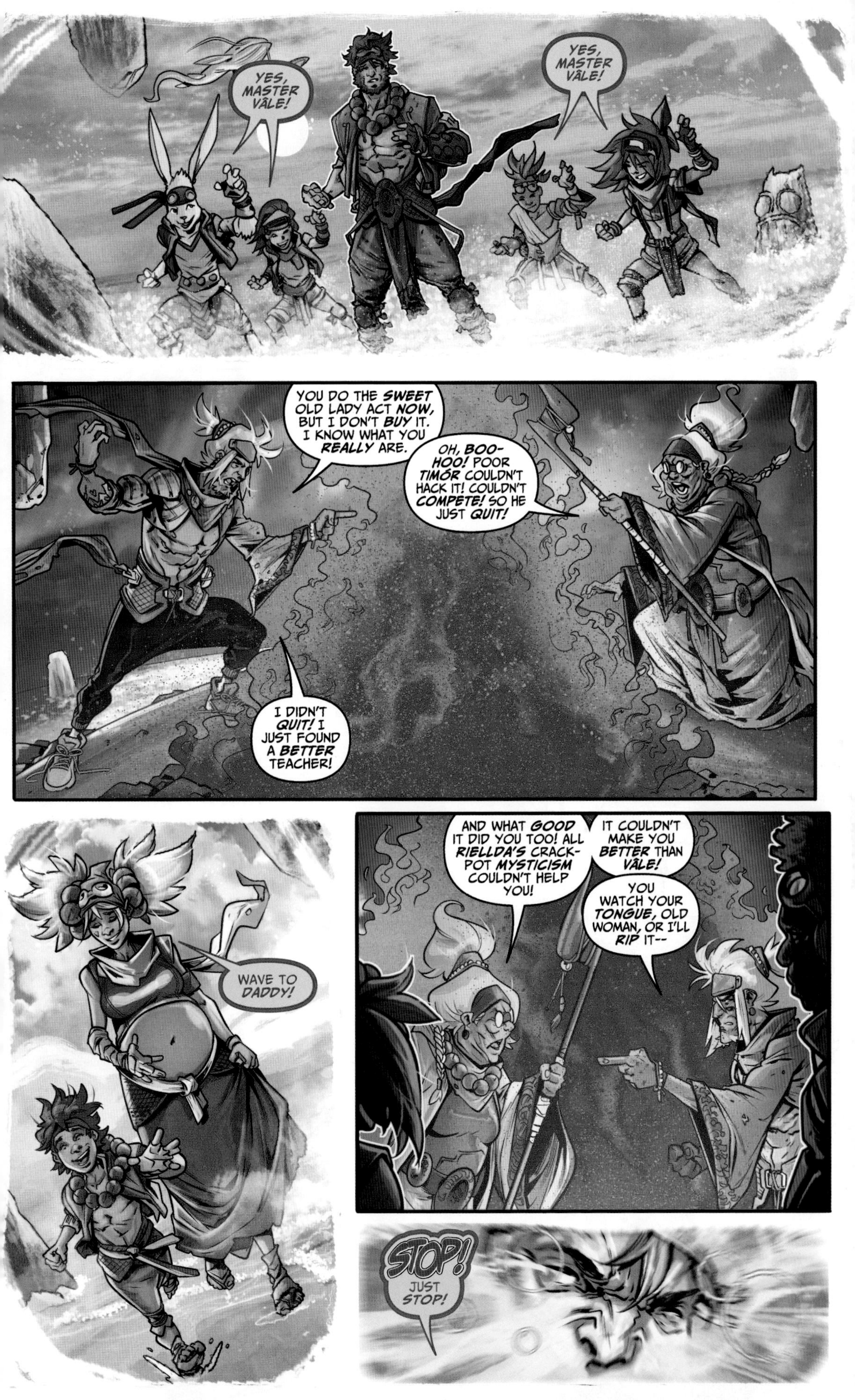
YES, MASTER VÂLE!
YES, MASTER VÂLE!
YOU DO THE SWEET OLD LADY ACT NOW, BUT I DON'T BUY IT. I KNOW WHAT YOU REALLY ARE.
OH, BOO-HOO! POOR TIMÓR COULDN'T HACK IT! COULDN'T COMPETE! SO HE JUST QUIT!
I DIDN'T QUIT! I JUST FOUND A BETTER TEACHER!
WAVE TO DADDY!
AND WHAT GOOD IT DID YOU TOO! ALL RIELLDA'S CRACK-POT MYSTICISM COULDN'T HELP YOU!
IT COULDN'T MAKE YOU BETTER THAN VÂLE!
YOU WATCH YOUR TONGUE, OLD WOMAN, OR I'LL RIP IT--
STOP! JUST STOP!

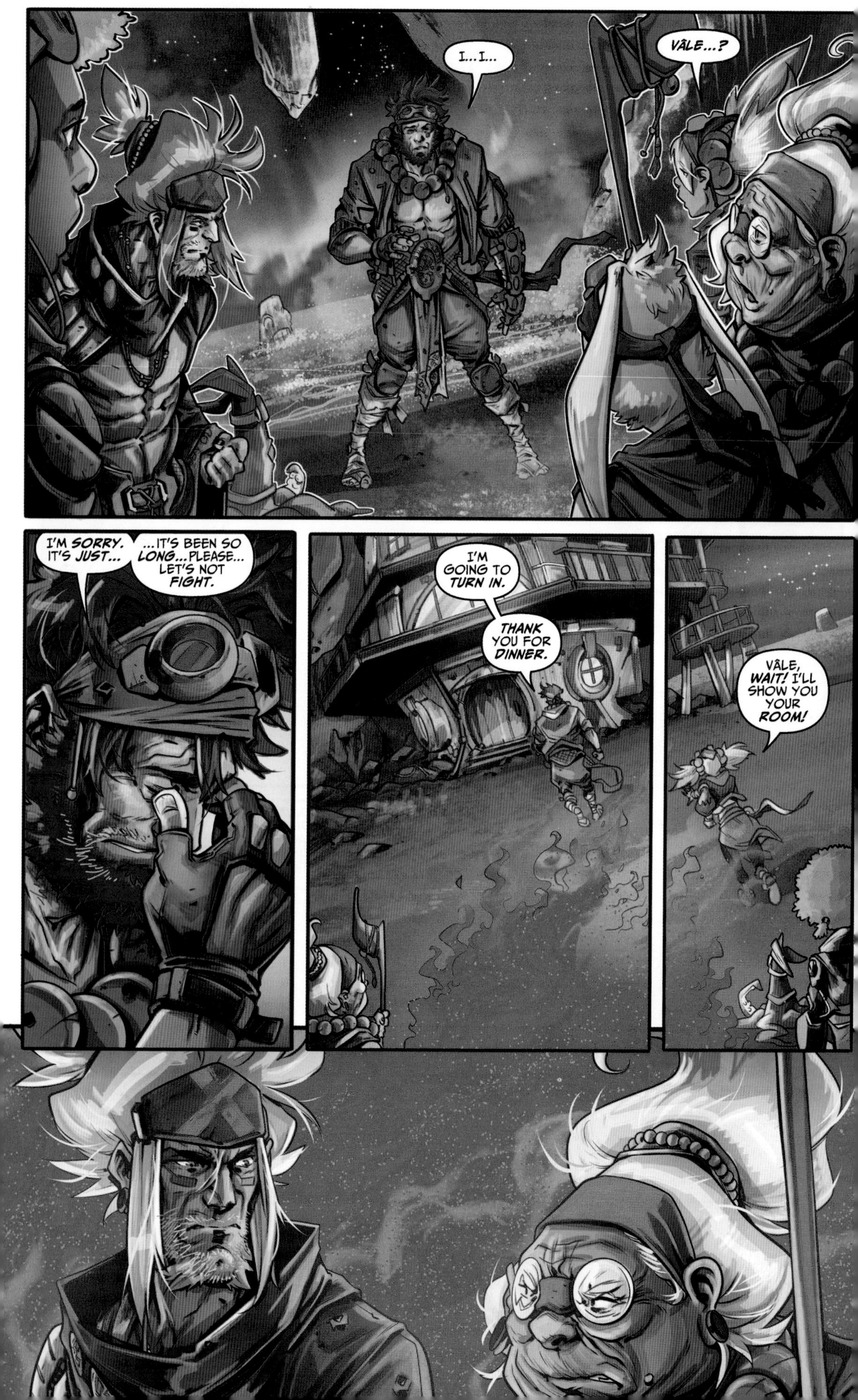
I... I...
VÂLE...?
I'M SORRY. IT'S JUST...
...IT'S BEEN SO LONG... PLEASE... LET'S NOT FIGHT.
I'M GOING TO TURN IN.
THANK YOU FOR DINNER.
VÂLE, WAIT! I'LL SHOW YOU YOUR ROOM!

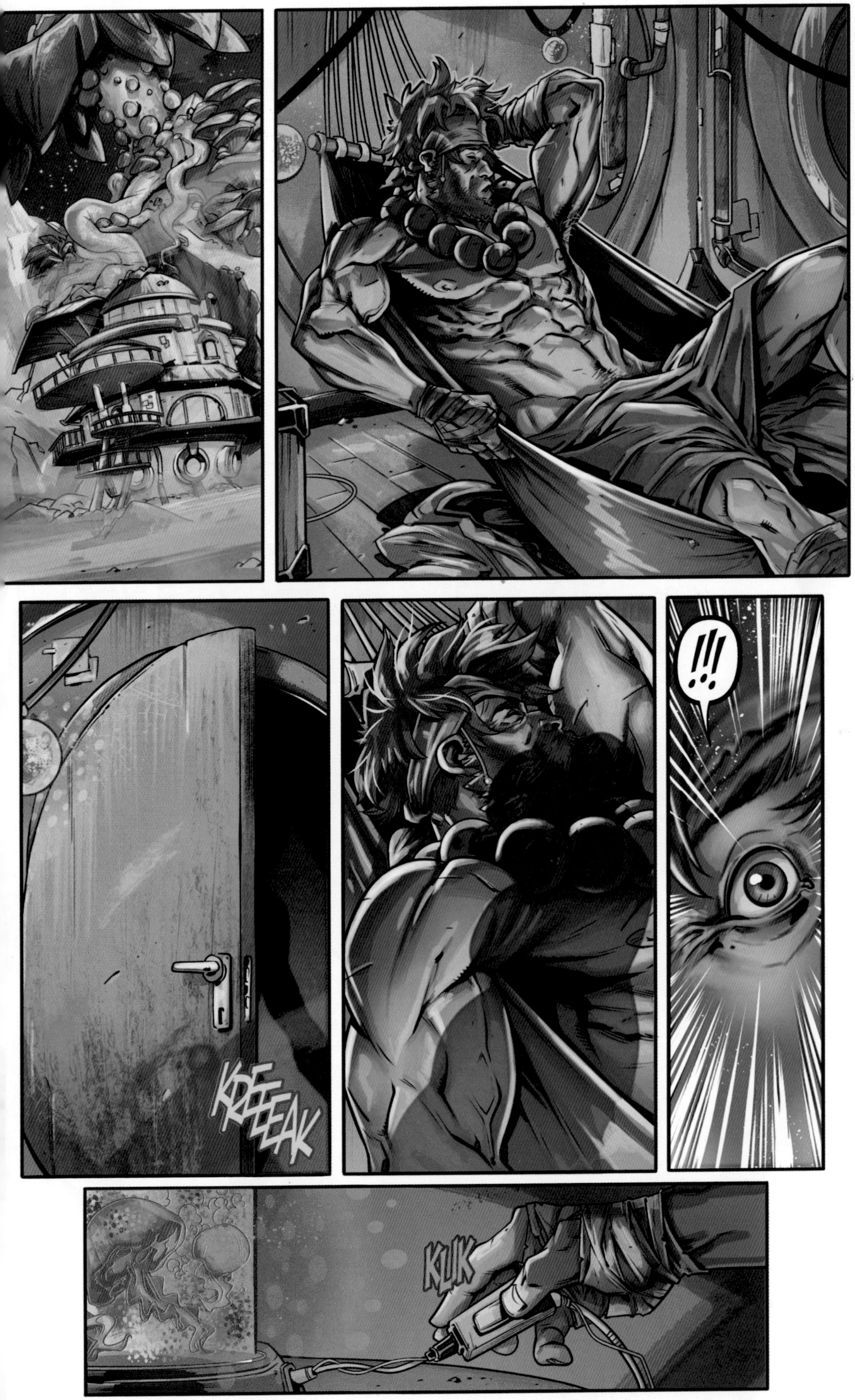
KREEEEAK
!!!
KLIK

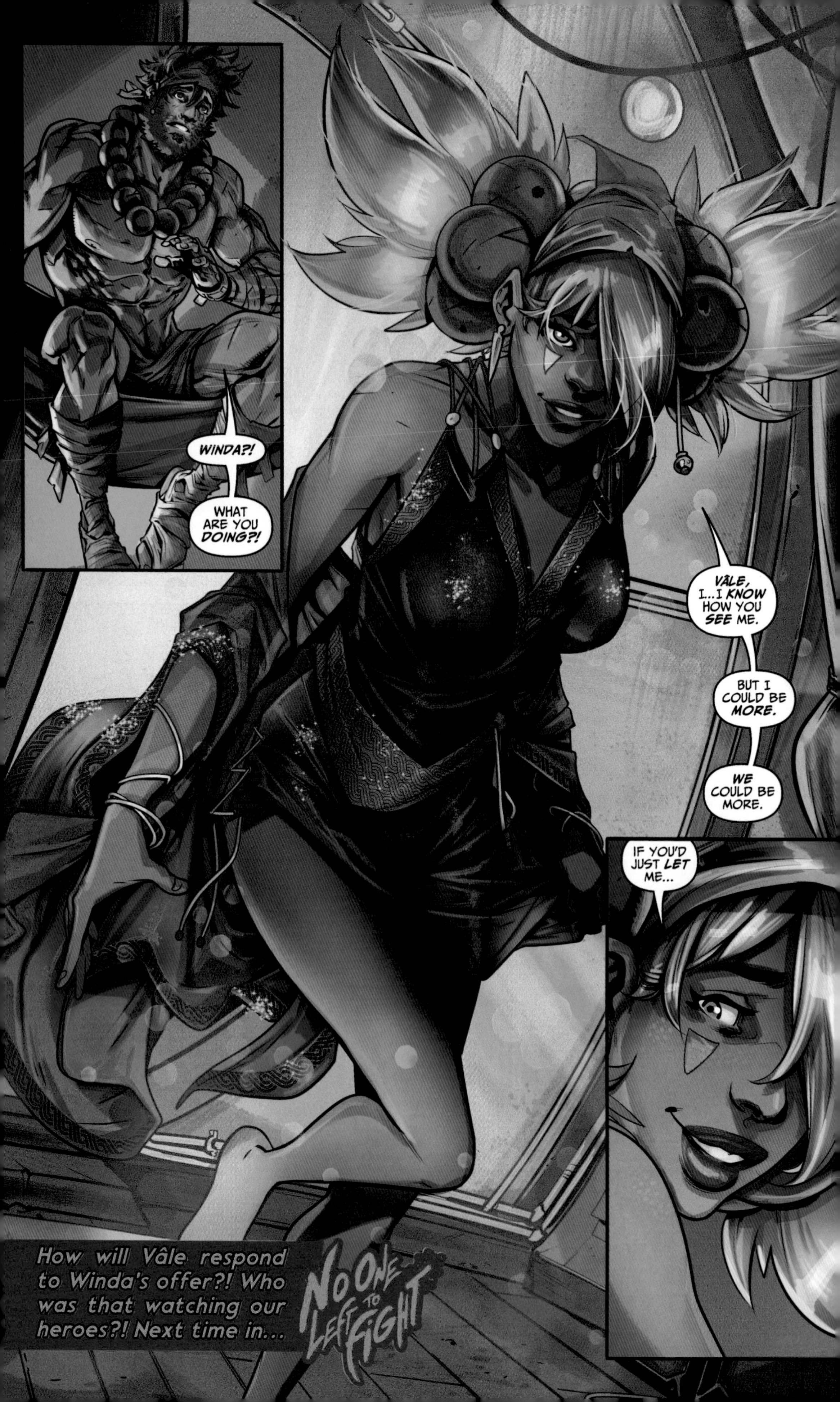
WINDA?!
WHAT ARE YOU DOING?!
VÂLE, I...I KNOW HOW YOU SEE ME.
BUT I COULD BE MORE.
WE COULD BE MORE.
IF YOU'D JUST LET ME...
How will Vâle respond to Winda's offer?! Who was that watching our heroes?! Next time in...
NO ONE LEFT TO FIGHT

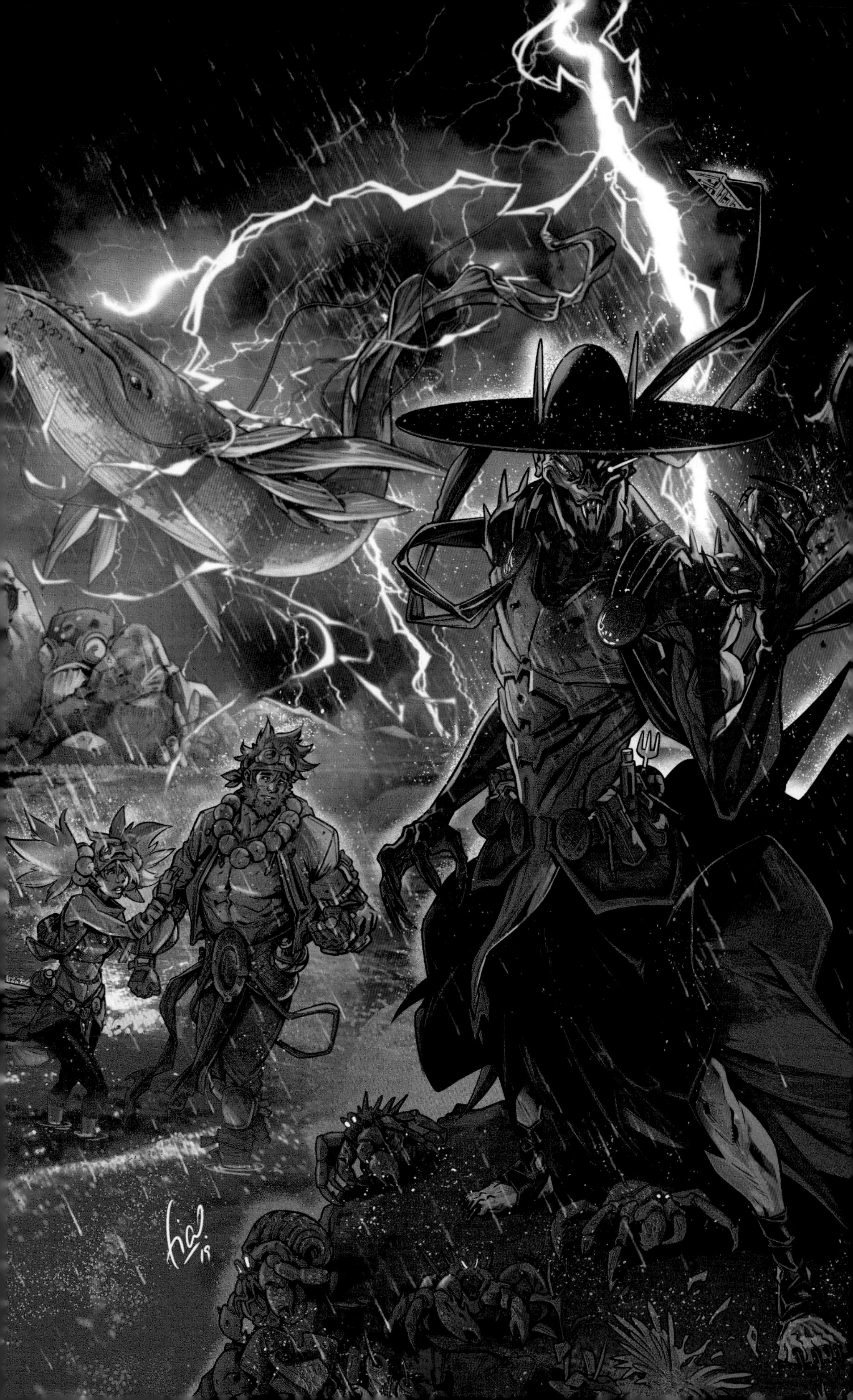

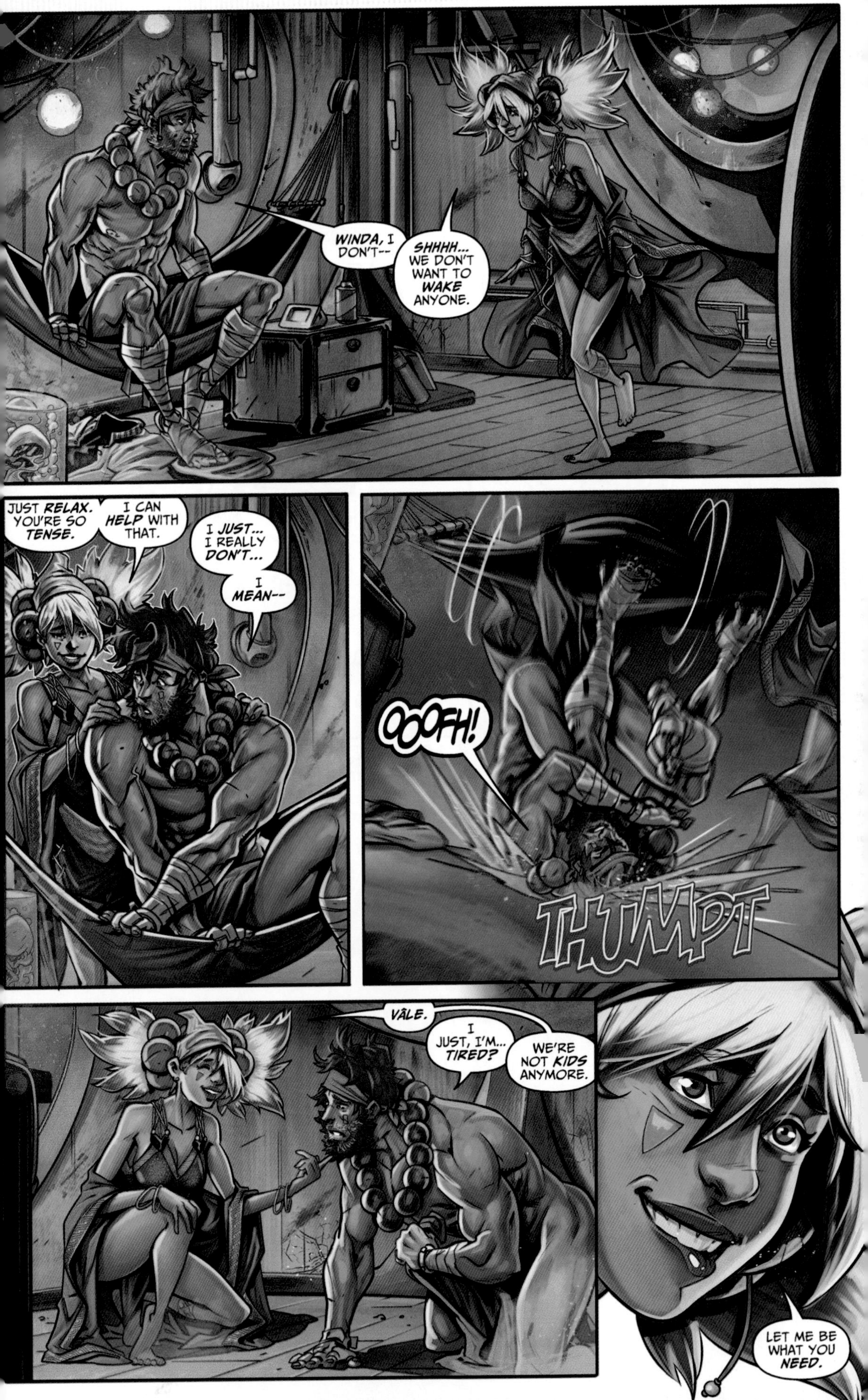
WINDA, I DON'T--
SHHHH... WE DON'T WANT TO WAKE ANYONE.
JUST RELAX. YOU'RE SO TENSE.
I CAN HELP WITH THAT.
I JUST... I REALLY DON'T...
I MEAN--
OOOFH!
THUMPT
VÂLE.
I JUST, I'M... TIRED?
WE'RE NOT KIDS ANYMORE.
LET ME BE WHAT YOU NEED.

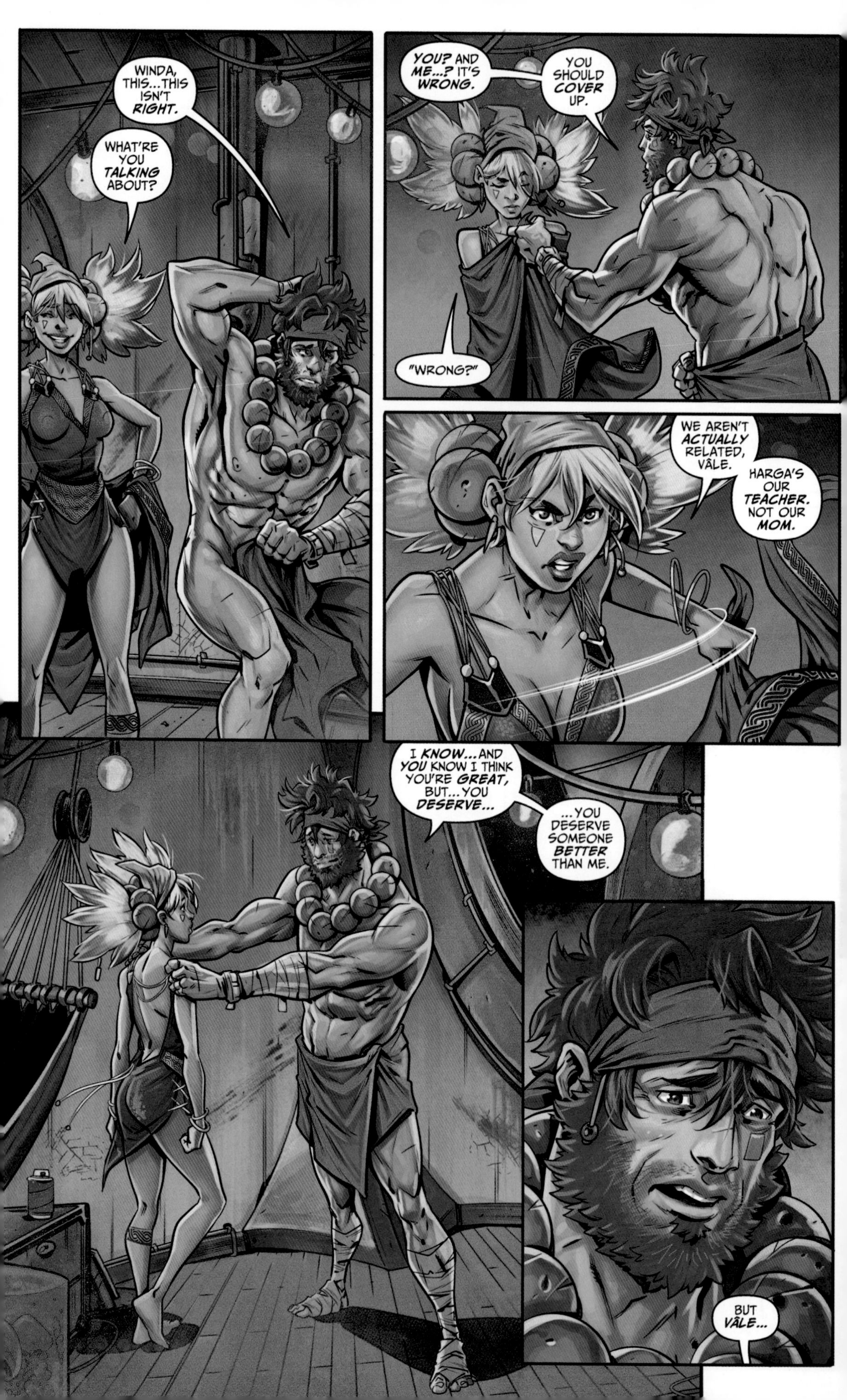
WINDA, THIS...THIS ISN'T RIGHT.
WHAT'RE YOU TALKING ABOUT?
YOU? AND ME...? IT'S WRONG.
YOU SHOULD COVER UP.
"WRONG?"
WE AREN'T ACTUALLY RELATED, VÂLE.
HARGA'S OUR TEACHER. NOT OUR MOM.
I KNOW...AND YOU KNOW I THINK YOU'RE GREAT, BUT...YOU DESERVE...
...YOU DESERVE SOMEONE BETTER THAN ME.
BUT VÂLE...

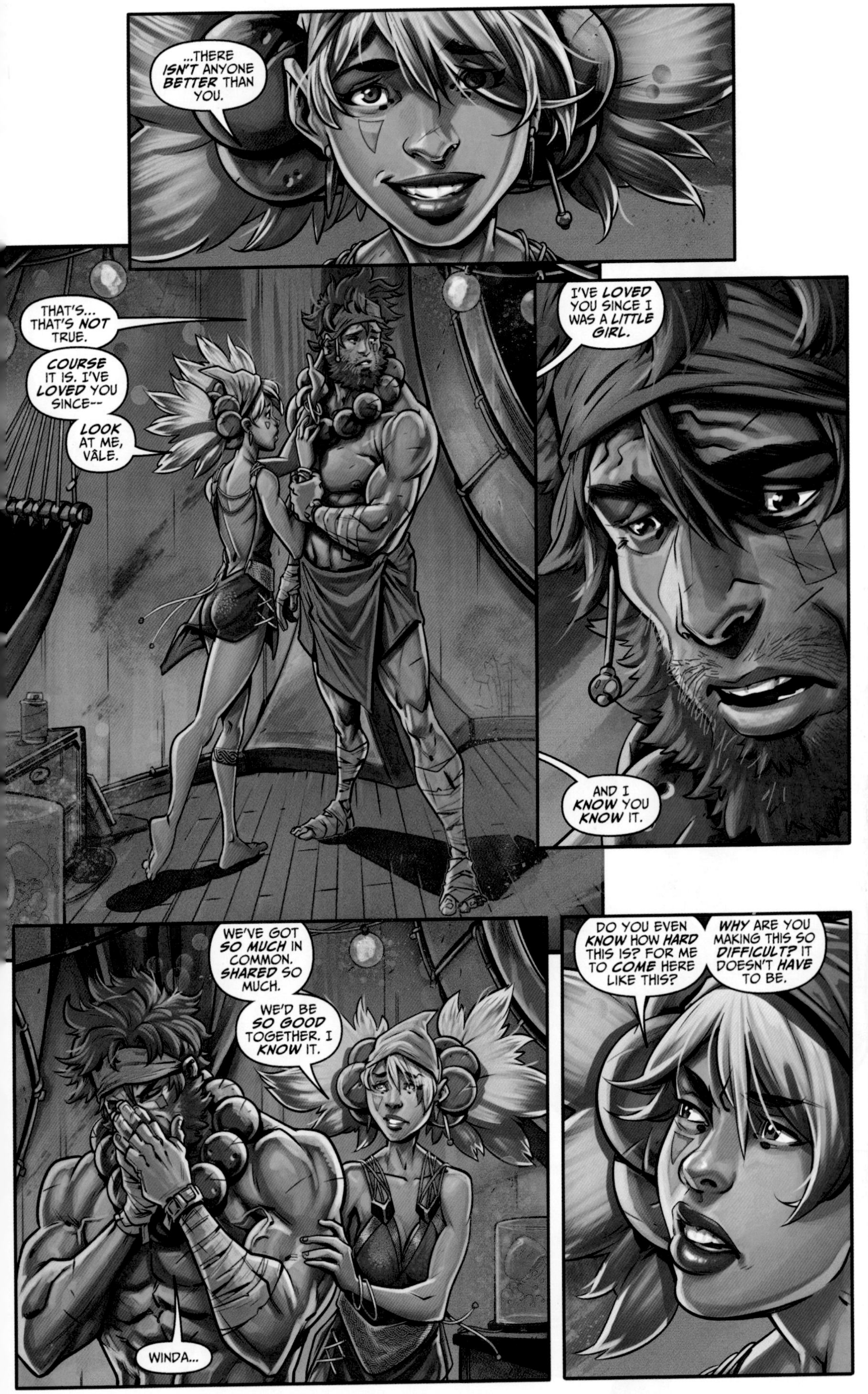
...THERE ISN'T ANYONE BETTER THAN YOU.
THAT'S... THAT'S NOT TRUE.
COURSE IT IS. I'VE LOVED YOU SINCE--
LOOK AT ME, VÂLE.
I'VE LOVED YOU SINCE I WAS A LITTLE GIRL.
AND I KNOW YOU KNOW IT.
WE'VE GOT SO MUCH IN COMMON. SHARED SO MUCH.
WE'D BE SO GOOD TOGETHER. I KNOW IT.
WINDA...
DO YOU EVEN KNOW HOW HARD THIS IS? FOR ME TO COME HERE LIKE THIS?
WHY ARE YOU MAKING THIS SO DIFFICULT? IT DOESN'T HAVE TO BE.

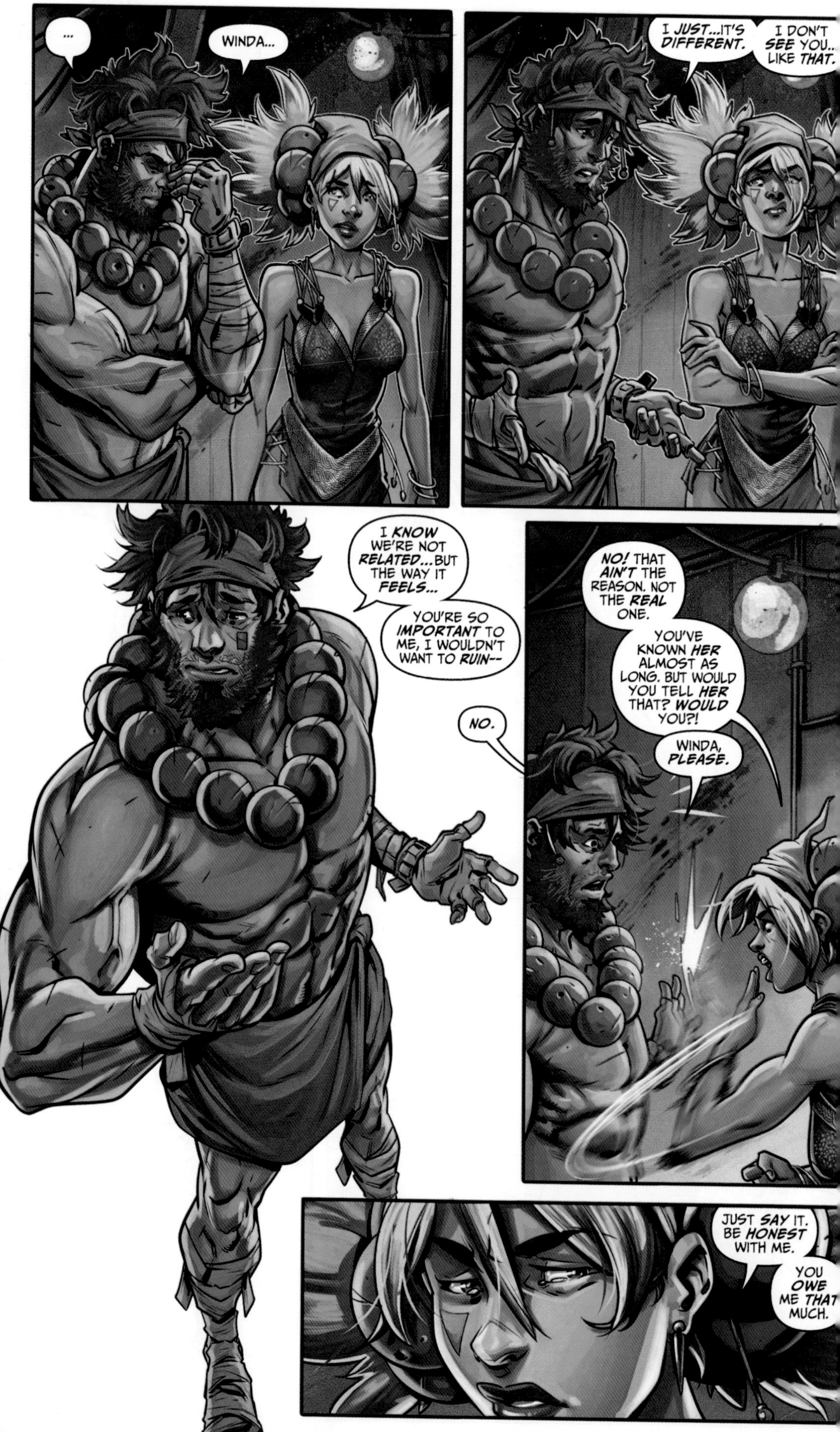
...
WINDA...
I JUST...IT'S DIFFERENT.
I DON'T SEE YOU.. LIKE THAT.
I KNOW WE'RE NOT RELATED...BUT THE WAY IT FEELS...
YOU'RE SO IMPORTANT TO ME, I WOULDN'T WANT TO RUIN--
NO! THAT AIN'T THE REASON. NOT THE REAL ONE.
YOU'VE KNOWN HER ALMOST AS LONG. BUT WOULD YOU TELL HER THAT? WOULD YOU?!
NO.
WINDA, PLEASE.
JUST SAY IT. BE HONEST WITH ME.
YOU OWE ME THAT MUCH.

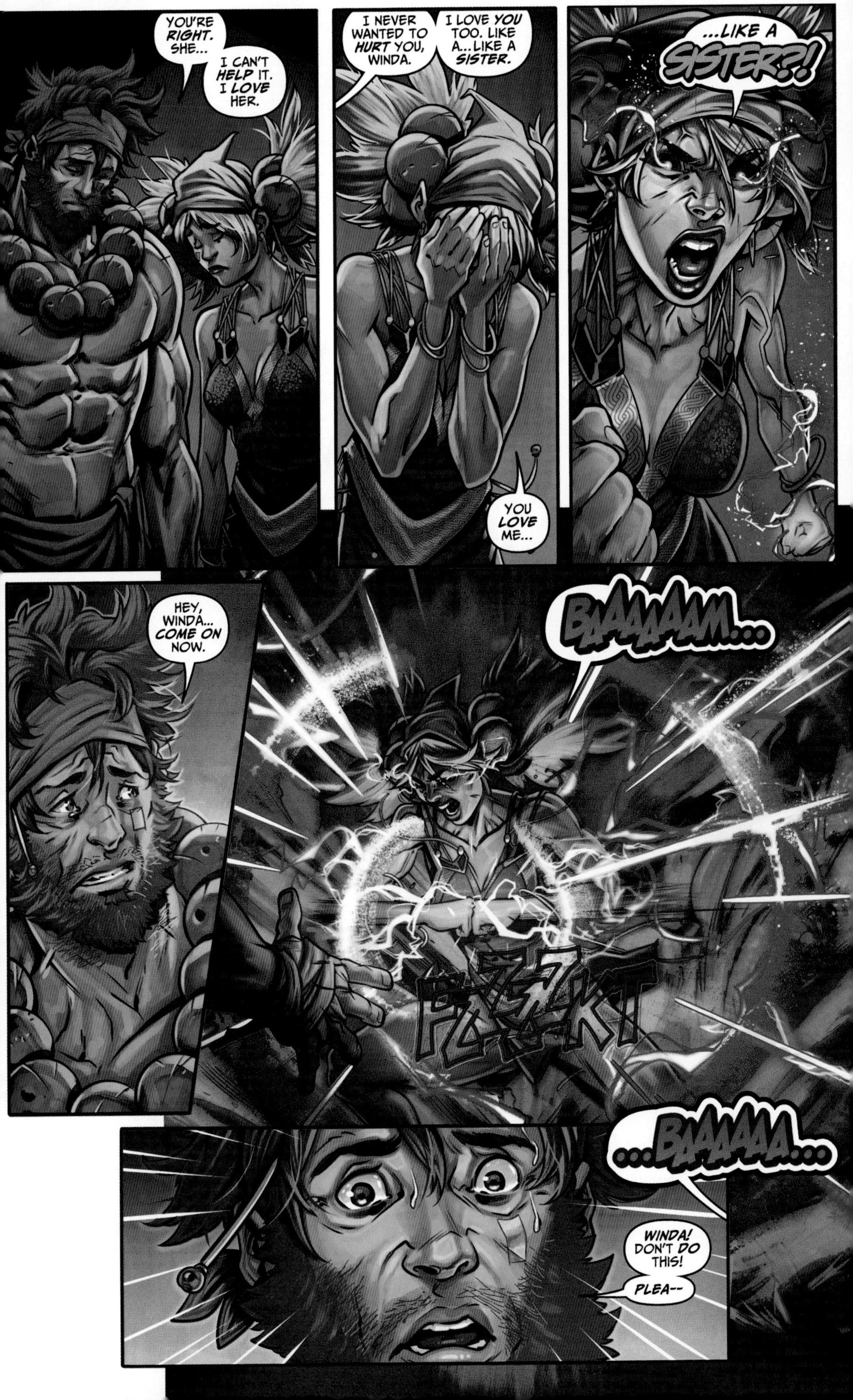
YOU'RE RIGHT. SHE...
I CAN'T HELP IT. I LOVE HER.
I NEVER WANTED TO HURT YOU, WINDA.
I LOVE YOU TOO. LIKE A...LIKE A SISTER.
YOU LOVE ME...
...LIKE A SISTER?!
HEY, WINDA... COME ON NOW.
BAAAAAM...
FZZZKT
...BAAAAA...
WINDA! DON'T DO THIS!
PLEA--

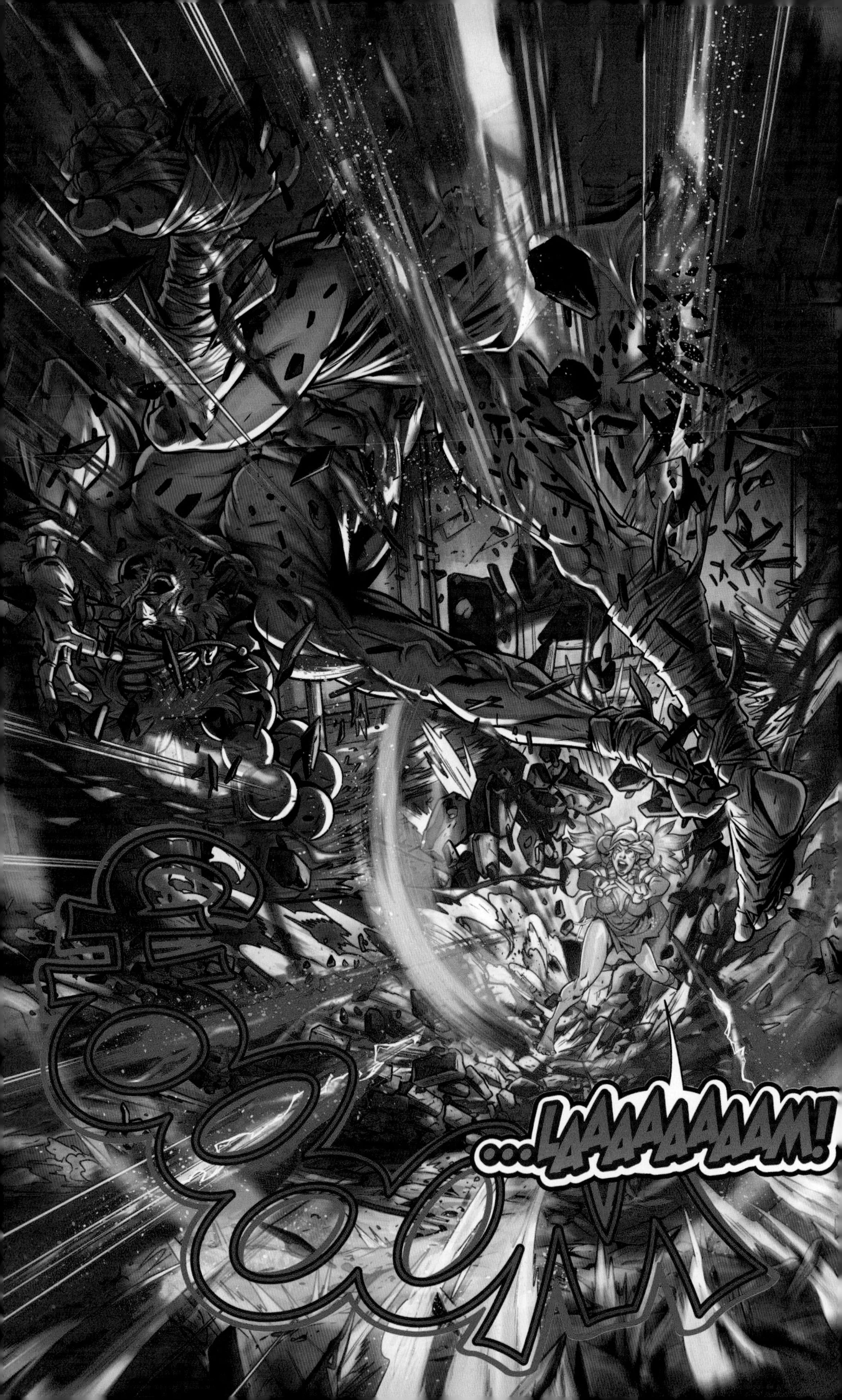
...LAAAAAAM!

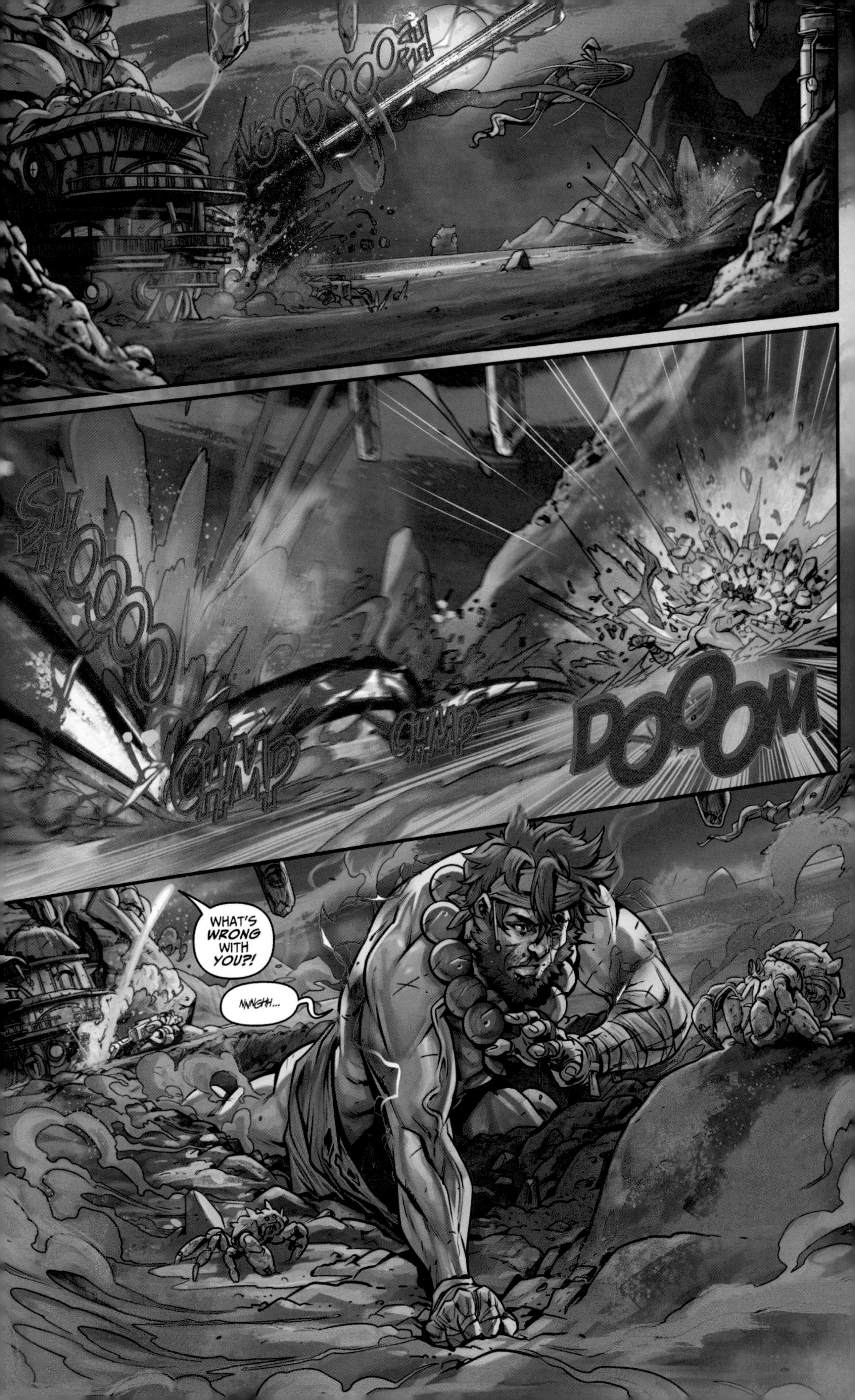
DOOOM
WHAT'S **WRONG** WITH **YOU?!**
NNNGHH...

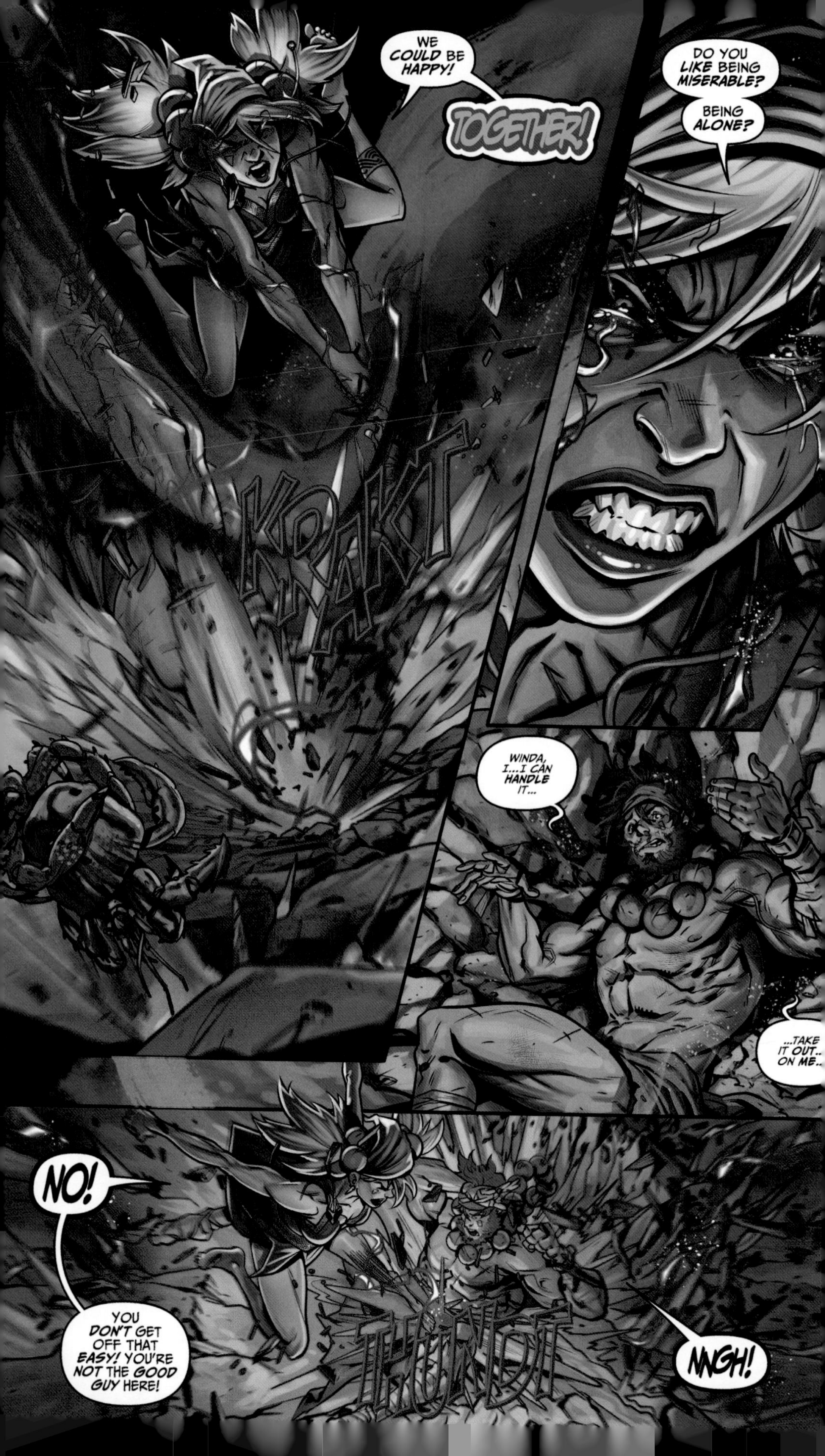
WE COULD BE HAPPY!
TOGETHER!
DO YOU LIKE BEING MISERABLE?
BEING ALONE?
KRAKT
WINDA, I...I CAN HANDLE IT...
...TAKE IT OUT... ON ME...
NO!
YOU DON'T GET OFF THAT EASY! YOU'RE NOT THE GOOD GUY HERE!
THUNDT
NNGH!

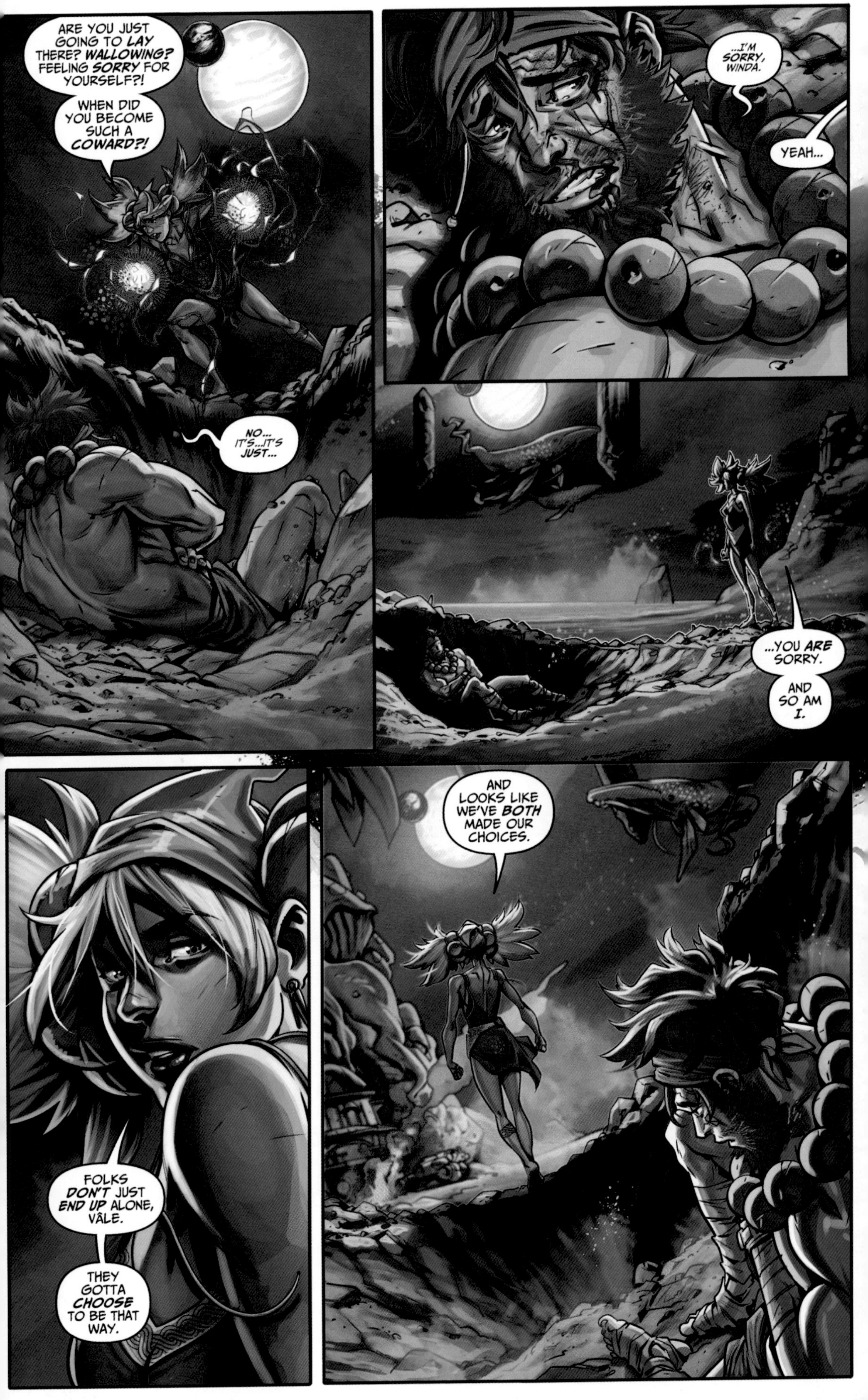
ARE YOU JUST GOING TO LAY THERE? WALLOWING? FEELING SORRY FOR YOURSELF?!
WHEN DID YOU BECOME SUCH A COWARD?!
NO... IT'S...IT'S JUST...
...I'M SORRY, WINDA.
YEAH...
...YOU ARE SORRY.
AND SO AM I.
FOLKS DON'T JUST END UP ALONE, VÂLE.
THEY GOTTA CHOOSE TO BE THAT WAY.
AND LOOKS LIKE WE'VE BOTH MADE OUR CHOICES.

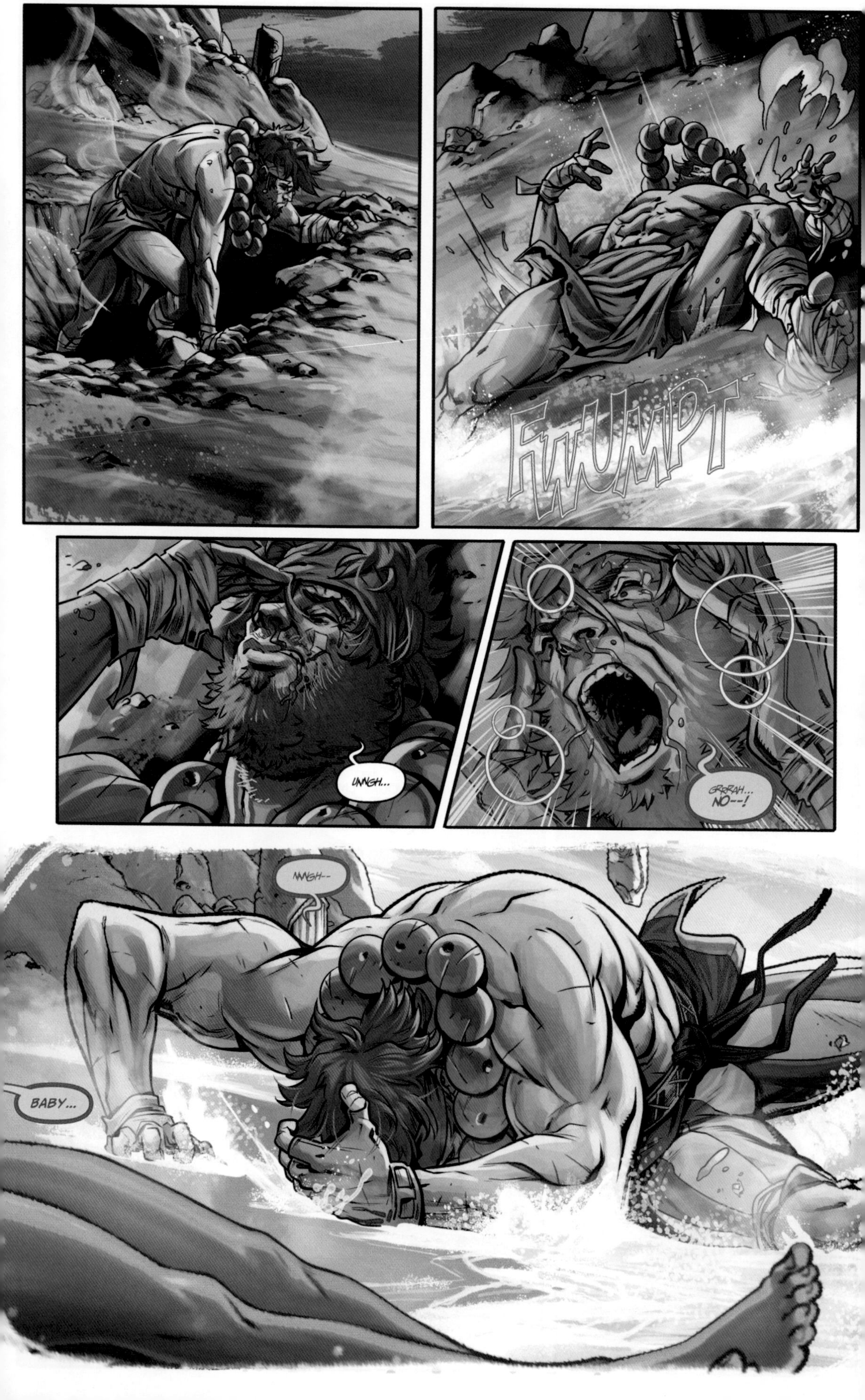
FWUMPT
UNNGH...
GRRRAH... NO--!
NNNGH--
BABY...

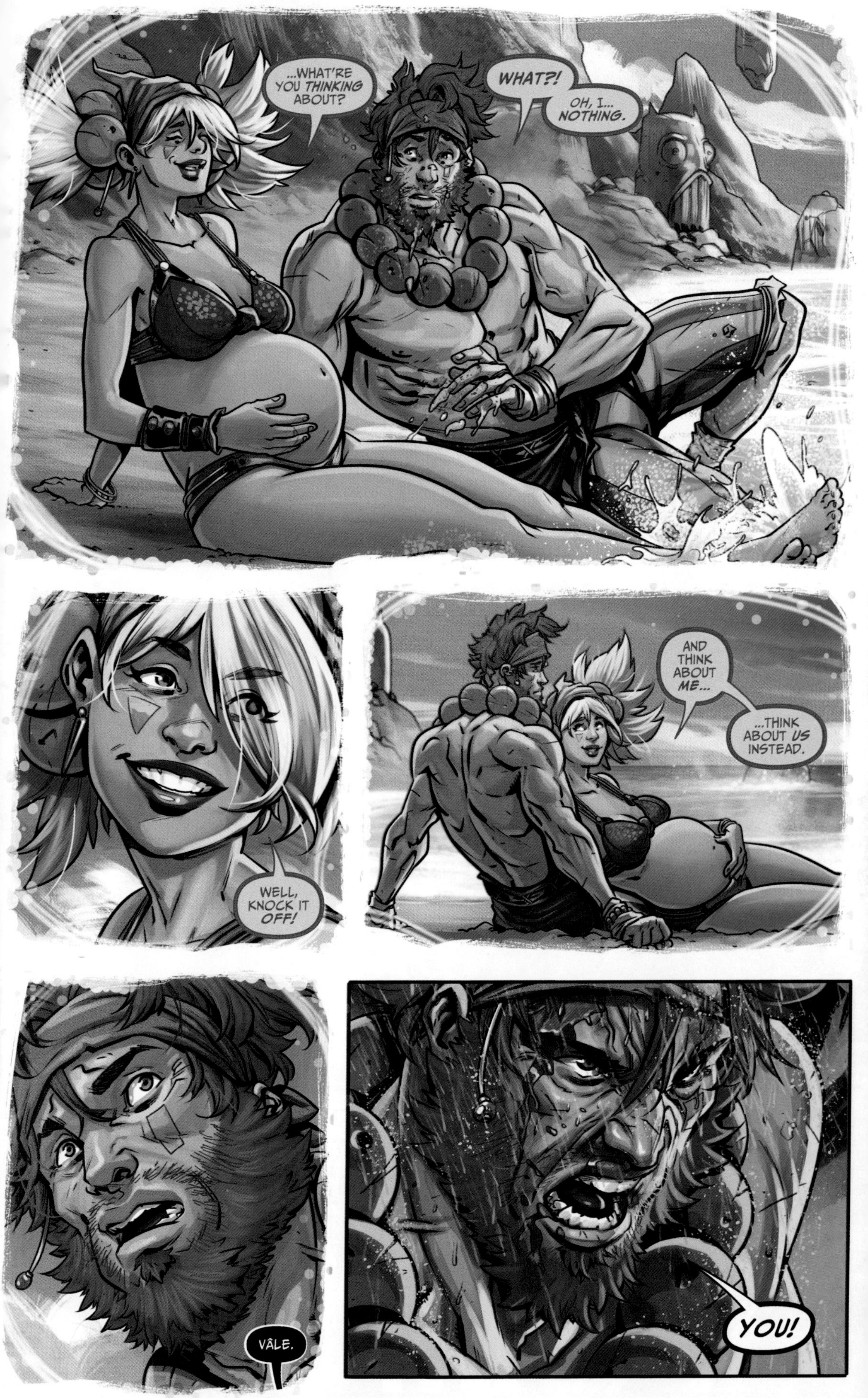
...WHAT'RE YOU *THINKING* ABOUT?
WHAT?!
OH, I... *NOTHING.*
WELL, KNOCK IT *OFF!*
AND THINK ABOUT *ME*...
...THINK ABOUT *US* INSTEAD.
VÂLE.
YOU!

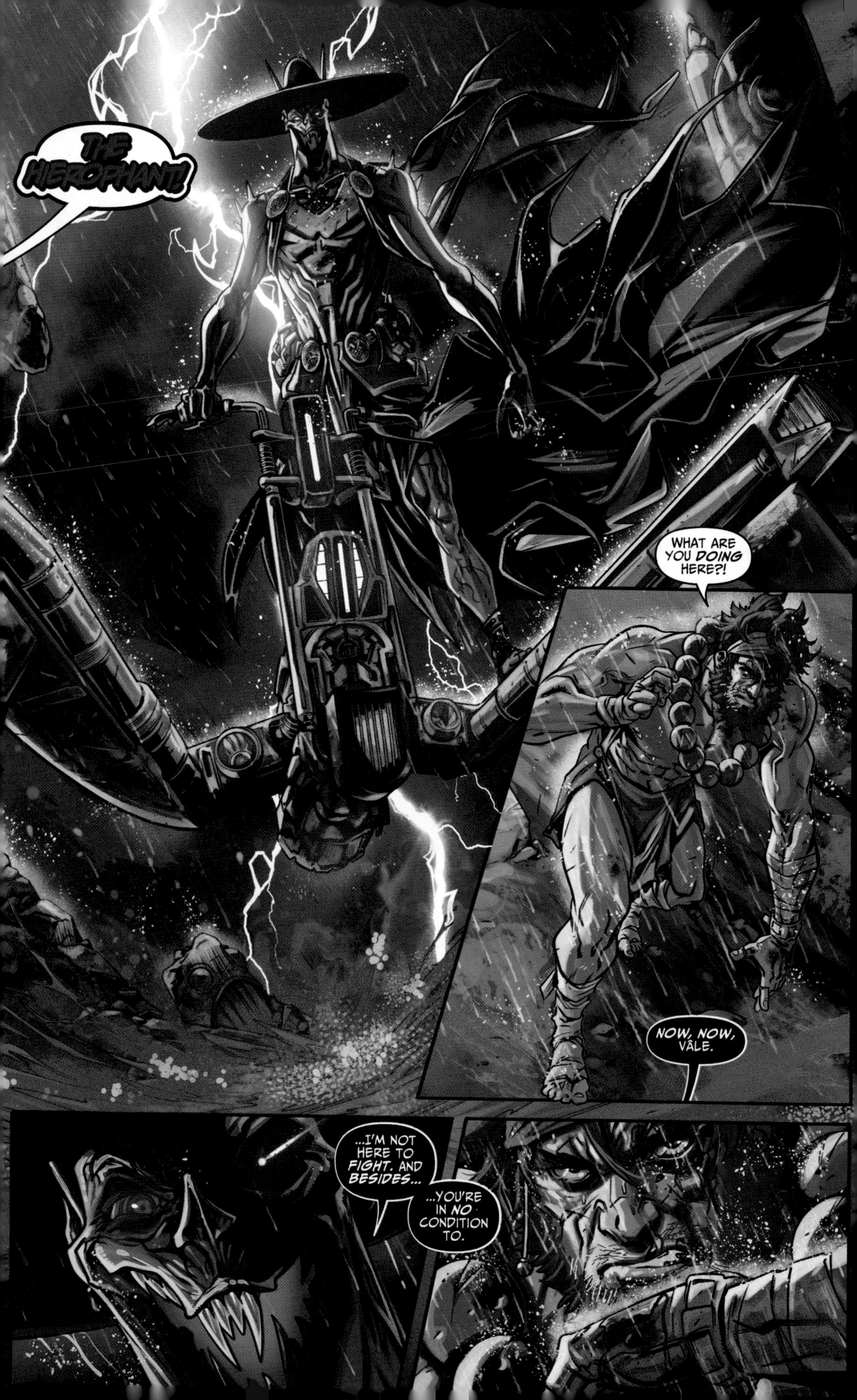
THE HIEROPHANT!
WHAT ARE YOU DOING HERE?!
NOW, NOW, VÂLE.
...I'M NOT HERE TO FIGHT. AND BESIDES...
...YOU'RE IN NO CONDITION TO.

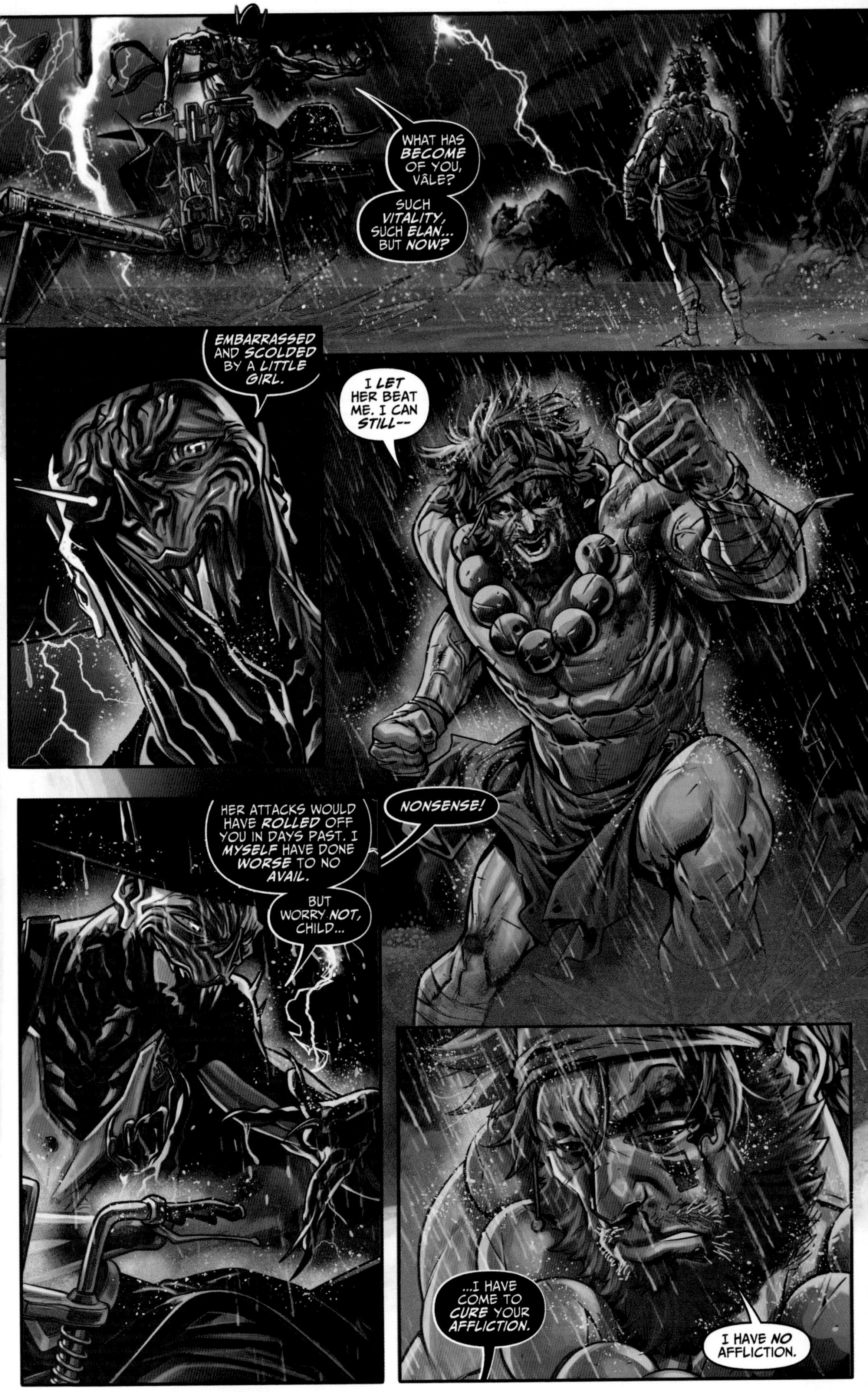
WHAT HAS BECOME OF YOU, VÂLE?
SUCH VITALITY, SUCH ELAN... BUT NOW?
EMBARRASSED AND SCOLDED BY A LITTLE GIRL.
I LET HER BEAT ME. I CAN STILL--
HER ATTACKS WOULD HAVE ROLLED OFF YOU IN DAYS PAST. I MYSELF HAVE DONE WORSE TO NO AVAIL.
NONSENSE!
BUT WORRY NOT, CHILD...
...I HAVE COME TO CURE YOUR AFFLICTION.
I HAVE NO AFFLICTION.

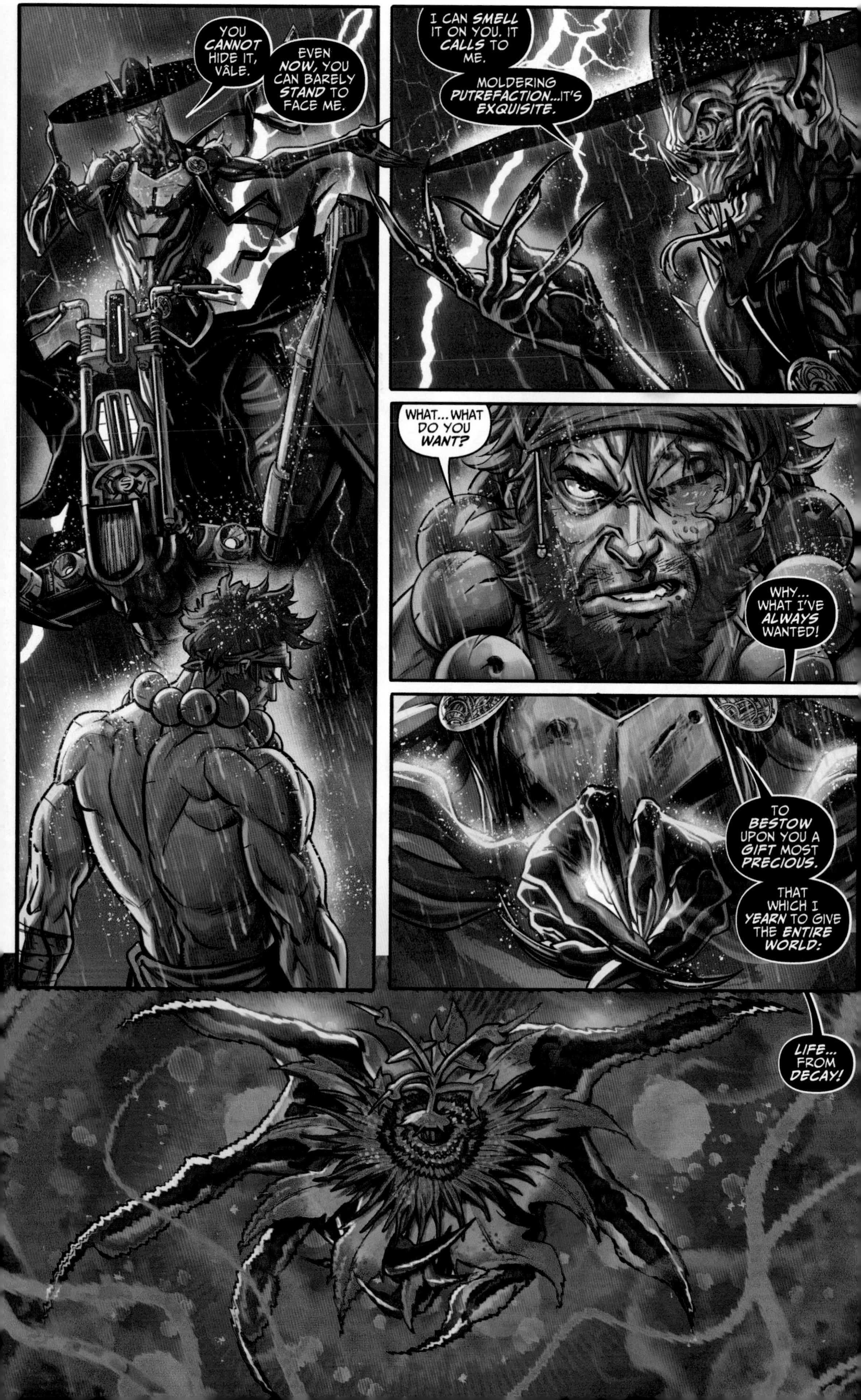
YOU CANNOT HIDE IT, VALE.
EVEN NOW, YOU CAN BARELY STAND TO FACE ME.
I CAN SMELL IT ON YOU. IT CALLS TO ME.
MOLDERING PUTREFACTION...IT'S EXQUISITE.
WHAT...WHAT DO YOU WANT?
WHY... WHAT I'VE ALWAYS WANTED!
TO BESTOW UPON YOU A GIFT MOST PRECIOUS.
THAT WHICH I YEARN TO GIVE THE ENTIRE WORLD:
LIFE... FROM DECAY!

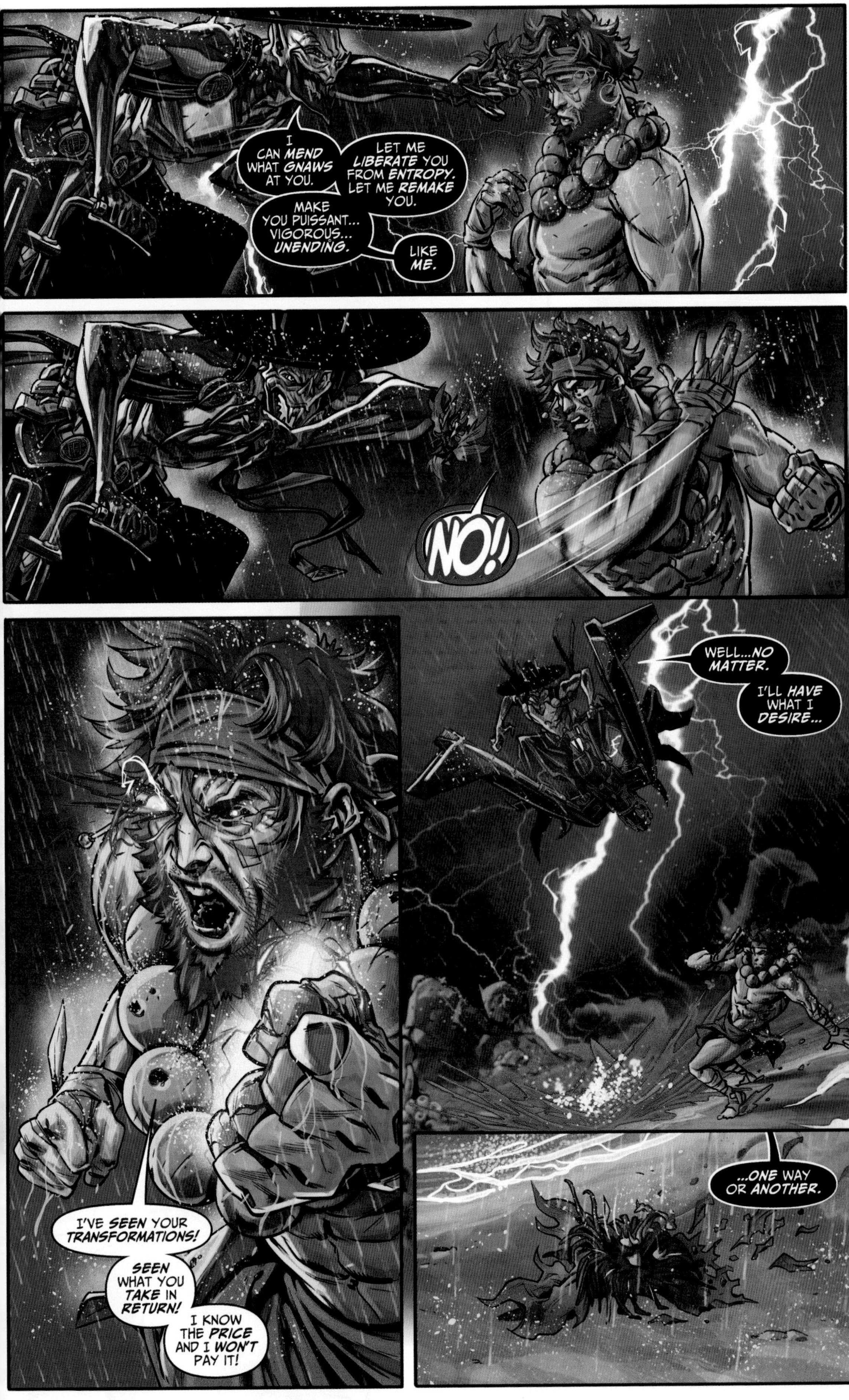
I CAN MEND WHAT GNAWS AT YOU.
LET ME LIBERATE YOU FROM ENTROPY. LET ME REMAKE YOU.
MAKE YOU PUISSANT... VIGOROUS... UNENDING.
LIKE ME.
NO!!
I'VE SEEN YOUR TRANSFORMATIONS!
SEEN WHAT YOU TAKE IN RETURN!
I KNOW THE PRICE AND I WON'T PAY IT!
WELL...NO MATTER.
I'LL HAVE WHAT I DESIRE...
...ONE WAY OR ANOTHER.

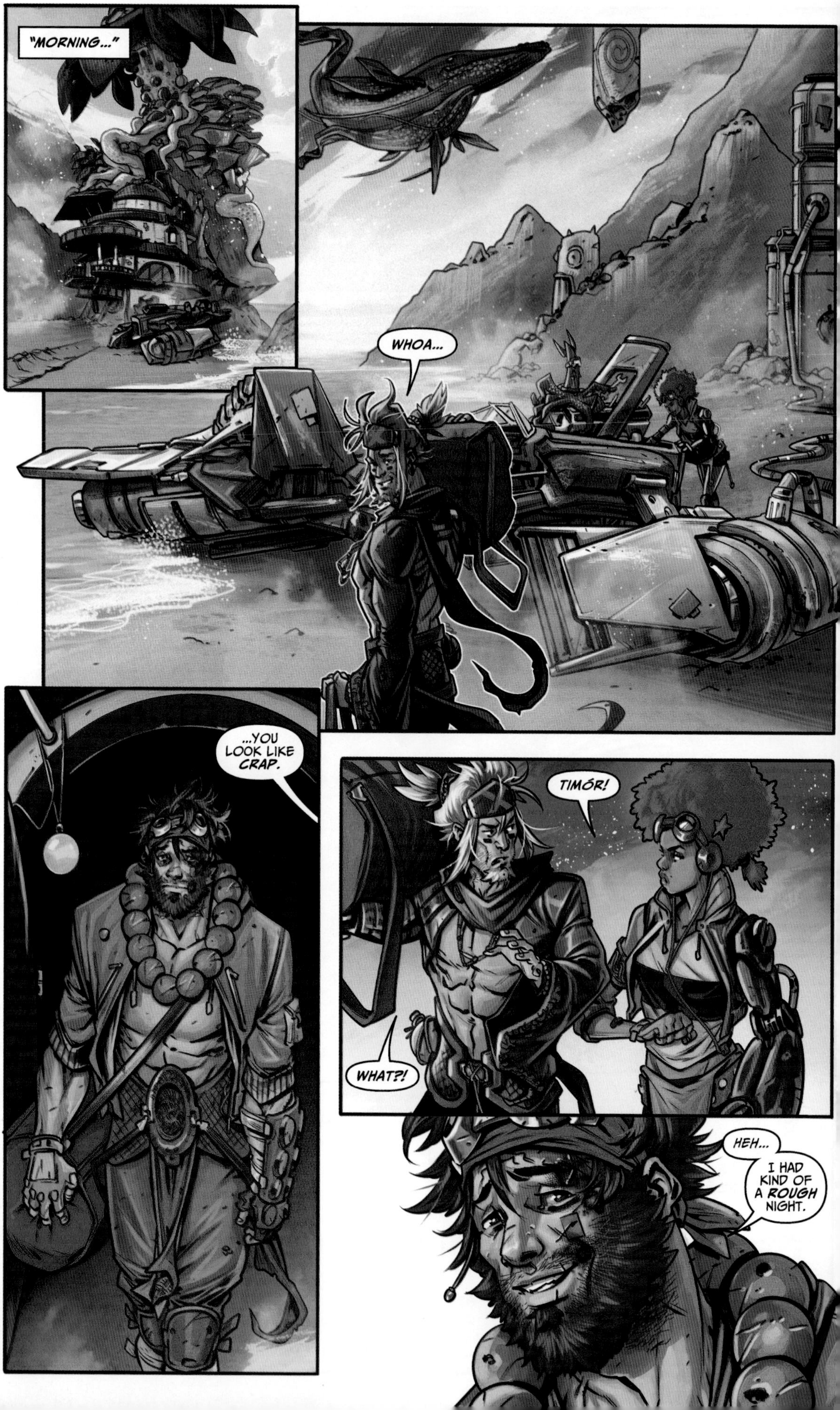
"MORNING..."
WHOA...
...YOU LOOK LIKE CRAP.
TIMÓR!
WHAT?!
HEH...
I HAD KIND OF A ROUGH NIGHT.

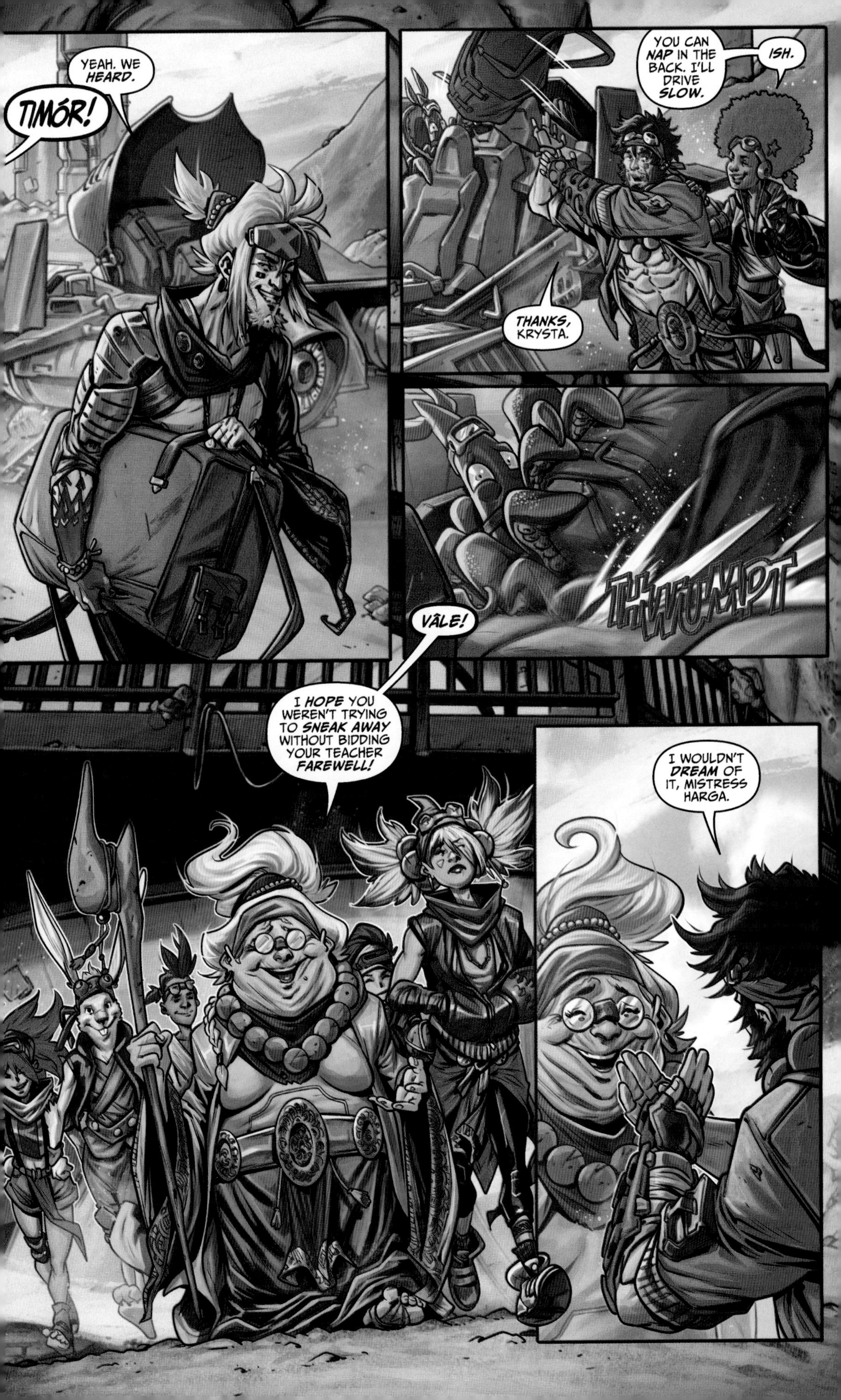

YEAH. WE HEARD.
TIMÓR!
YOU CAN NAP IN THE BACK. I'LL DRIVE SLOW.
ISH.
THANKS, KRYSTA.
THWUMPT
VÂLE!
I HOPE YOU WEREN'T TRYING TO SNEAK AWAY WITHOUT BIDDING YOUR TEACHER FAREWELL!
I WOULDN'T DREAM OF IT, MISTRESS HARGA.

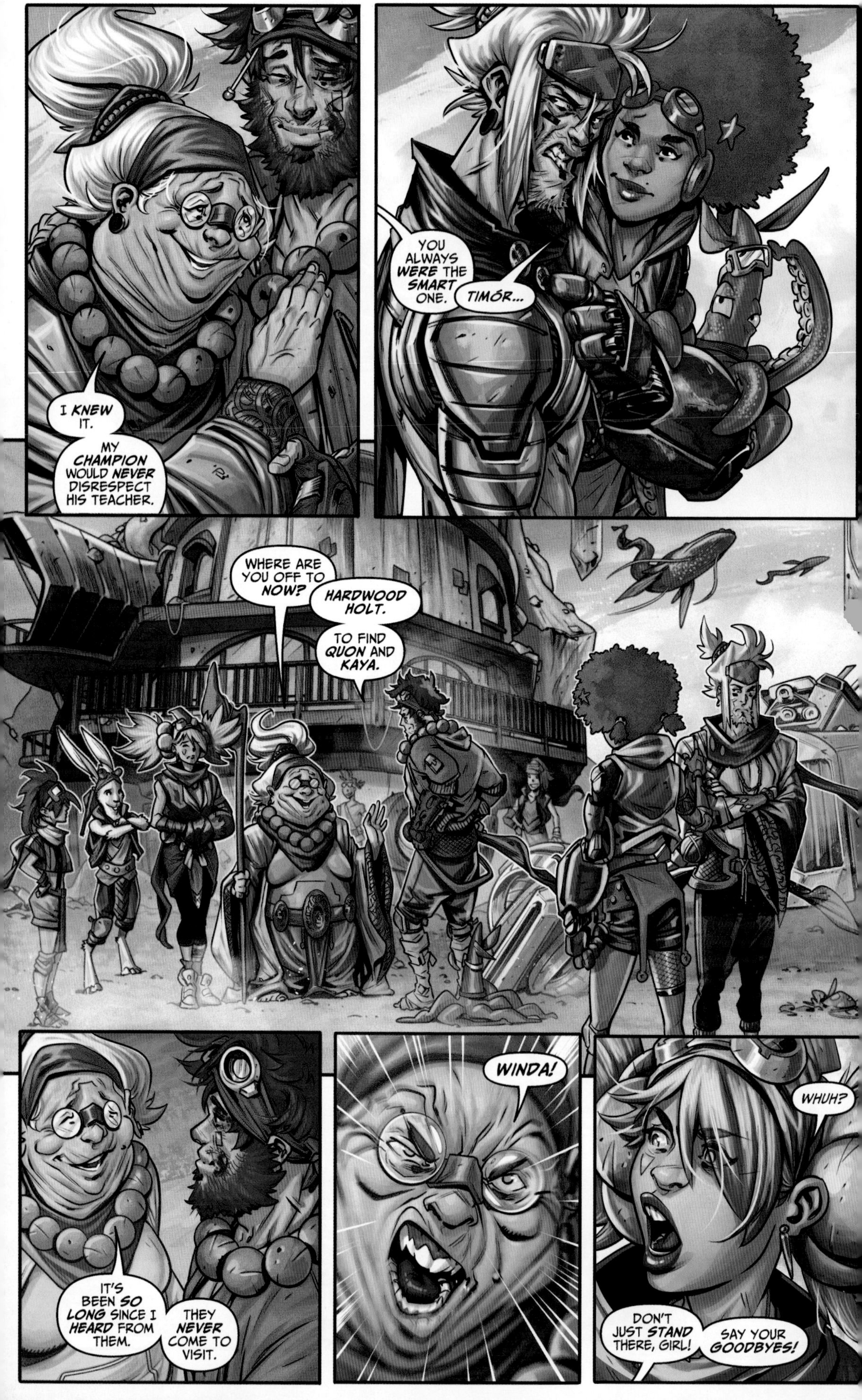

I KNEW IT.
MY CHAMPION WOULD NEVER DISRESPECT HIS TEACHER.
YOU ALWAYS WERE THE SMART ONE.
TIMÓR...
WHERE ARE YOU OFF TO NOW?
HARDWOOD HOLT.
TO FIND QUON AND KAYA.
IT'S BEEN SO LONG SINCE I HEARD FROM THEM.
THEY NEVER COME TO VISIT.
WINDA!
WHUH?
DON'T JUST STAND THERE, GIRL!
SAY YOUR GOODBYES!

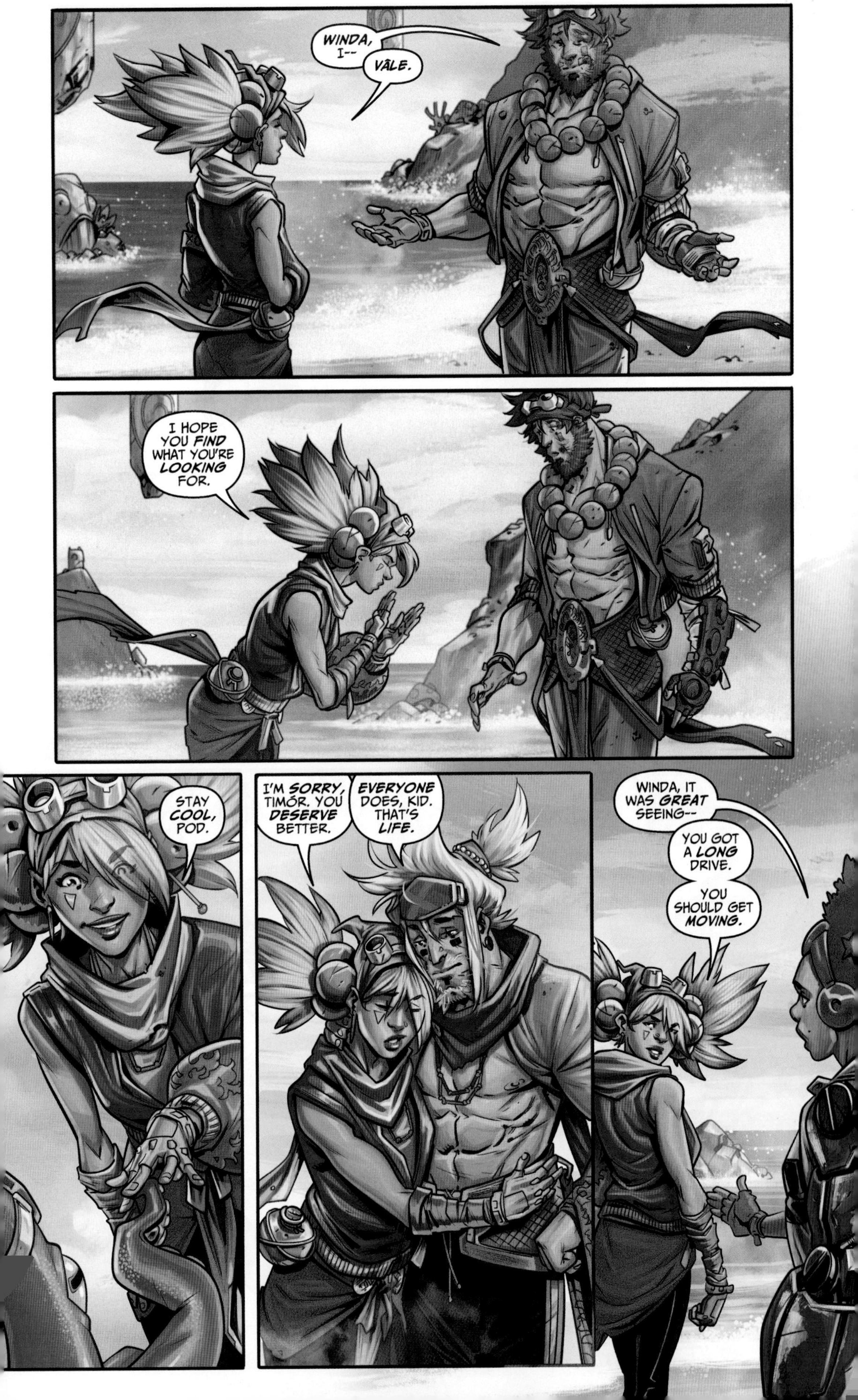
WINDA, I--
VALE.
I HOPE YOU FIND WHAT YOU'RE LOOKING FOR.
STAY COOL, POD.
I'M SORRY, TIMÓR. YOU DESERVE BETTER.
EVERYONE DOES, KID. THAT'S LIFE.
WINDA, IT WAS GREAT SEEING--
YOU GOT A LONG DRIVE.
YOU SHOULD GET MOVING.

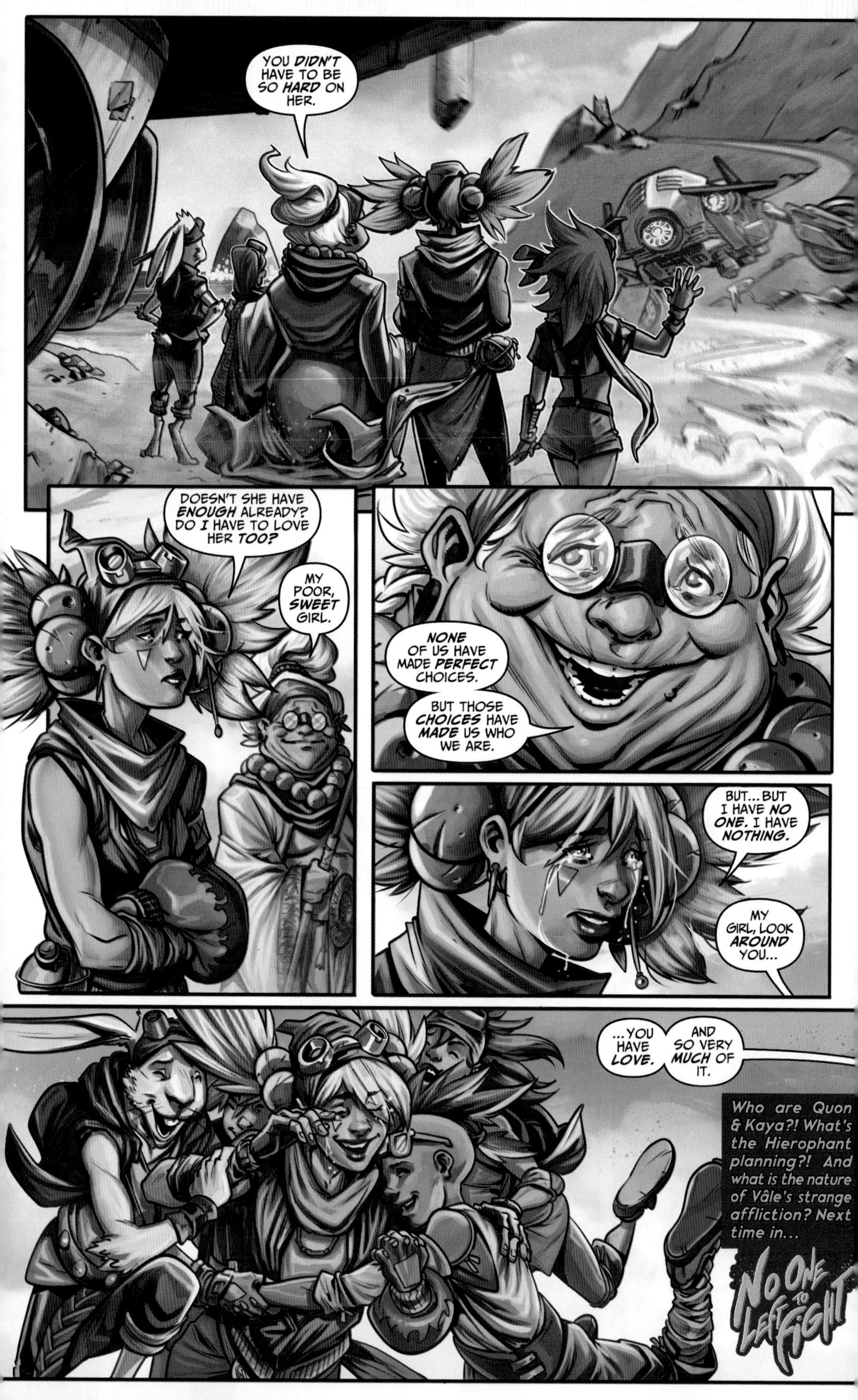
YOU DIDN'T HAVE TO BE SO HARD ON HER.
DOESN'T SHE HAVE ENOUGH ALREADY? DO I HAVE TO LOVE HER TOO?
MY POOR, SWEET GIRL.
NONE OF US HAVE MADE PERFECT CHOICES.
BUT THOSE CHOICES HAVE MADE US WHO WE ARE.
BUT... BUT I HAVE NO ONE. I HAVE NOTHING.
MY GIRL, LOOK AROUND YOU...
...YOU HAVE LOVE.
AND SO VERY MUCH OF IT.
Who are Quon & Kaya?! What's the Hierophant planning?! And what is the nature of Vâle's strange affliction? Next time in...
NO ONE LEFT TO FIGHT

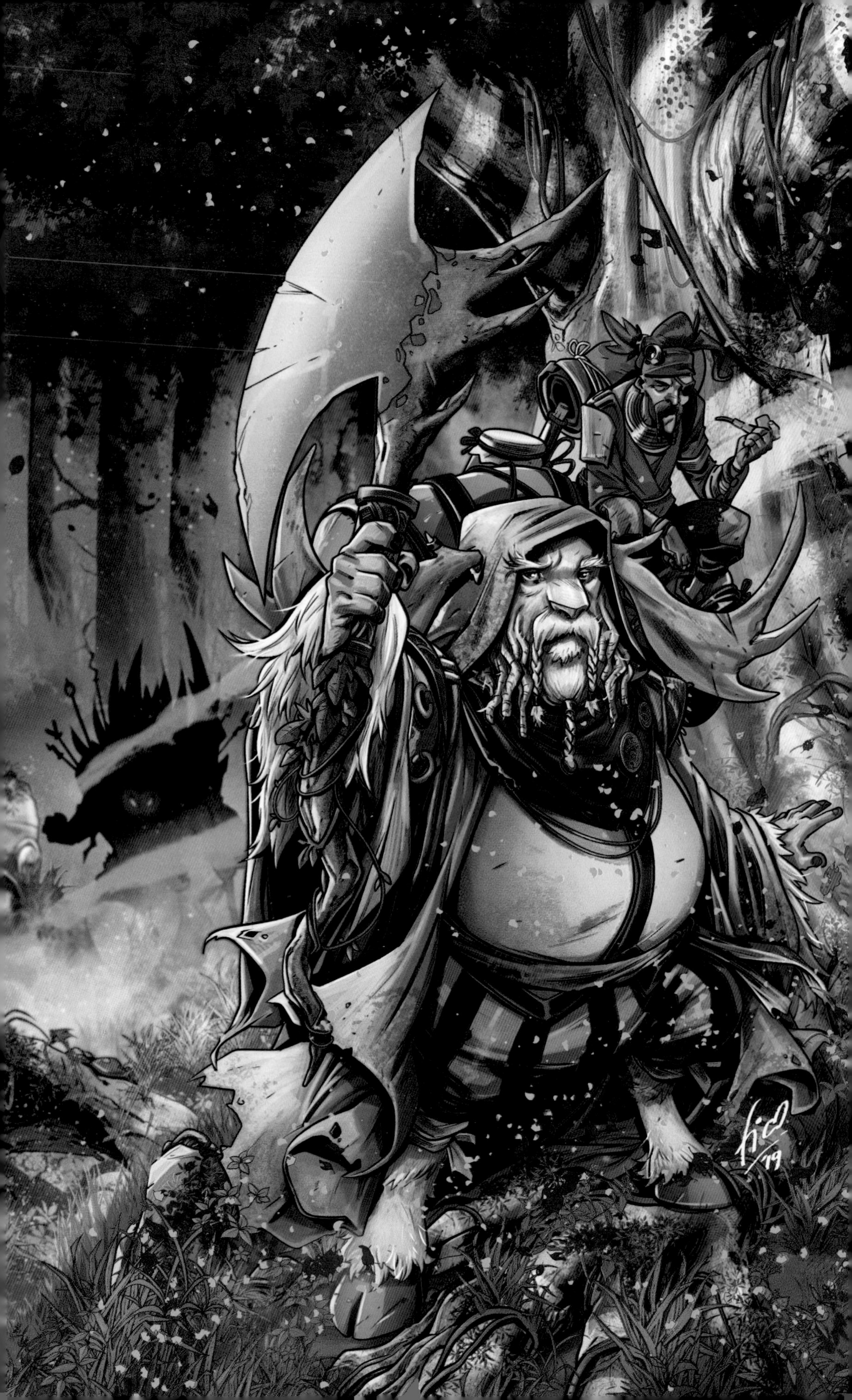

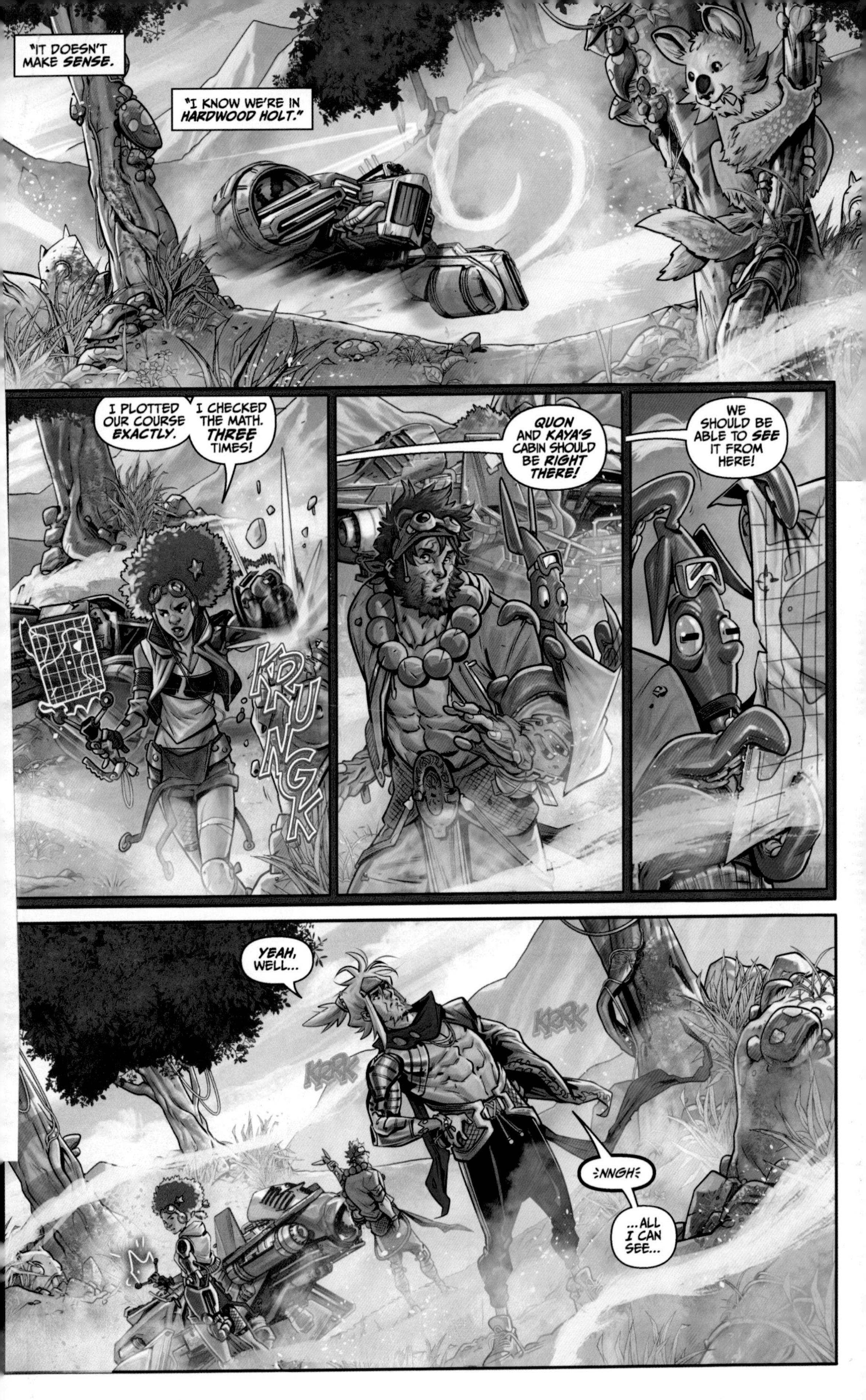

"IT DOESN'T MAKE SENSE.
"I KNOW WE'RE IN HARDWOOD HOLT."
I PLOTTED OUR COURSE EXACTLY.
I CHECKED THE MATH. THREE TIMES!
KRUNGK
QUON AND KAYA'S CABIN SHOULD BE RIGHT THERE!
WE SHOULD BE ABLE TO SEE IT FROM HERE!
YEAH, WELL...
KRRK
KRRK
NNGH
...ALL I CAN SEE...

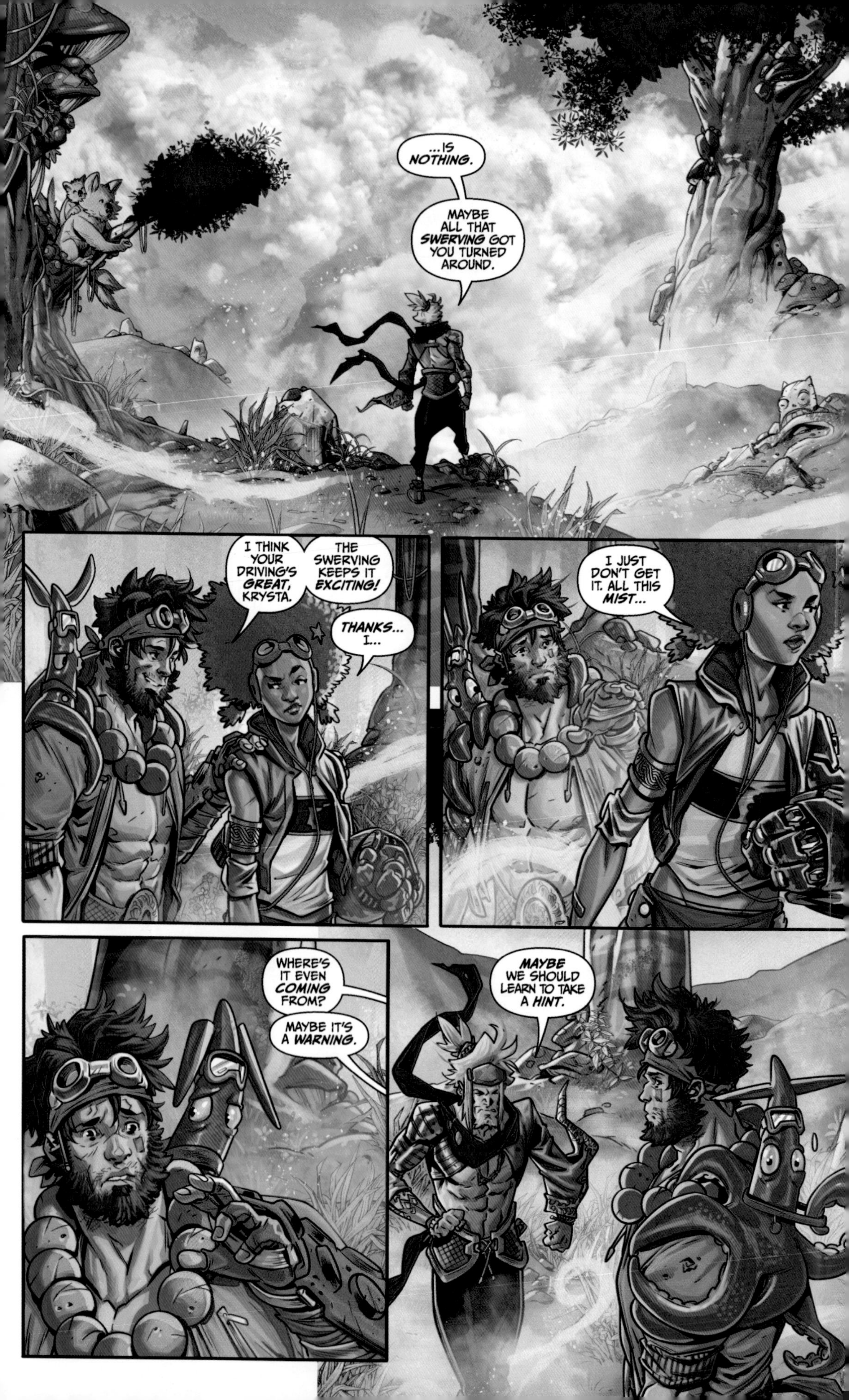

...IS NOTHING.
MAYBE ALL THAT SWERVING GOT YOU TURNED AROUND.
I THINK YOUR DRIVING'S GREAT, KRYSTA.
THE SWERVING KEEPS IT EXCITING!
THANKS... I...
I JUST DON'T GET IT. ALL THIS MIST...
WHERE'S IT EVEN COMING FROM?
MAYBE IT'S A WARNING.
MAYBE WE SHOULD LEARN TO TAKE A HINT.

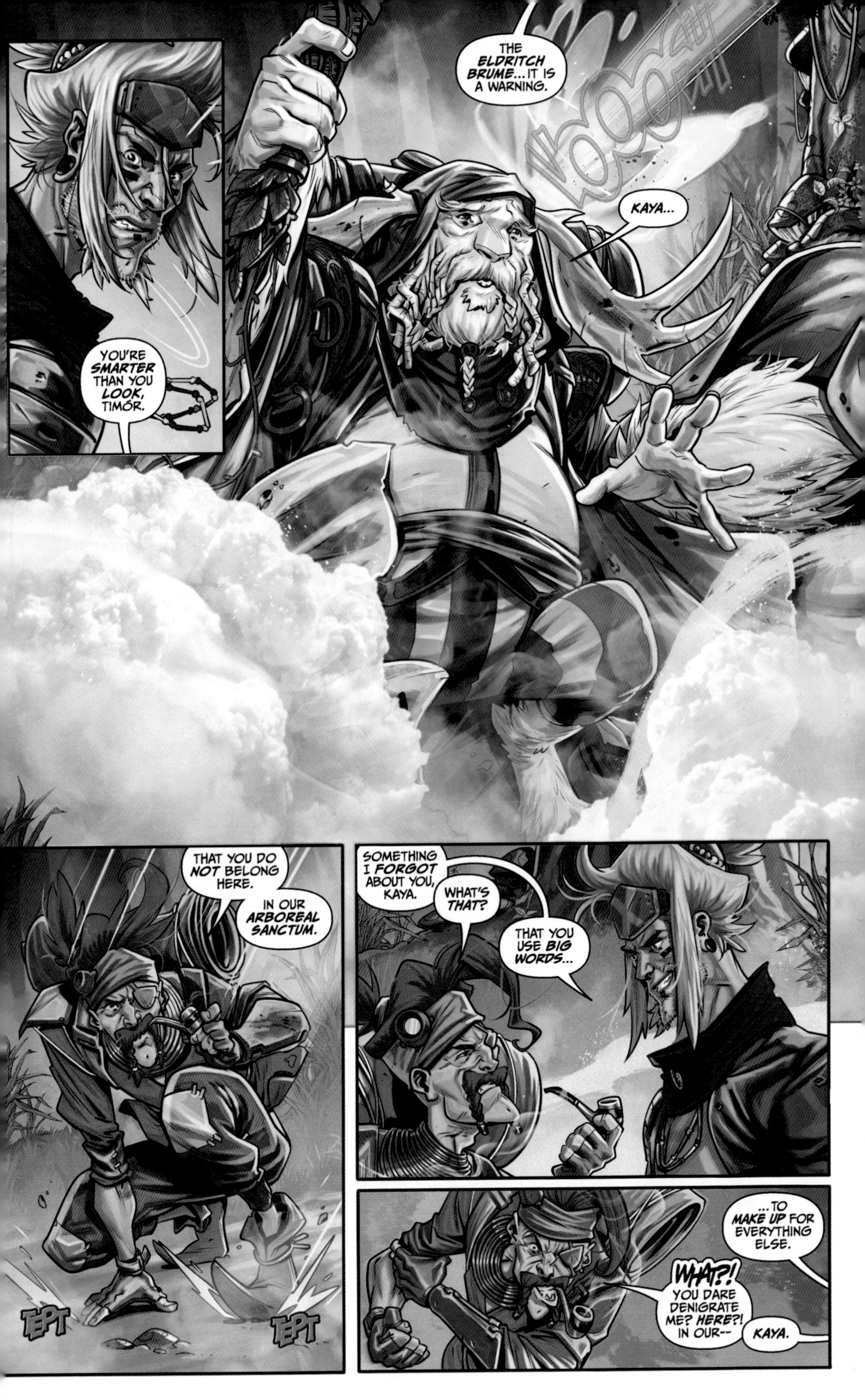

THE ELDRITCH BRUME... IT IS A WARNING.
YOU'RE SMARTER THAN YOU LOOK, TIMÓR.
KAYA...
THAT YOU DO NOT BELONG HERE.
IN OUR ARBOREAL SANCTUM.
TEPT
TEPT
SOMETHING I FORGOT ABOUT YOU, KAYA.
WHAT'S THAT?
THAT YOU USE BIG WORDS...
...TO MAKE UP FOR EVERYTHING ELSE.
WHAT?! YOU DARE DENIGRATE ME? HERE?! IN OUR--
KAYA.

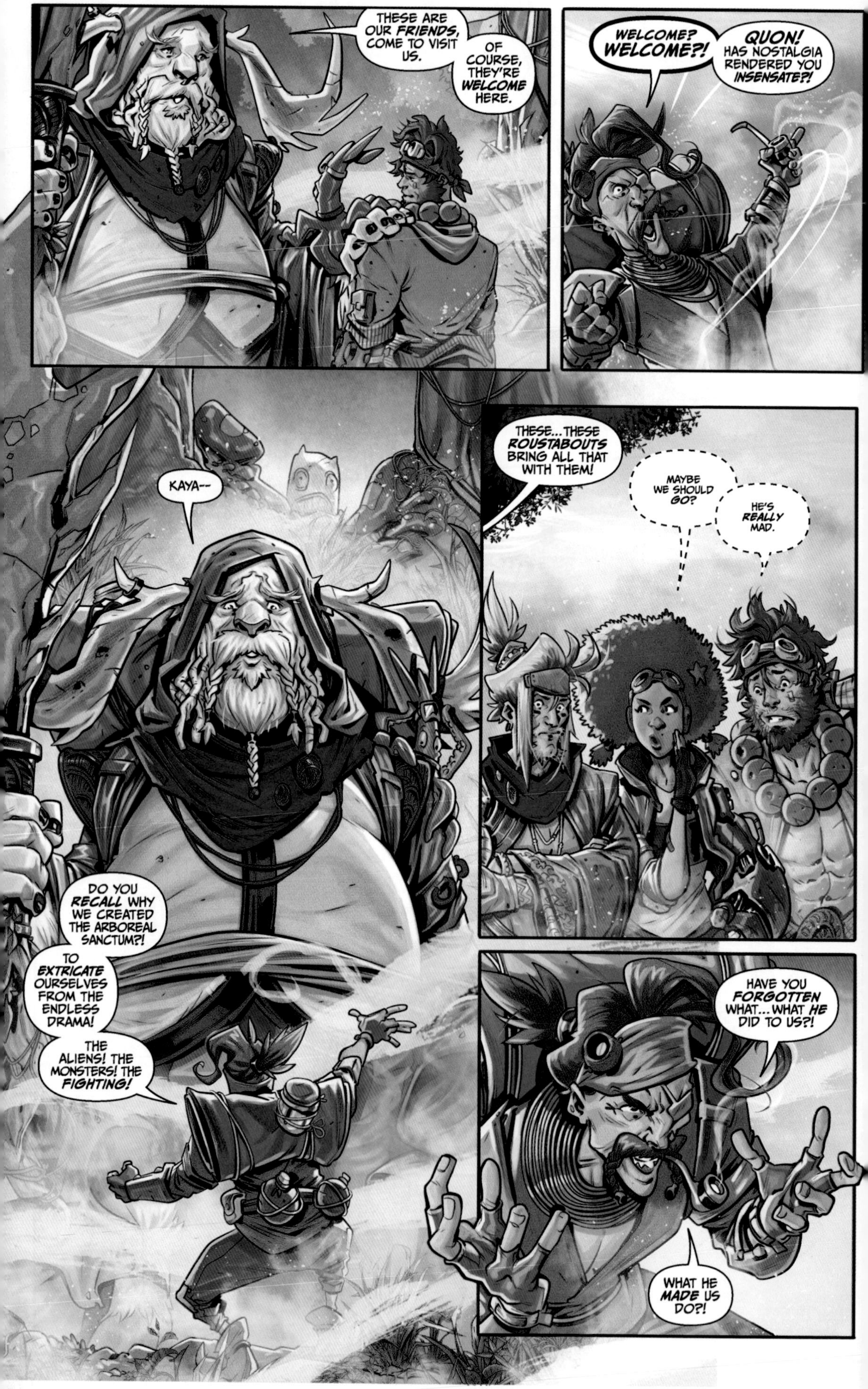

THESE ARE OUR FRIENDS, COME TO VISIT US.
OF COURSE, THEY'RE WELCOME HERE.
WELCOME? WELCOME?!
QUON! HAS NOSTALGIA RENDERED YOU INSENSATE?!
KAYA--
DO YOU RECALL WHY WE CREATED THE ARBOREAL SANCTUM?!
TO EXTRICATE OURSELVES FROM THE ENDLESS DRAMA!
THE ALIENS! THE MONSTERS! THE FIGHTING!
THESE... THESE ROUSTABOUTS BRING ALL THAT WITH THEM!
MAYBE WE SHOULD GO?
HE'S REALLY MAD.
HAVE YOU FORGOTTEN WHAT... WHAT HE DID TO US?!
WHAT HE MADE US DO?!

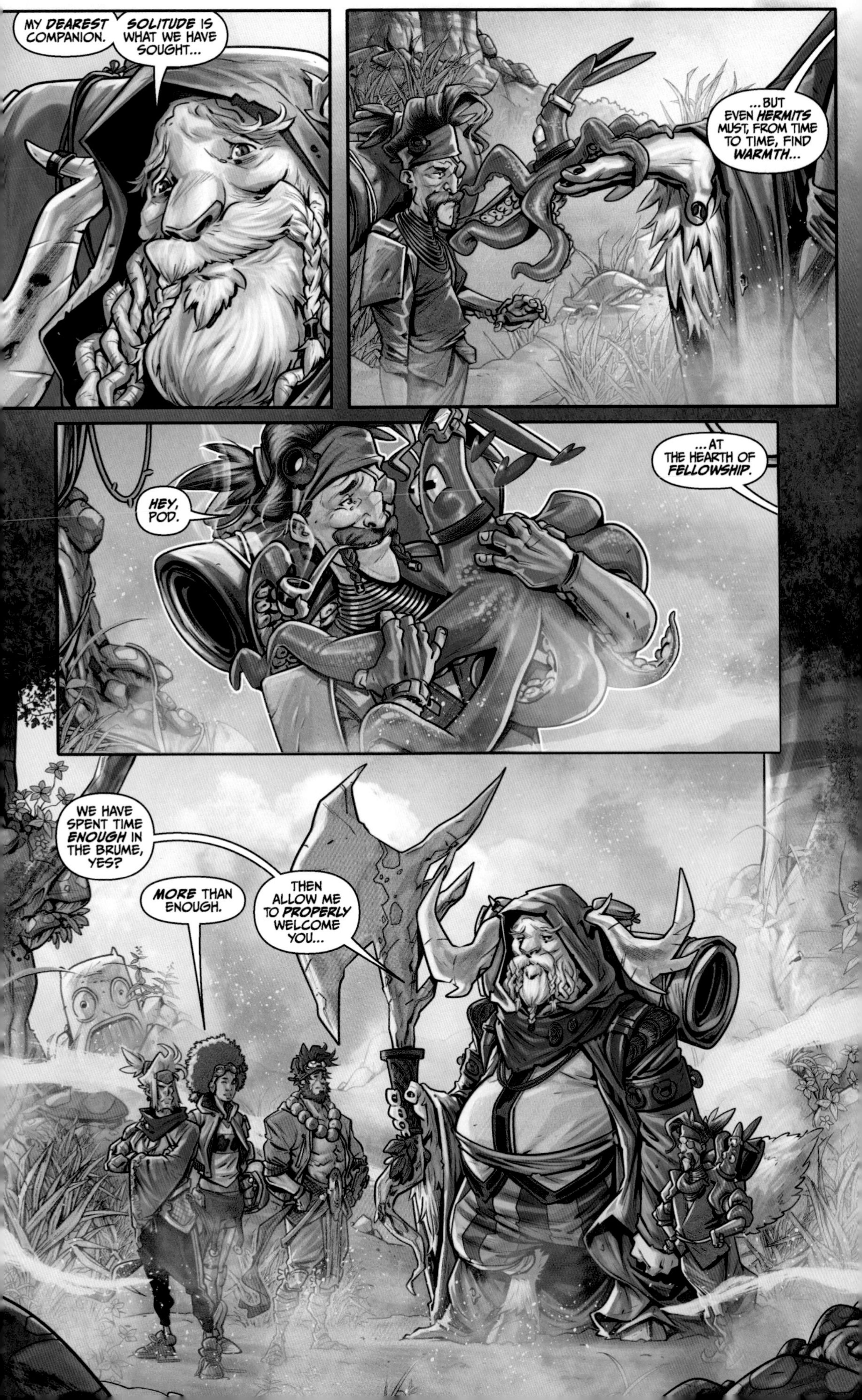

MY DEAREST COMPANION.
SOLITUDE IS WHAT WE HAVE SOUGHT...
...BUT EVEN HERMITS MUST, FROM TIME TO TIME, FIND WARMTH...
...AT THE HEARTH OF FELLOWSHIP.
HEY, POD.
WE HAVE SPENT TIME ENOUGH IN THE BRUME, YES?
MORE THAN ENOUGH.
THEN ALLOW ME TO PROPERLY WELCOME YOU...

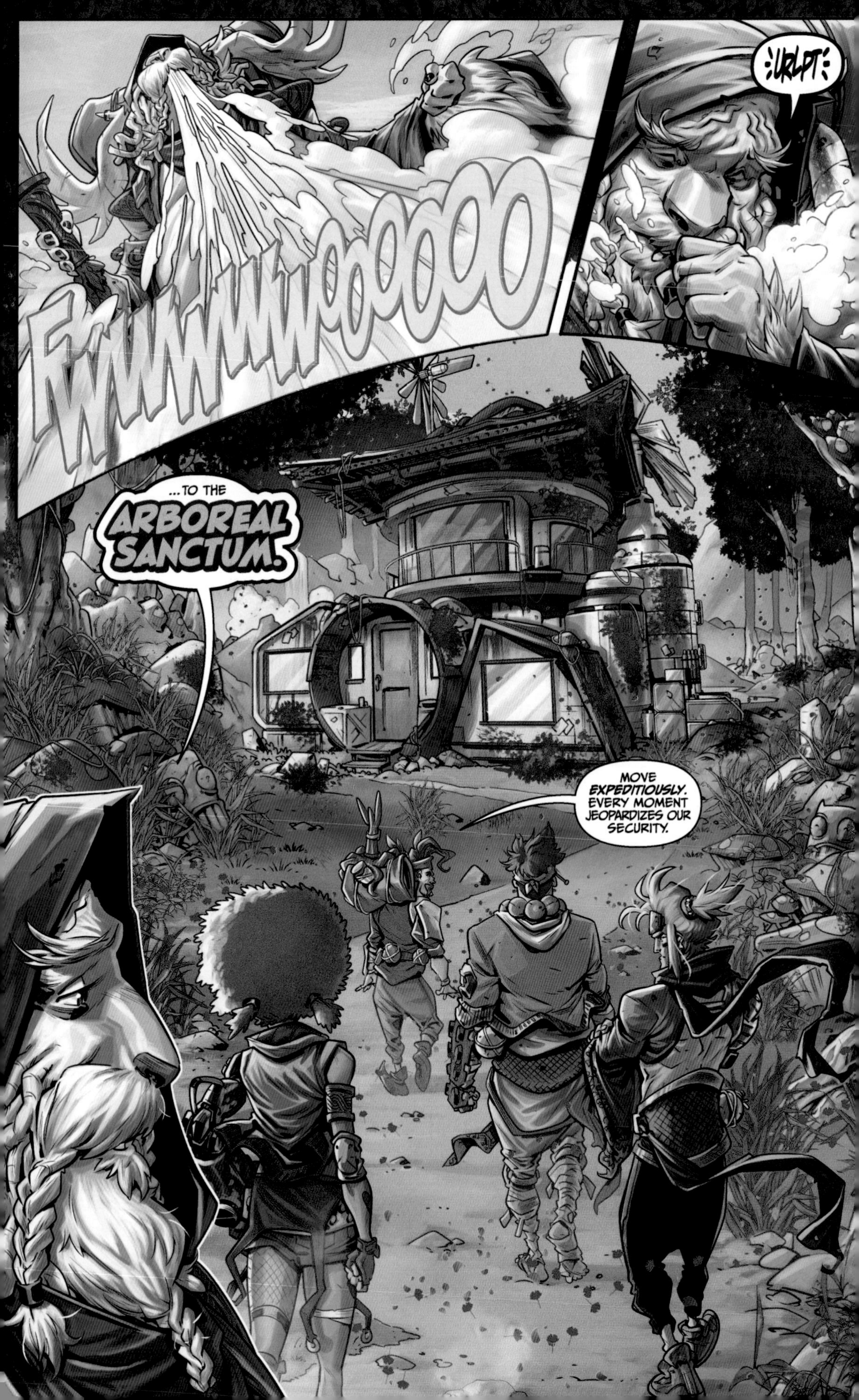
FWWWWWOOOOOO
URLPT
...TO THE ARBOREAL SANCTUM.
MOVE EXPEDITIOUSLY. EVERY MOMENT JEOPARDIZES OUR SECURITY.

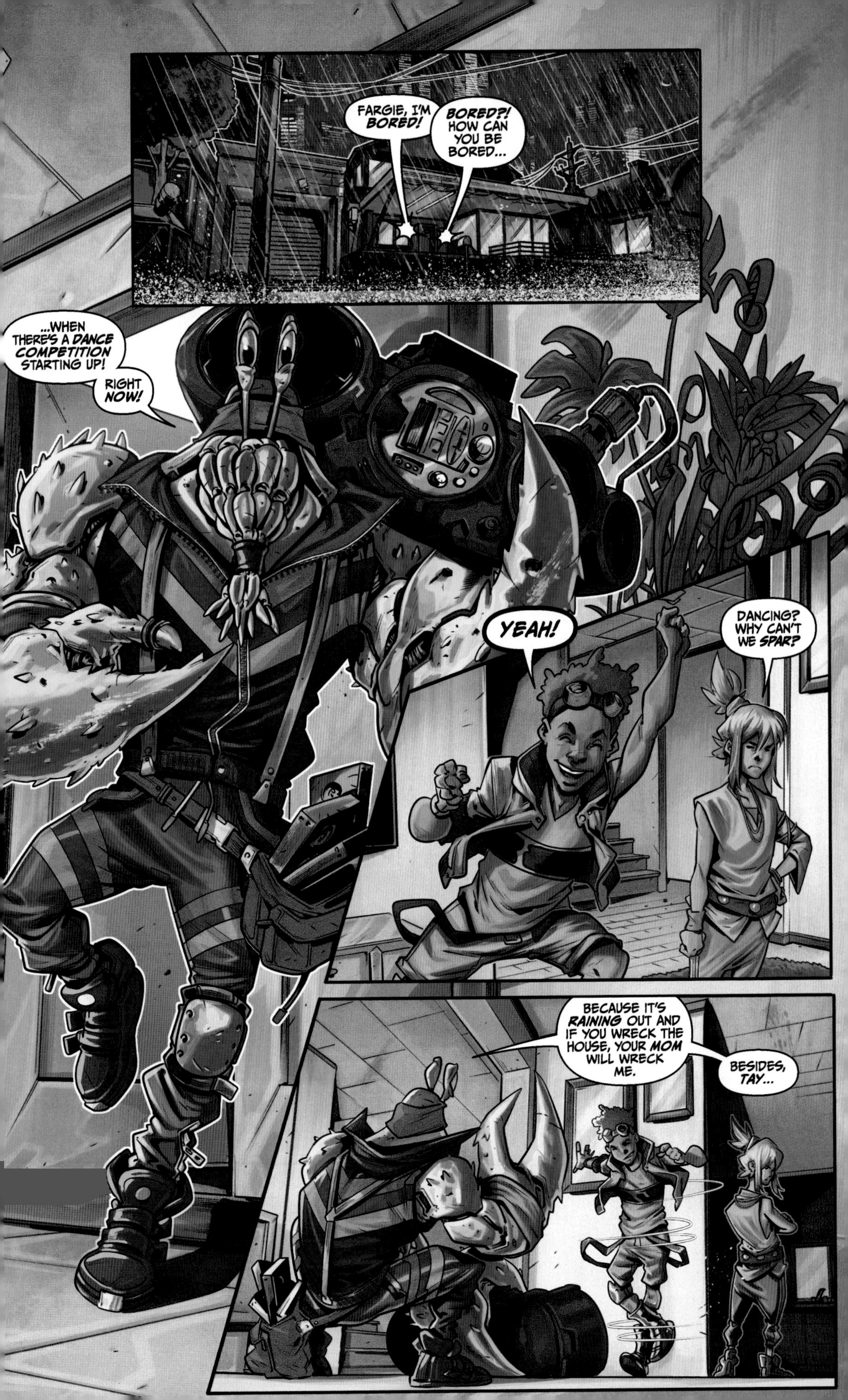
FARGIE, I'M BORED!
BORED?! HOW CAN YOU BE BORED...
...WHEN THERE'S A DANCE COMPETITION STARTING UP!
RIGHT NOW!
YEAH!
DANCING? WHY CAN'T WE SPAR?
BECAUSE IT'S RAINING OUT AND IF YOU WRECK THE HOUSE, YOUR MOM WILL WRECK ME.
BESIDES, TAY...

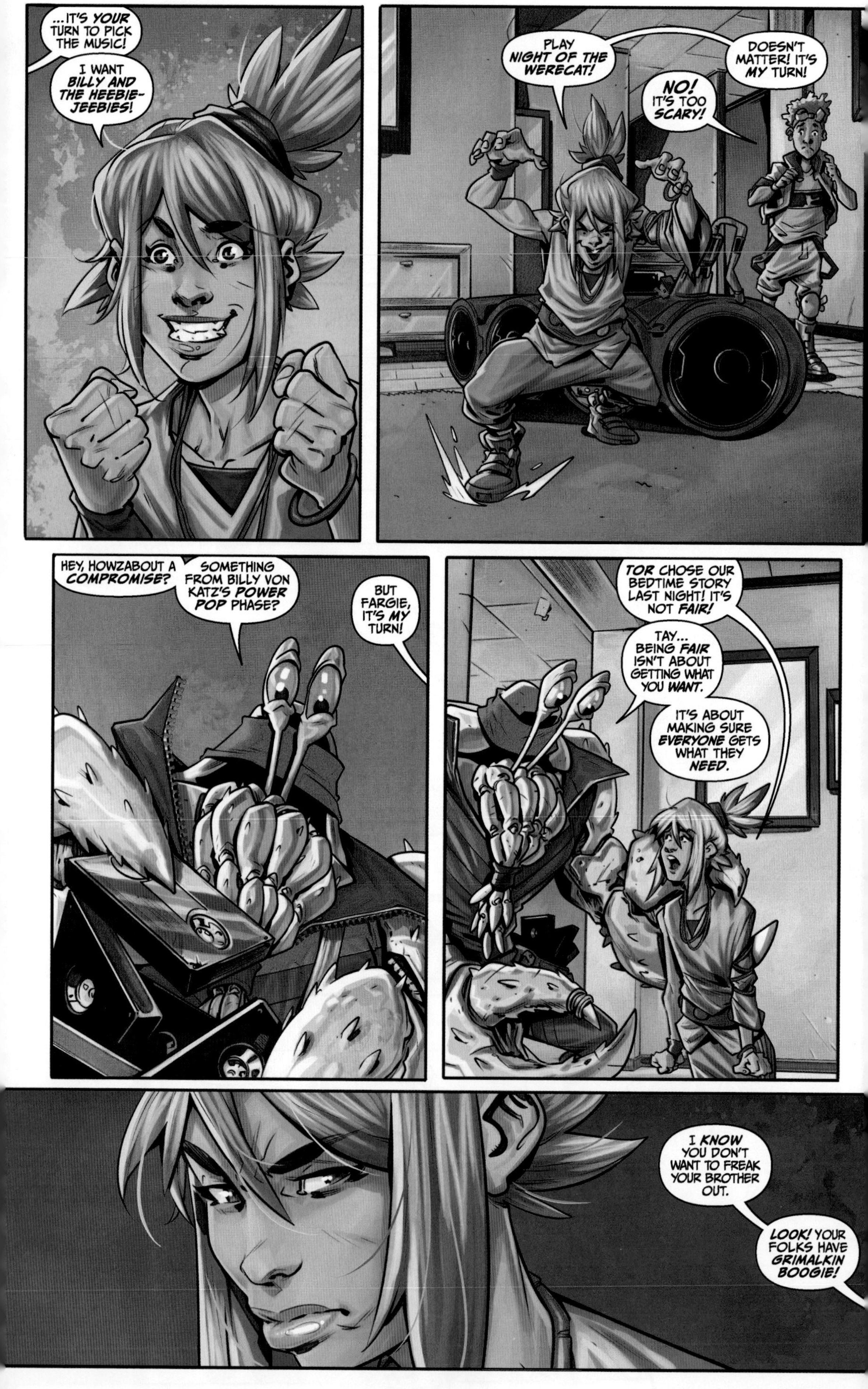
...IT'S *YOUR* TURN TO PICK THE MUSIC!
I WANT *BILLY AND THE HEEBIE-JEEBIES!*
PLAY *NIGHT OF THE WERECAT!*
DOESN'T MATTER! IT'S *MY* TURN!
NO! IT'S TOO *SCARY!*
HEY, HOWZABOUT A *COMPROMISE?*
SOMETHING FROM BILLY VON KATZ'S *POWER POP* PHASE?
BUT FARGIE, IT'S *MY* TURN!
TOR CHOSE OUR BEDTIME STORY LAST NIGHT! IT'S NOT *FAIR!*
TAY... BEING *FAIR* ISN'T ABOUT GETTING WHAT YOU *WANT*.
IT'S ABOUT MAKING SURE *EVERYONE* GETS WHAT THEY *NEED*.
I *KNOW* YOU DON'T WANT TO FREAK YOUR BROTHER OUT.
LOOK! YOUR FOLKS HAVE *GRIMALKIN BOOGIE!*

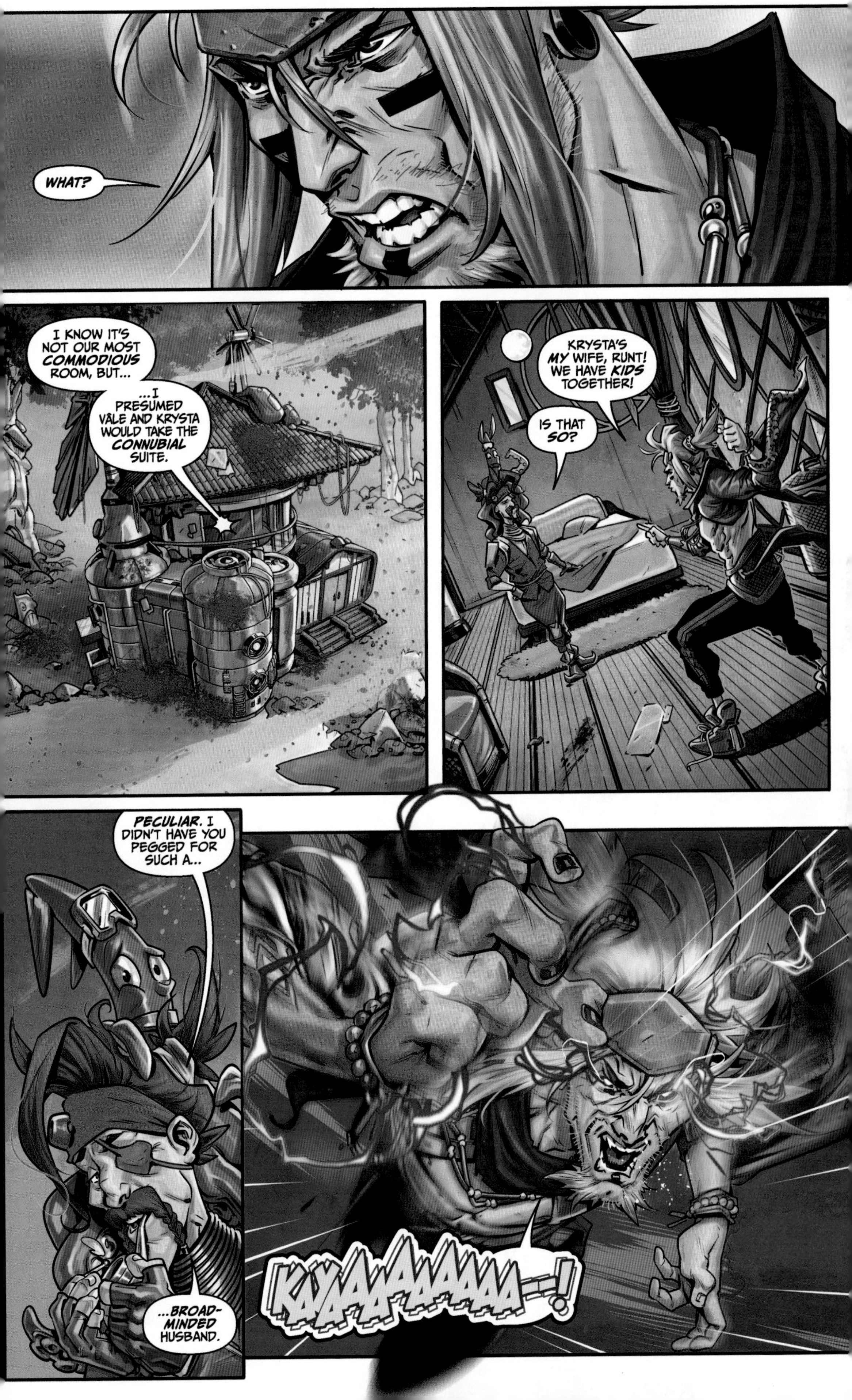
WHAT?
I KNOW IT'S NOT OUR MOST COMMODIOUS ROOM, BUT...
...I PRESUMED VALE AND KRYSTA WOULD TAKE THE CONNUBIAL SUITE.
KRYSTA'S MY WIFE, RUNT! WE HAVE KIDS TOGETHER!
IS THAT SO?
PECULIAR. I DIDN'T HAVE YOU PEGGED FOR SUCH A...
...BROAD-MINDED HUSBAND.
KYAAAAAAAAAA--!

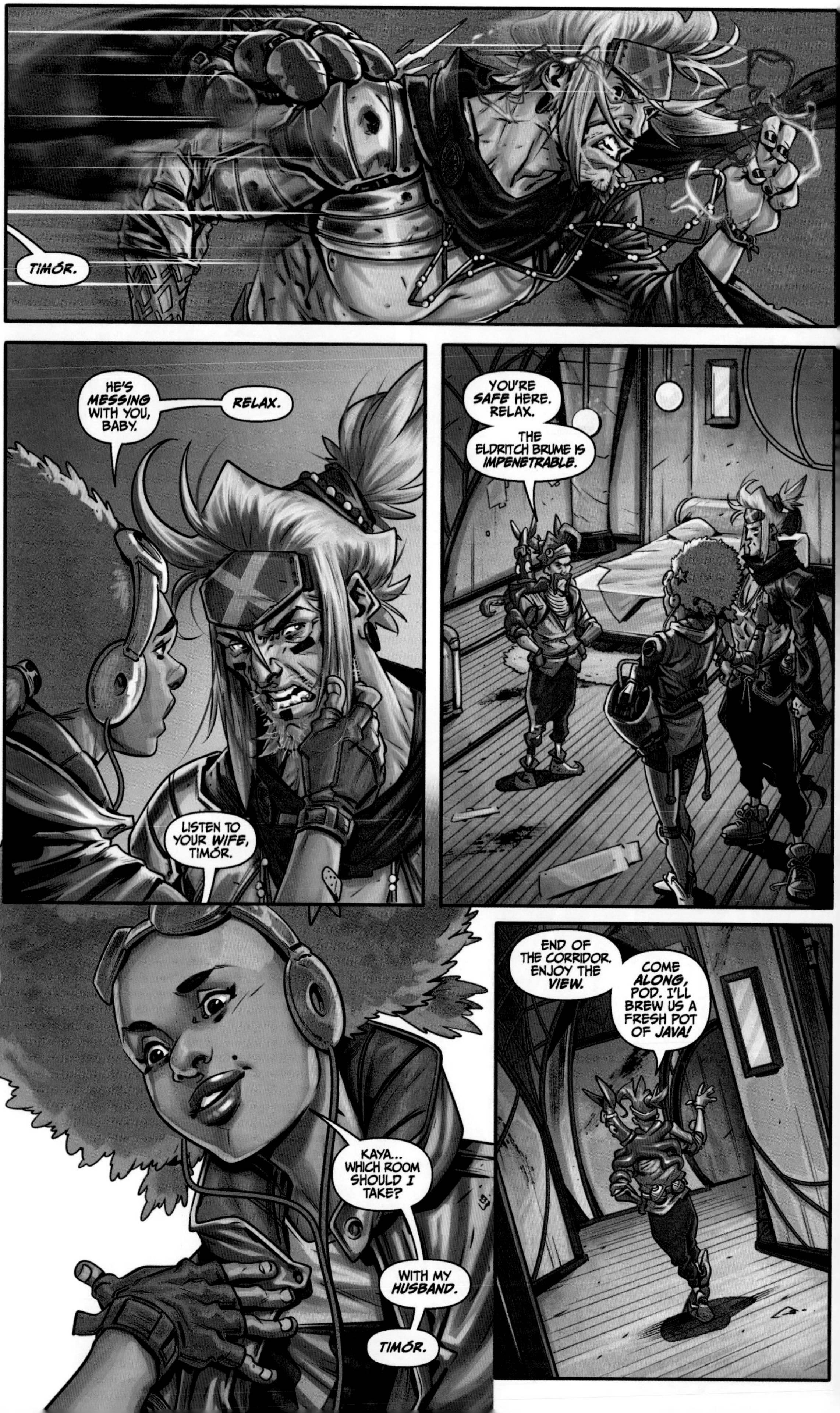
TIMÓR.
HE'S MESSING WITH YOU, BABY.
RELAX.
LISTEN TO YOUR WIFE, TIMÓR.
YOU'RE SAFE HERE. RELAX.
THE ELDRITCH BRUME IS IMPENETRABLE.
KAYA... WHICH ROOM SHOULD I TAKE?
WITH MY HUSBAND.
TIMÓR.
END OF THE CORRIDOR. ENJOY THE VIEW.
COME ALONG, POD. I'LL BREW US A FRESH POT OF JAVA!

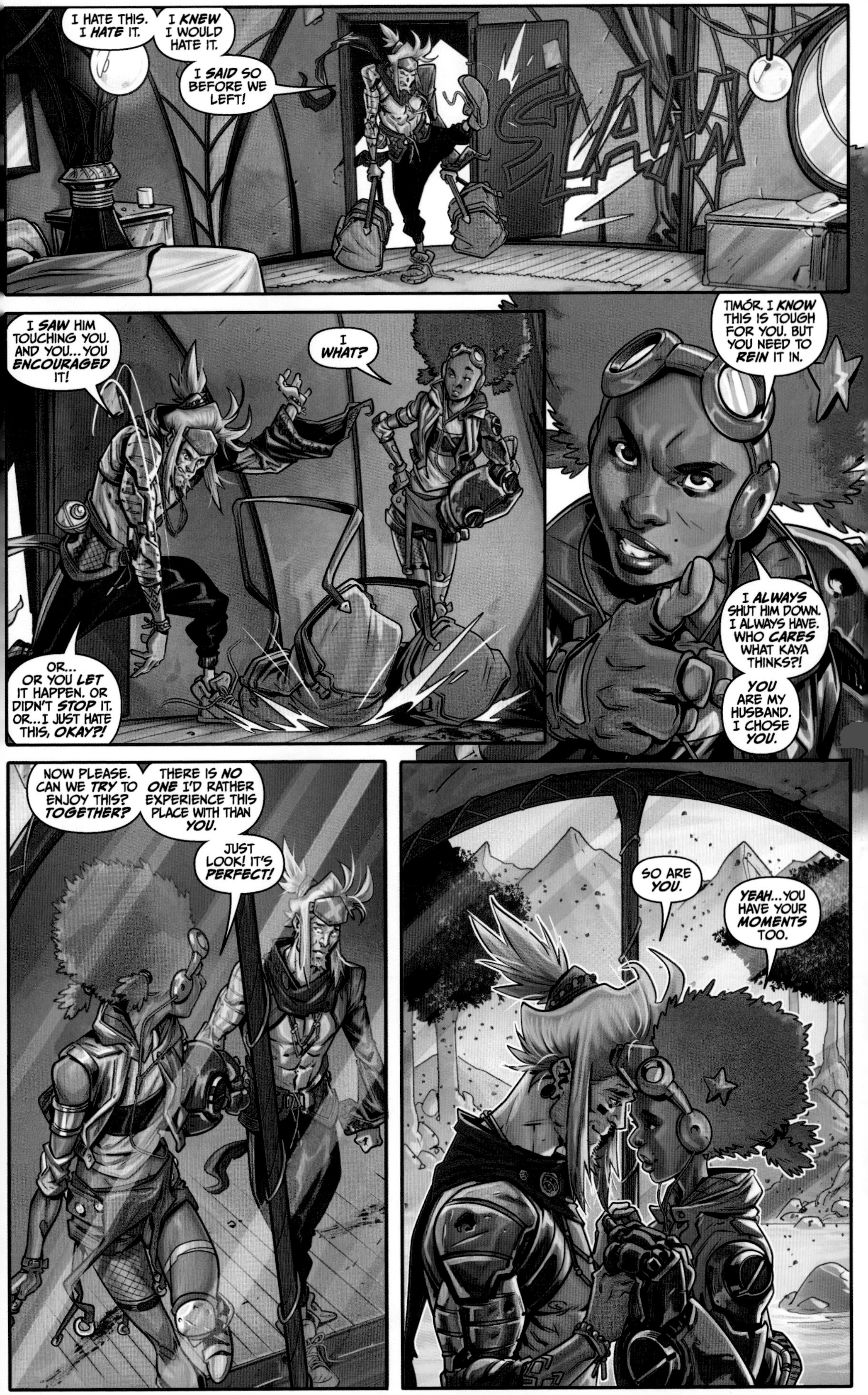
I HATE THIS. I *HATE* IT.
I *KNEW* I WOULD HATE IT.
I *SAID* SO BEFORE WE LEFT!
SLAM
I *SAW* HIM TOUCHING YOU. AND YOU...YOU *ENCOURAGED* IT!
I *WHAT?*
OR... OR YOU *LET* IT HAPPEN. OR DIDN'T *STOP* IT. OR...I JUST HATE THIS, *OKAY?!*
TIMÓR, I *KNOW* THIS IS TOUGH FOR YOU. BUT YOU NEED TO *REIN* IT IN.
I *ALWAYS* SHUT HIM DOWN. I ALWAYS HAVE. WHO *CARES* WHAT KAYA THINKS?!
YOU ARE MY HUSBAND. I CHOSE *YOU*.
NOW PLEASE. CAN WE *TRY* TO ENJOY THIS? *TOGETHER?*
THERE IS *NO ONE* I'D RATHER EXPERIENCE THIS PLACE WITH THAN *YOU*.
JUST LOOK! IT'S *PERFECT!*
SO ARE *YOU*.
YEAH...YOU HAVE YOUR *MOMENTS* TOO.

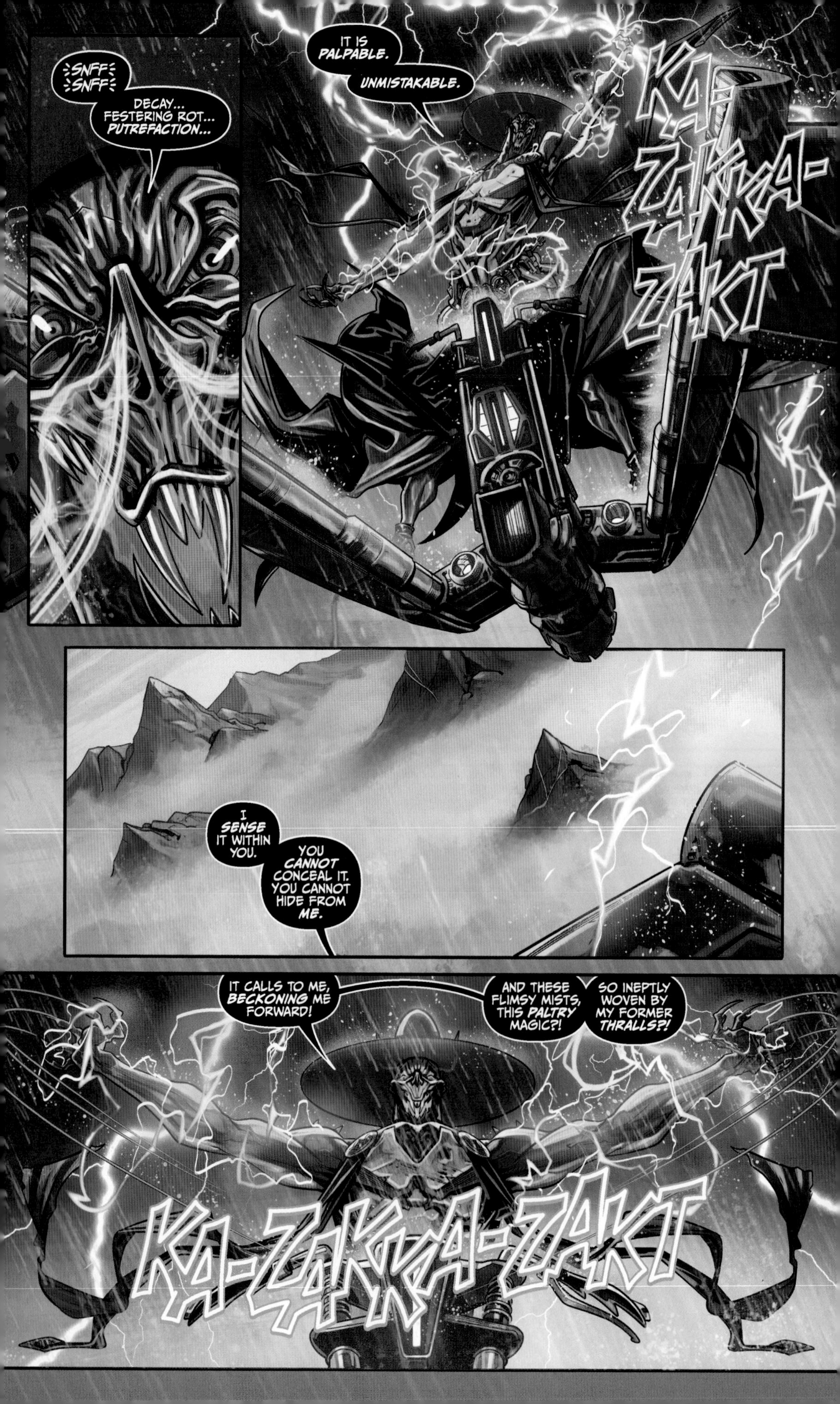
SNFF SNFF
DECAY... FESTERING ROT... PUTREFACTION...
IT IS PALPABLE.
UNMISTAKABLE.
KA-ZAKKA-ZAKT
I SENSE IT WITHIN YOU.
YOU CANNOT CONCEAL IT. YOU CANNOT HIDE FROM ME.
IT CALLS TO ME, BECKONING ME FORWARD!
AND THESE FLIMSY MISTS, THIS PALTRY MAGIC?!
SO INEPTLY WOVEN BY MY FORMER THRALLS?!
KA-ZAKKA-ZAKT

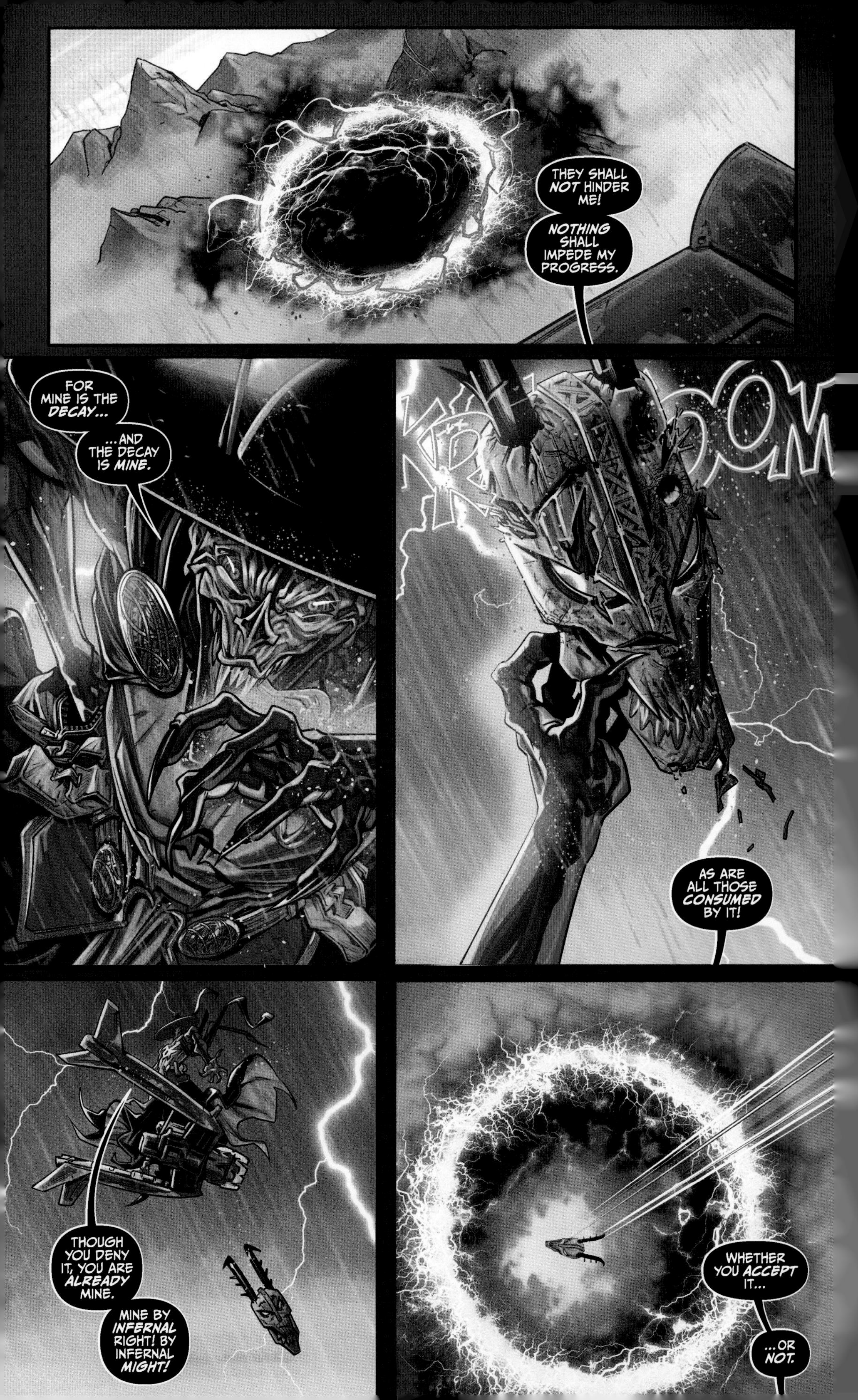
THEY SHALL NOT HINDER ME!
NOTHING SHALL IMPEDE MY PROGRESS.
FOR MINE IS THE DECAY...
...AND THE DECAY IS MINE.
AS ARE ALL THOSE CONSUMED BY IT!
THOUGH YOU DENY IT, YOU ARE ALREADY MINE.
MINE BY INFERNAL RIGHT! BY INFERNAL MIGHT!
WHETHER YOU ACCEPT IT...
...OR NOT.

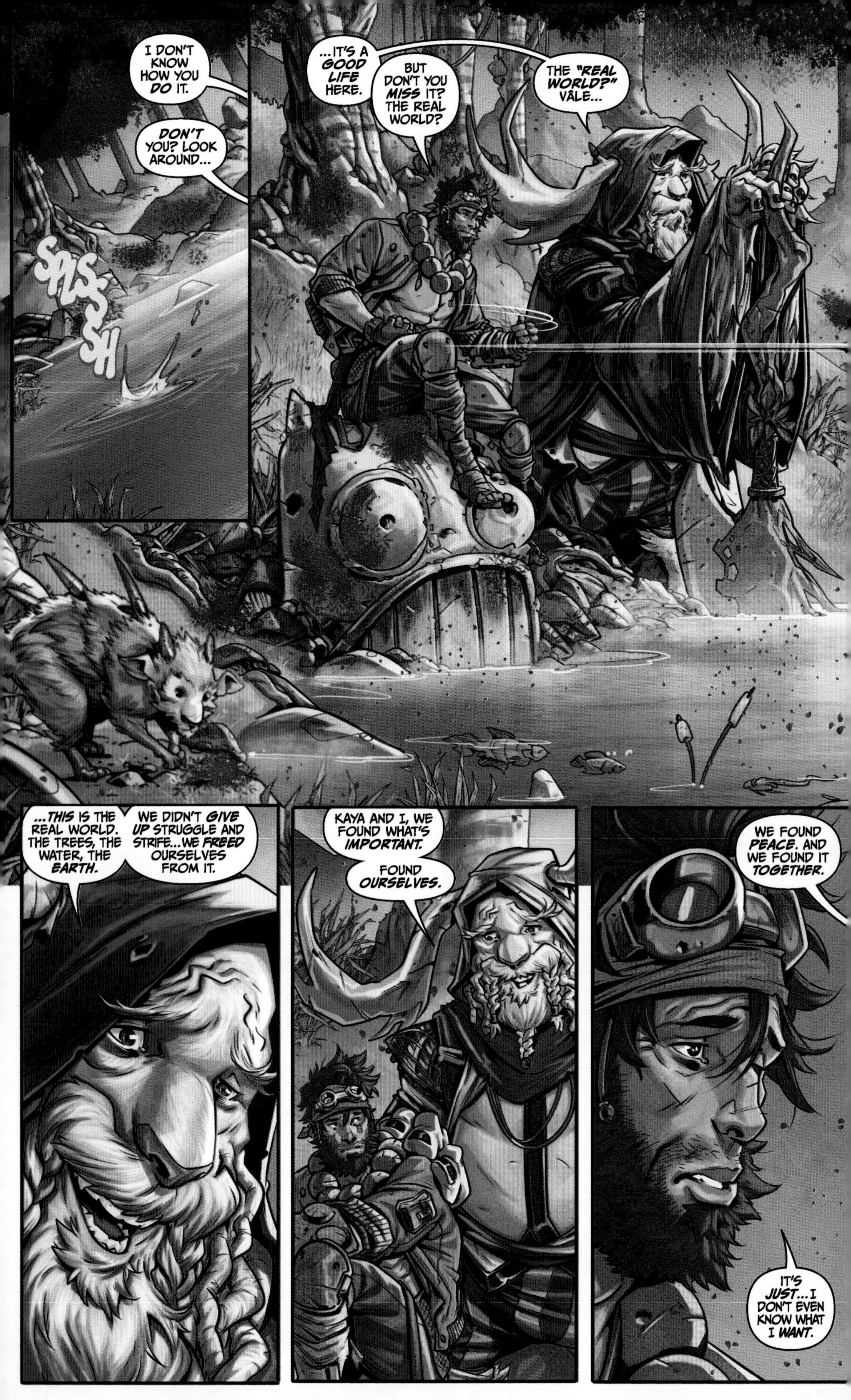
I DON'T KNOW HOW YOU DO IT.
DON'T YOU? LOOK AROUND...
SPLSSSH
...IT'S A GOOD LIFE HERE.
BUT DON'T YOU MISS IT? THE REAL WORLD?
THE "REAL WORLD?" VÂLE...
...THIS IS THE REAL WORLD. THE TREES, THE WATER, THE EARTH.
WE DIDN'T GIVE UP STRUGGLE AND STRIFE...WE FREED OURSELVES FROM IT.
KAYA AND I, WE FOUND WHAT'S IMPORTANT.
FOUND OURSELVES.
WE FOUND PEACE. AND WE FOUND IT TOGETHER.
IT'S JUST...I DON'T EVEN KNOW WHAT I WANT.

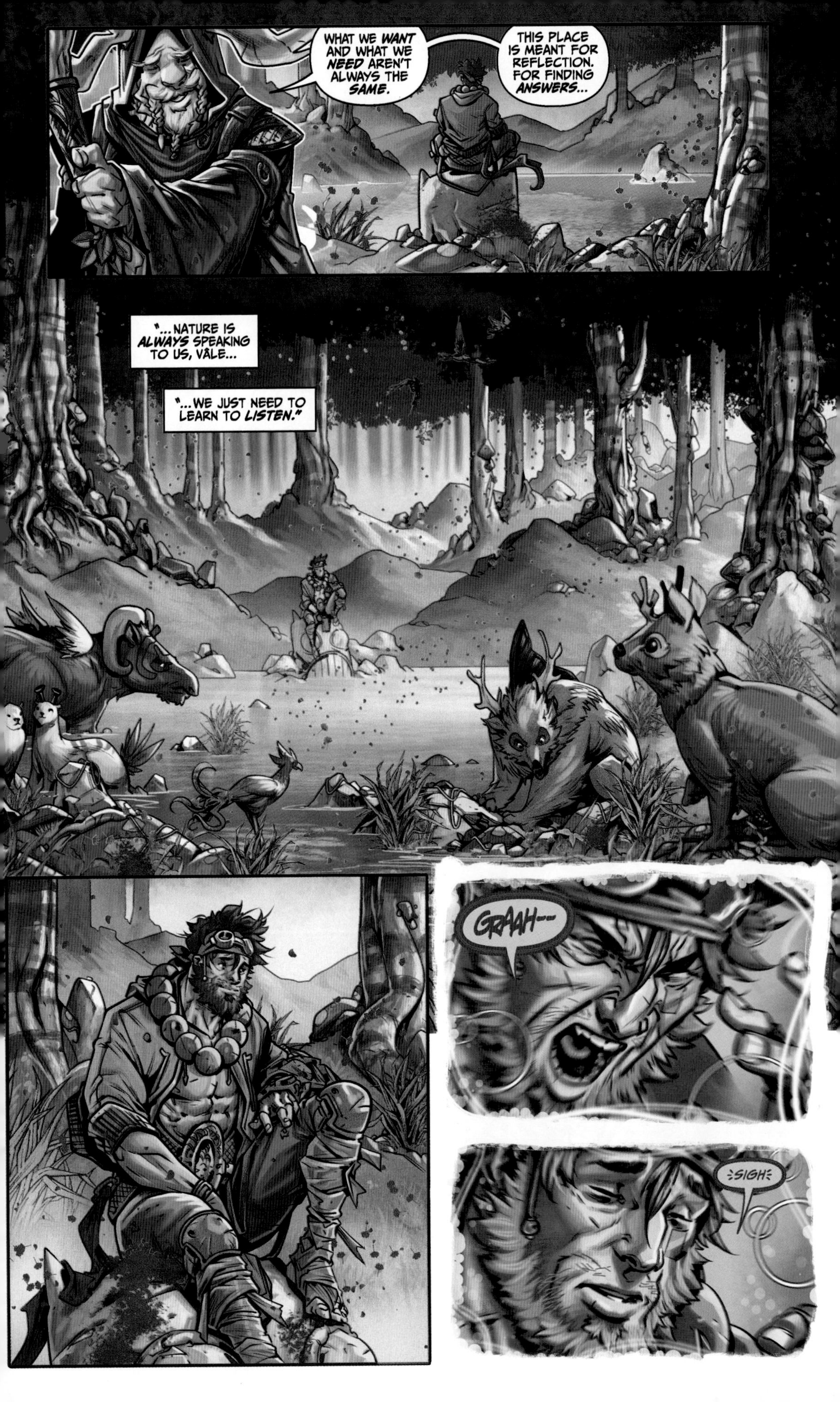
WHAT WE WANT AND WHAT WE NEED AREN'T ALWAYS THE SAME.
THIS PLACE IS MEANT FOR REFLECTION. FOR FINDING ANSWERS...
"...NATURE IS ALWAYS SPEAKING TO US, VÅLE...
"...WE JUST NEED TO LEARN TO LISTEN."
GRAAH--
SIGH

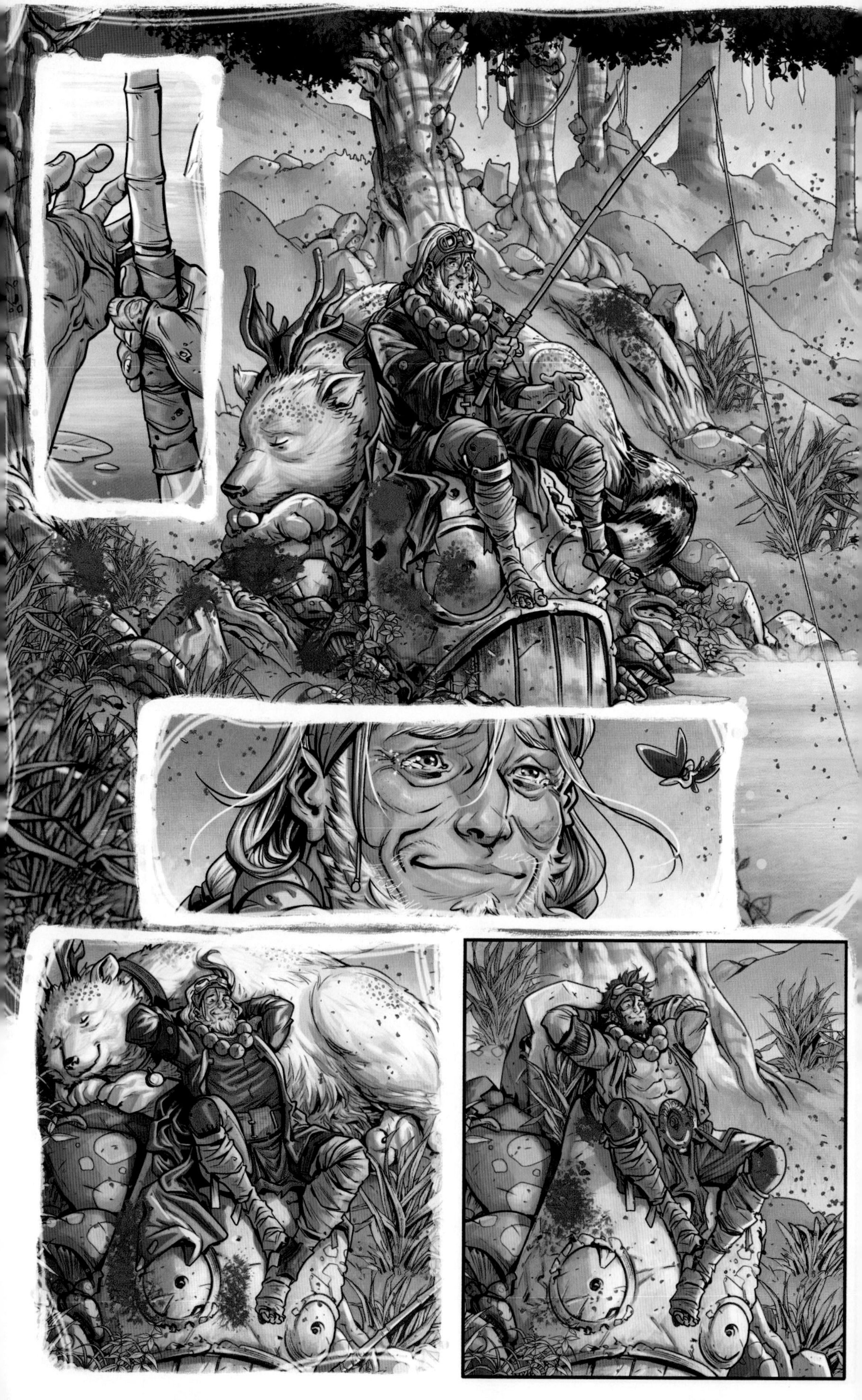

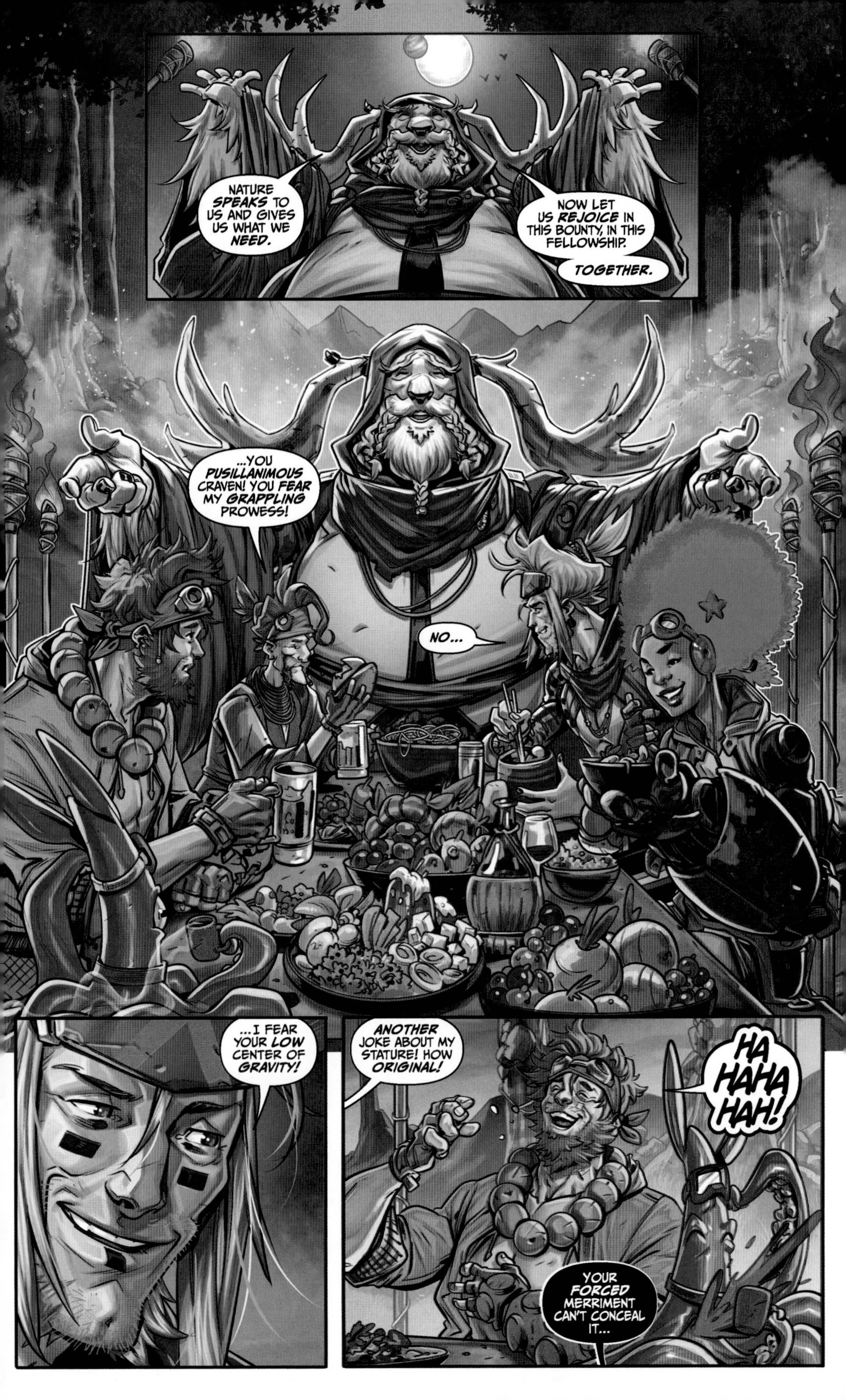
NATURE SPEAKS TO US AND GIVES US WHAT WE NEED.
NOW LET US REJOICE IN THIS BOUNTY, IN THIS FELLOWSHIP.
TOGETHER.
...YOU PUSILLANIMOUS CRAVEN! YOU FEAR MY GRAPPLING PROWESS!
NO...
...I FEAR YOUR LOW CENTER OF GRAVITY!
ANOTHER JOKE ABOUT MY STATURE! HOW ORIGINAL!
HA HAHA HAH!
YOUR FORCED MERRIMENT CAN'T CONCEAL IT...

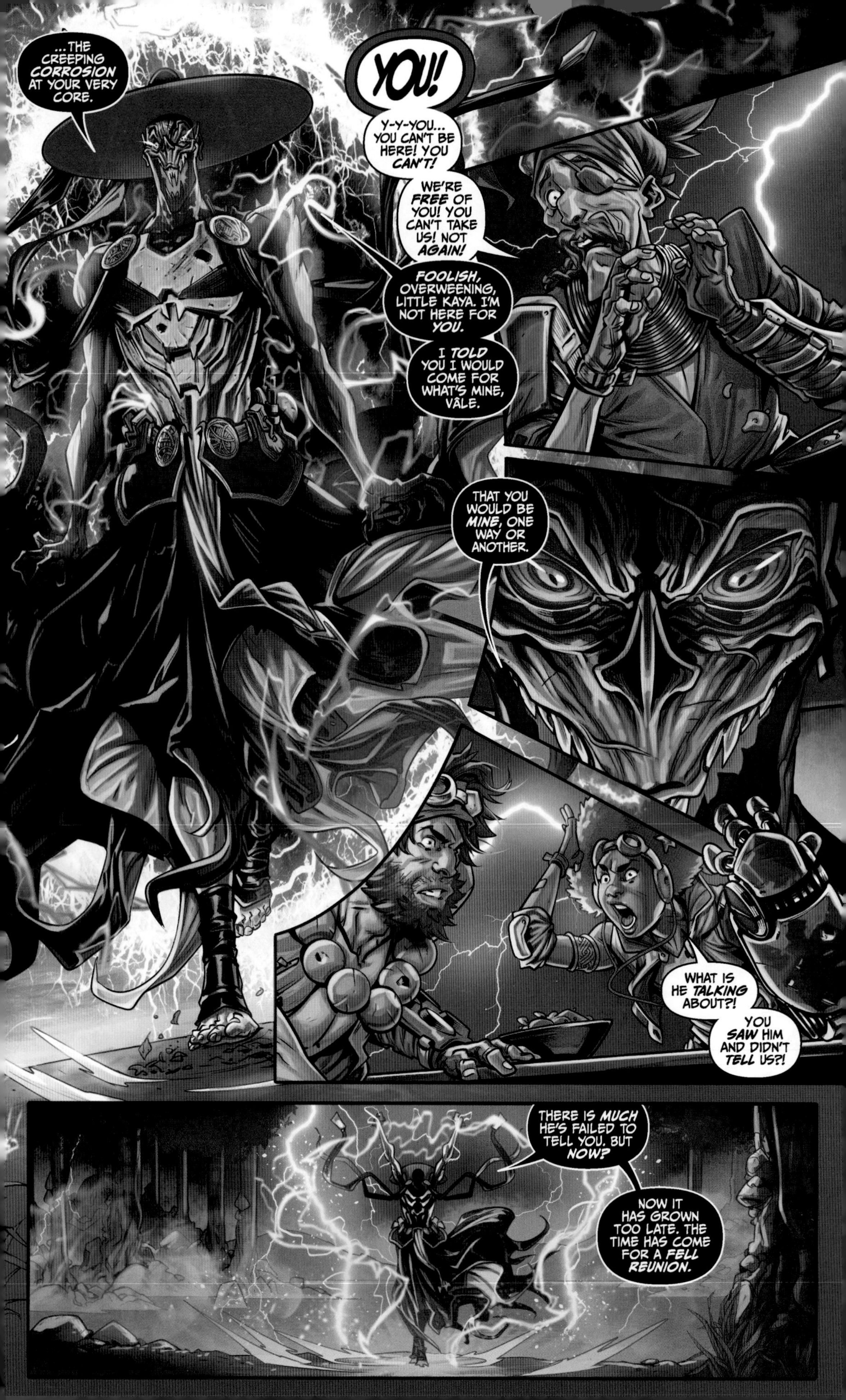
...THE CREEPING CORROSION AT YOUR VERY CORE.
YOU!
Y-Y-YOU... YOU CAN'T BE HERE! YOU CAN'T!
WE'RE FREE OF YOU! YOU CAN'T TAKE US! NOT AGAIN!
FOOLISH, OVERWEENING, LITTLE KAYA. I'M NOT HERE FOR YOU.
I TOLD YOU I WOULD COME FOR WHAT'S MINE, VÂLE.
THAT YOU WOULD BE MINE, ONE WAY OR ANOTHER.
WHAT IS HE TALKING ABOUT?!
YOU SAW HIM AND DIDN'T TELL US?!
THERE IS MUCH HE'S FAILED TO TELL YOU. BUT NOW?
NOW IT HAS GROWN TOO LATE. THE TIME HAS COME FOR A FELL REUNION.

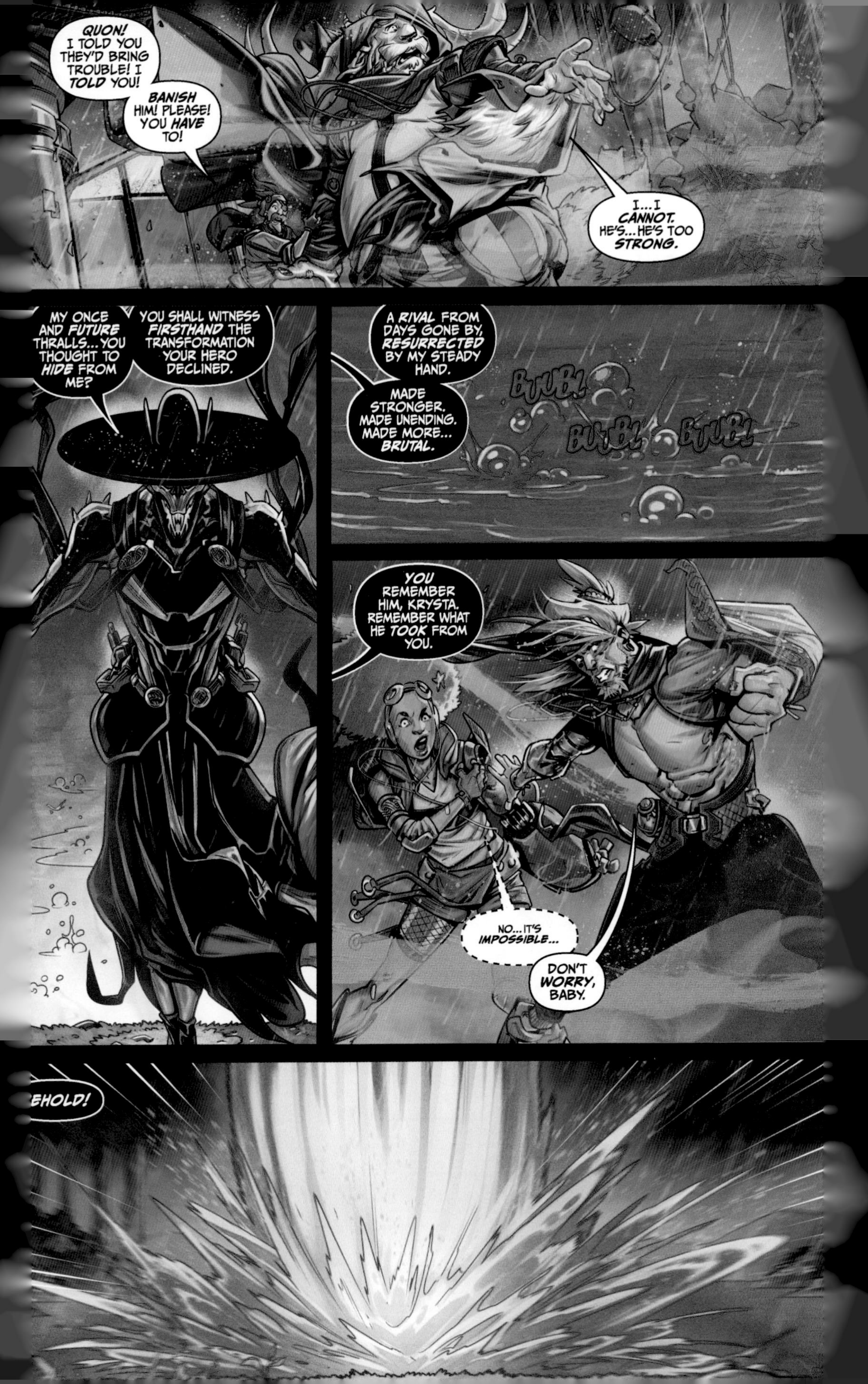
QUON! I TOLD YOU THEY'D BRING TROUBLE! I TOLD YOU!
BANISH HIM! PLEASE! YOU HAVE TO!
I...I CANNOT. HE'S...HE'S TOO STRONG.
MY ONCE AND FUTURE THRALLS...YOU THOUGHT TO HIDE FROM ME?
YOU SHALL WITNESS FIRSTHAND THE TRANSFORMATION YOUR HERO DECLINED.
A RIVAL FROM DAYS GONE BY, RESURRECTED BY MY STEADY HAND.
MADE STRONGER. MADE UNENDING. MADE MORE... BRUTAL.
BLUBL
BLUBL
BLUBL
YOU REMEMBER HIM, KRYSTA. REMEMBER WHAT HE TOOK FROM YOU.
NO...IT'S IMPOSSIBLE...
DON'T WORRY, BABY.
EHOLD!

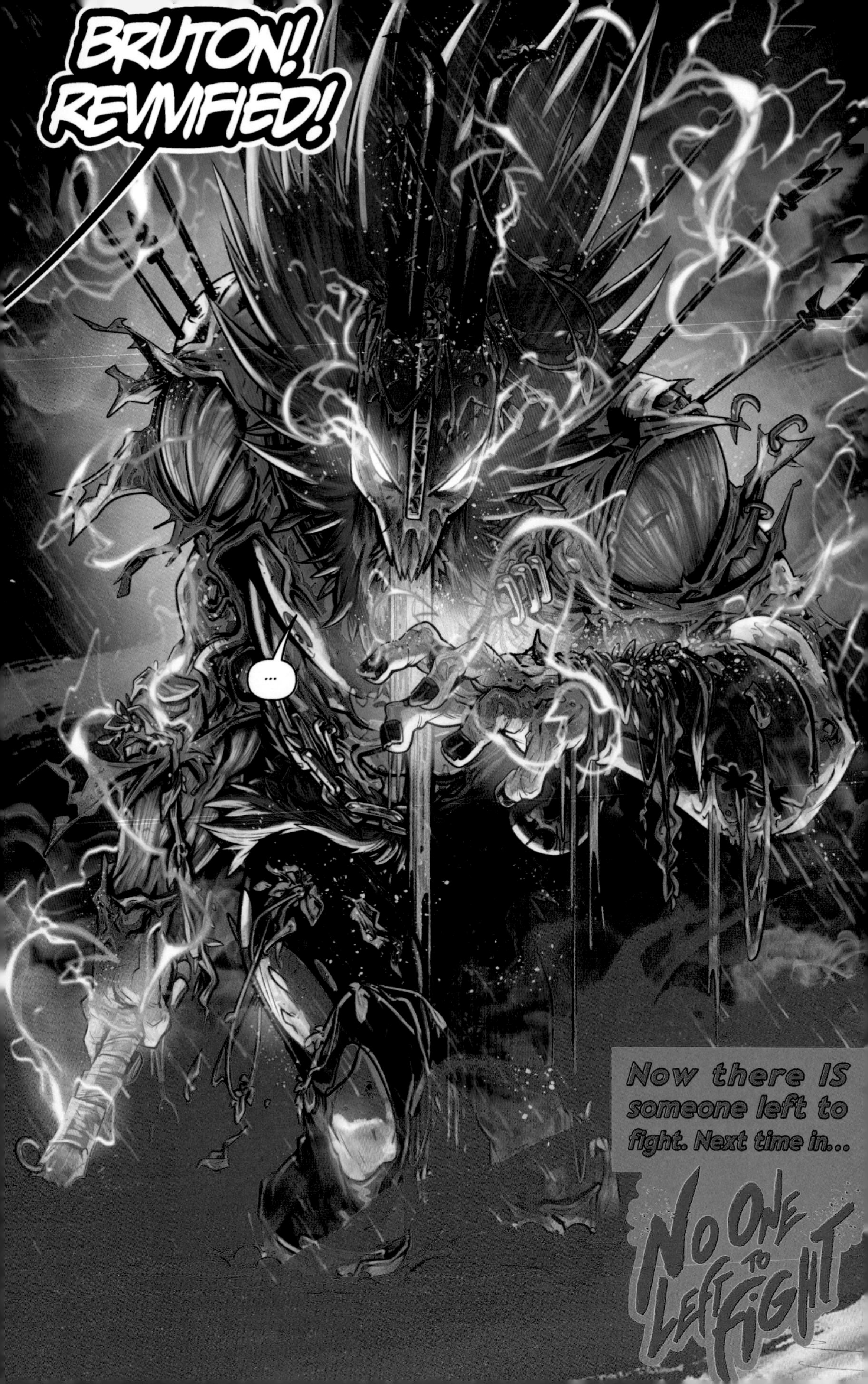
BRUTON! REVIVIFIED!
...
Now there IS someone left to fight. Next time in...
NO ONE LEFT TO FIGHT

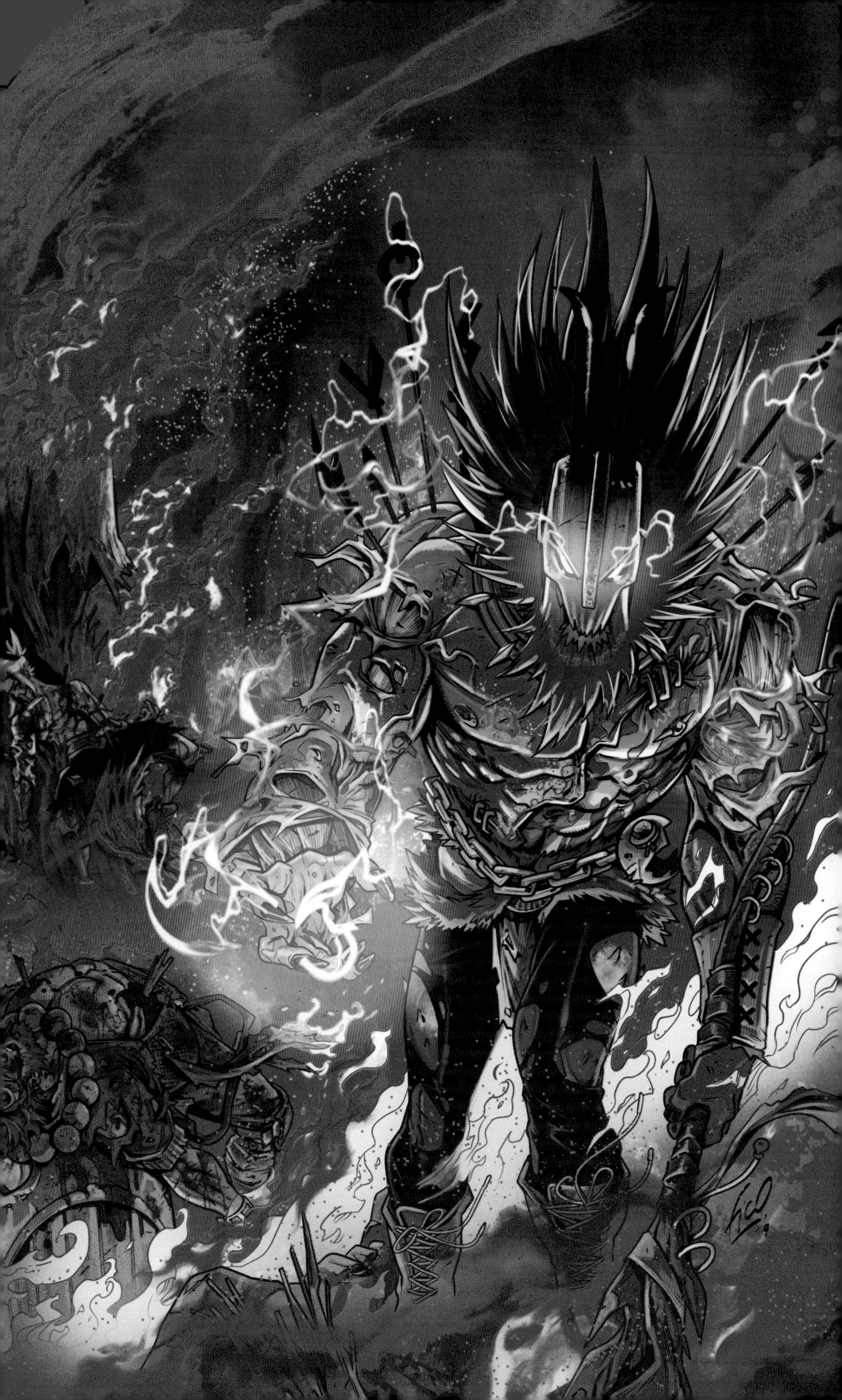

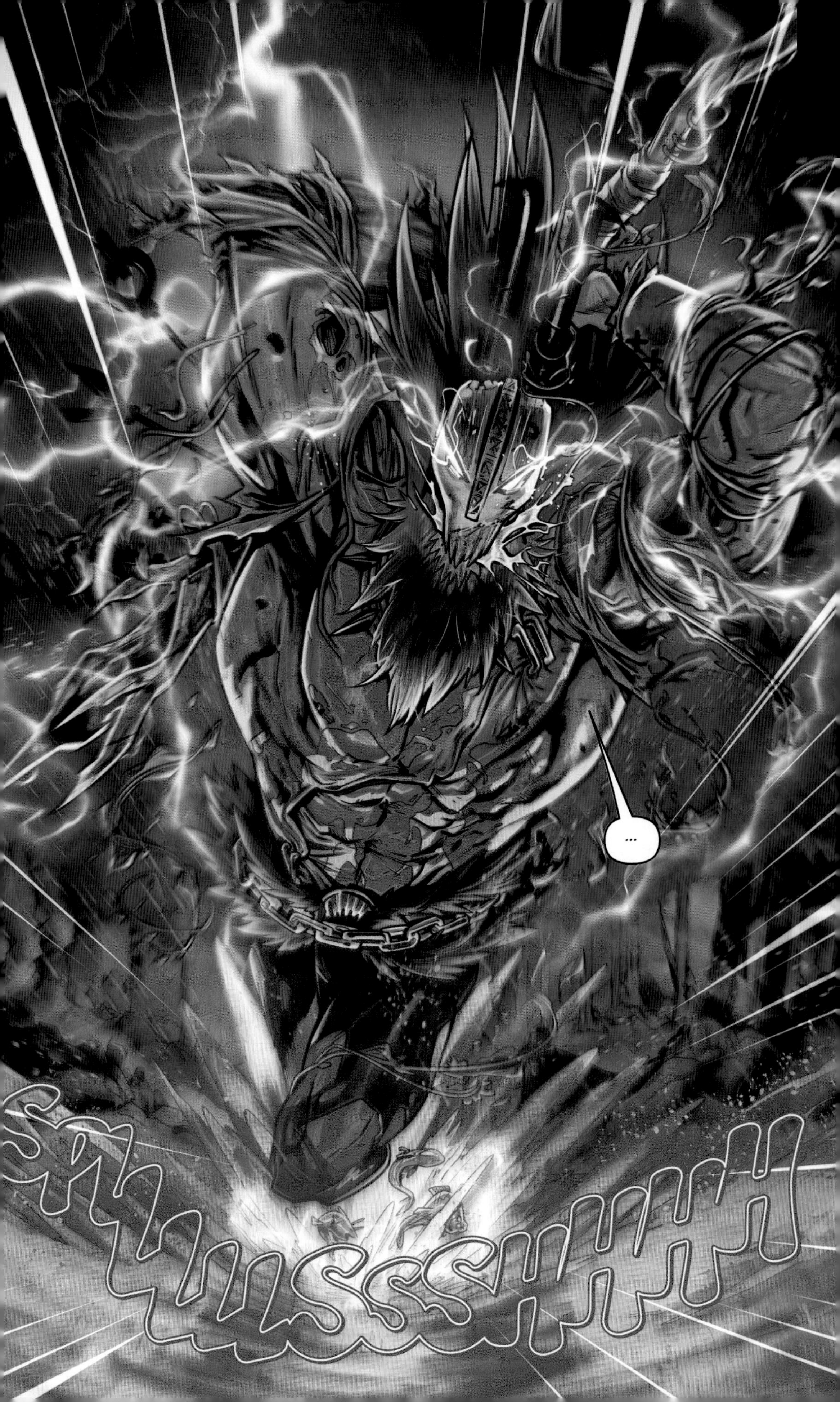
...
SHHHUSSSHHHHH

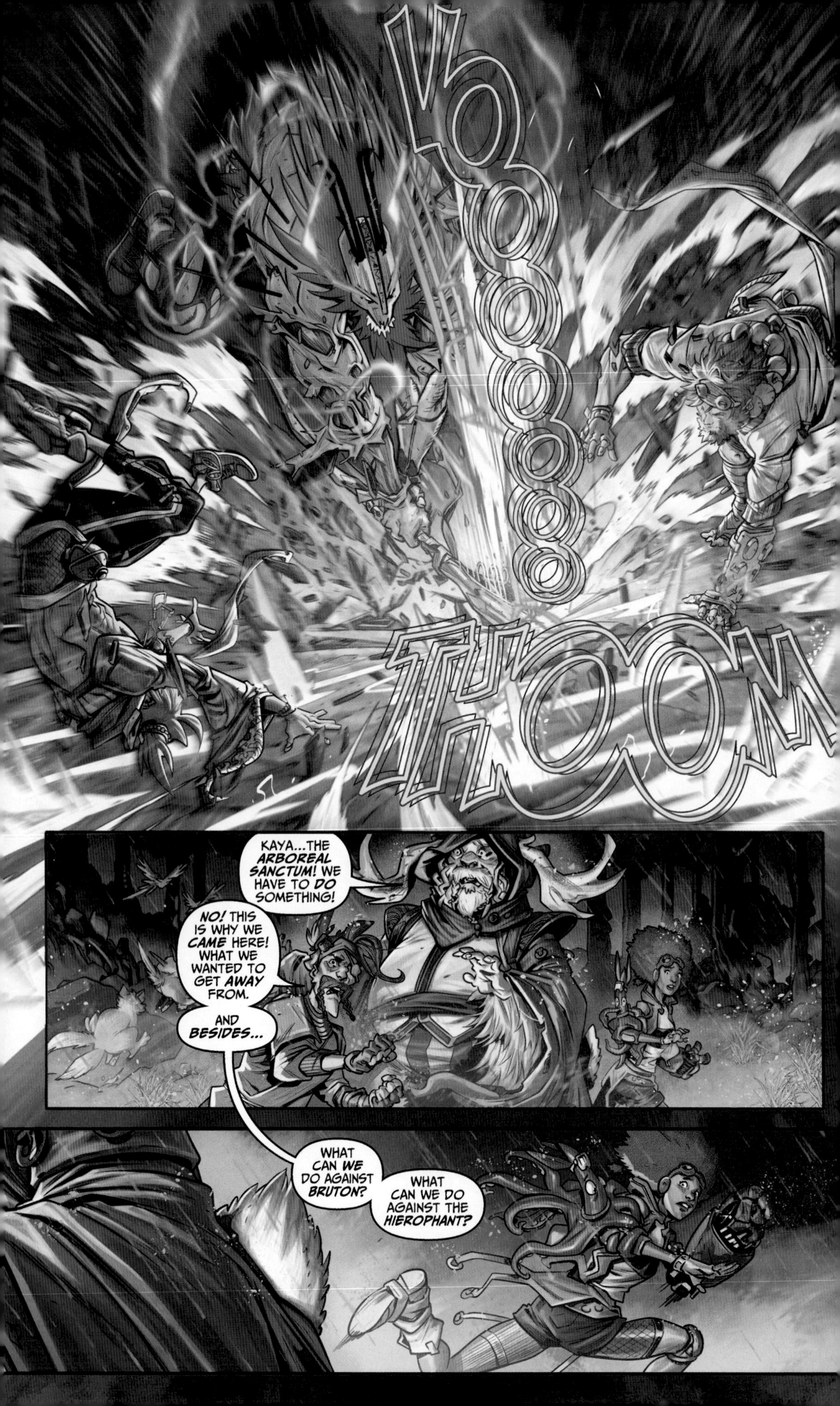
VOOOOOOOO
THOOM
KAYA...THE ARBOREAL SANCTUM! WE HAVE TO DO SOMETHING!
NO! THIS IS WHY WE CAME HERE! WHAT WE WANTED TO GET AWAY FROM.
AND BESIDES...
WHAT CAN WE DO AGAINST BRUTON?
WHAT CAN WE DO AGAINST THE HIEROPHANT?

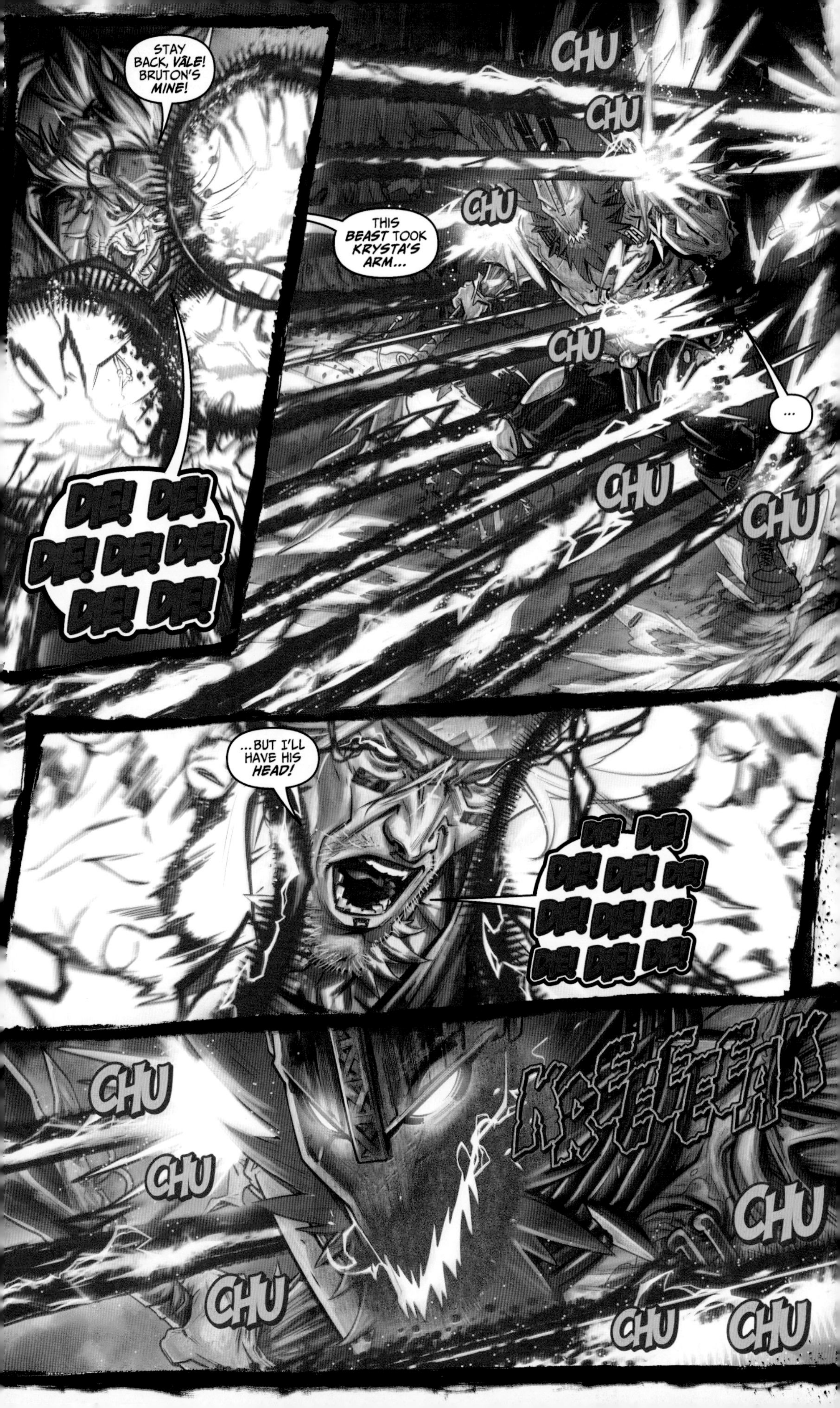
STAY BACK, VALE! BRUTON'S MINE!
CHU
CHU
CHU
THIS BEAST TOOK KRYSTA'S ARM...
CHU
...
CHU
CHU
DIE! DIE! DIE! DIE! DIE! DIE! DIE!
...BUT I'LL HAVE HIS HEAD!
DIE! DIE! DIE! DIE! DIE! DIE! DIE! DIE! DIE! DIE! DIE!
CHU
KREEEEEAK
CHU
CHU
CHU
CHU
CHU

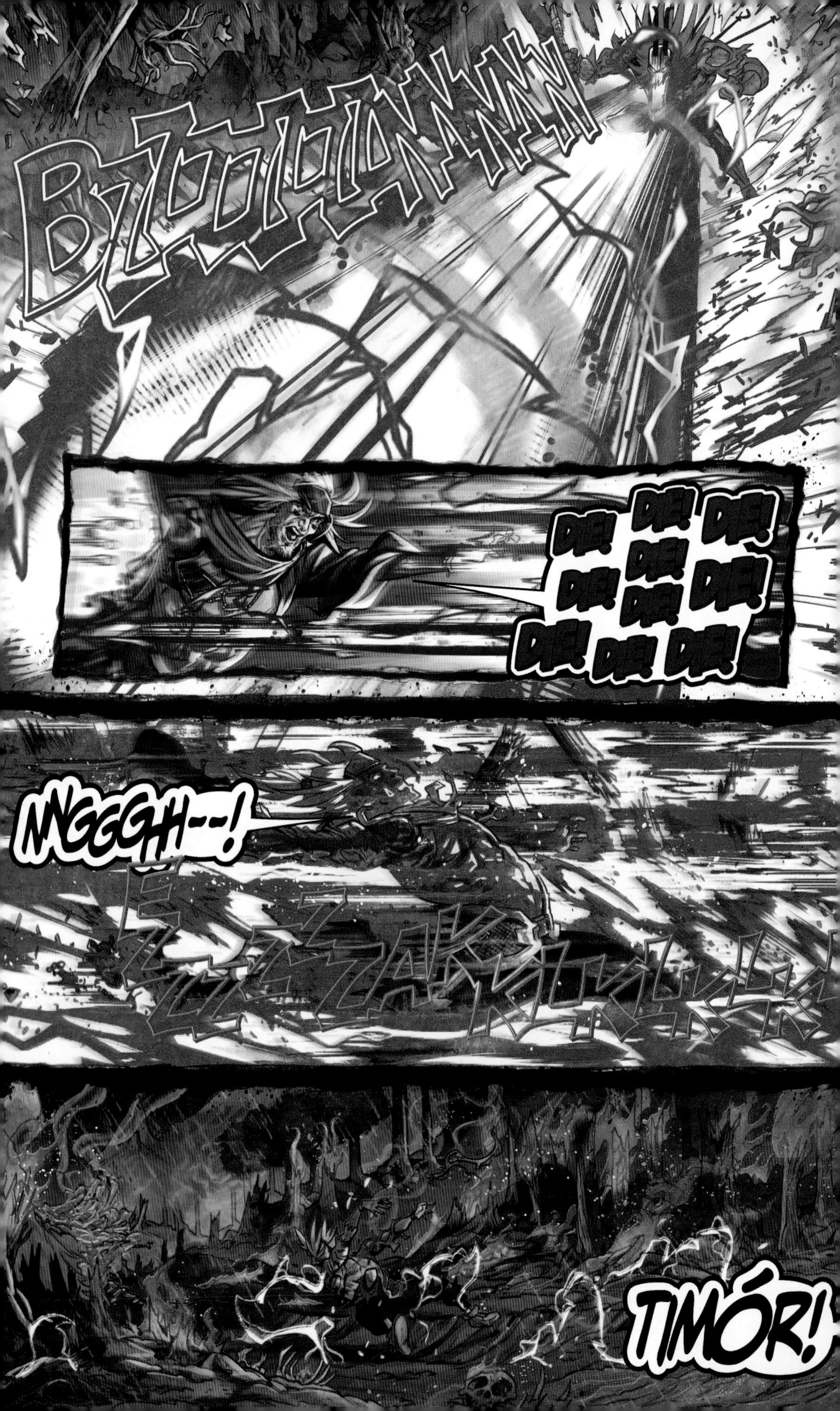
BZZOOOOOAAAWWWN
DIE! DIE! DIE! DIE! DIE! DIE! DIE! DIE! DIE! DIE! DIE!
NNGGGH--!
TIMÓR!

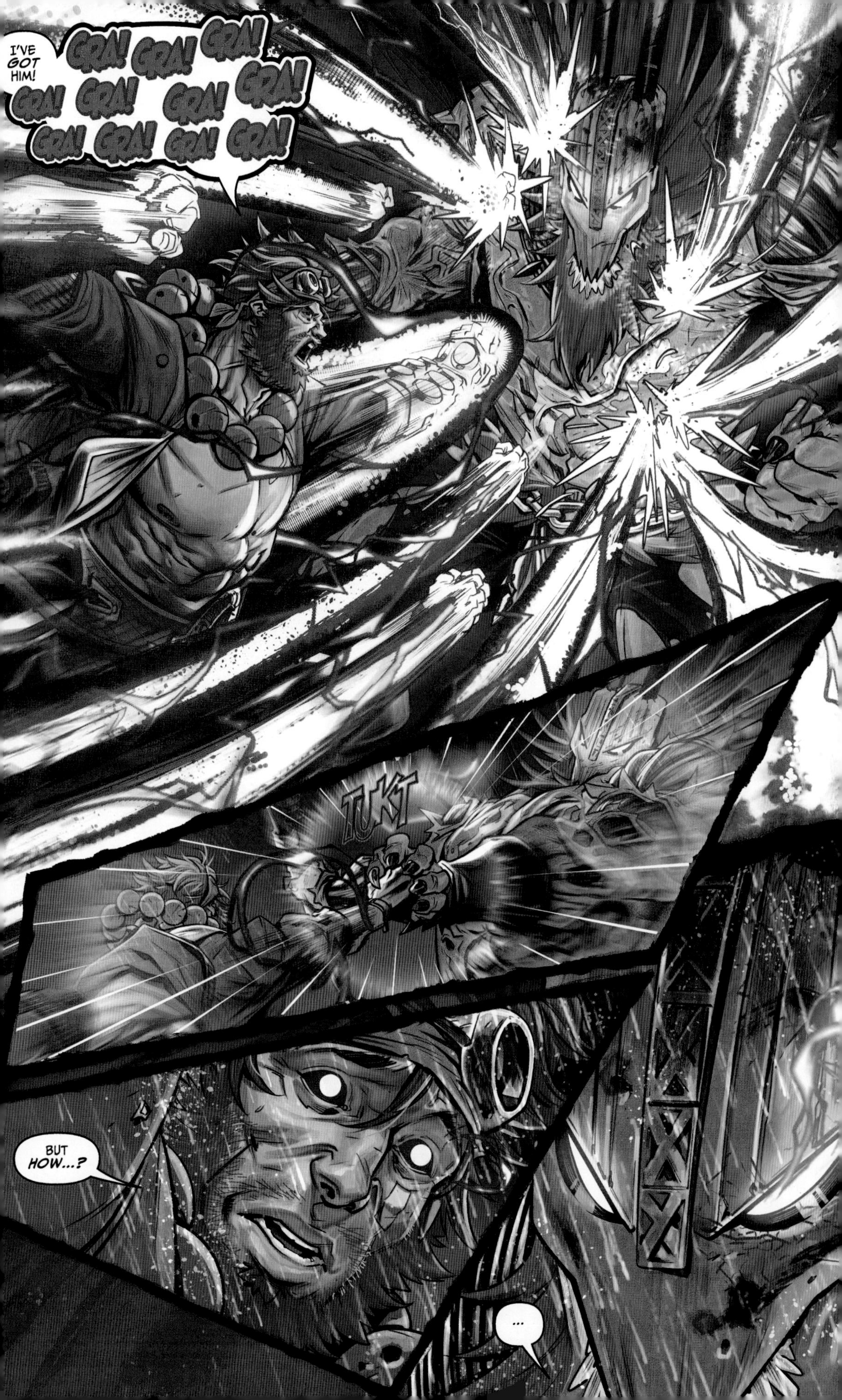
I'VE GOT HIM!
GRA! GRA! GRA! GRA! GRA! GRA! GRA! GRA! GRA! GRA! GRA!
TUKT
BUT HOW...?
...

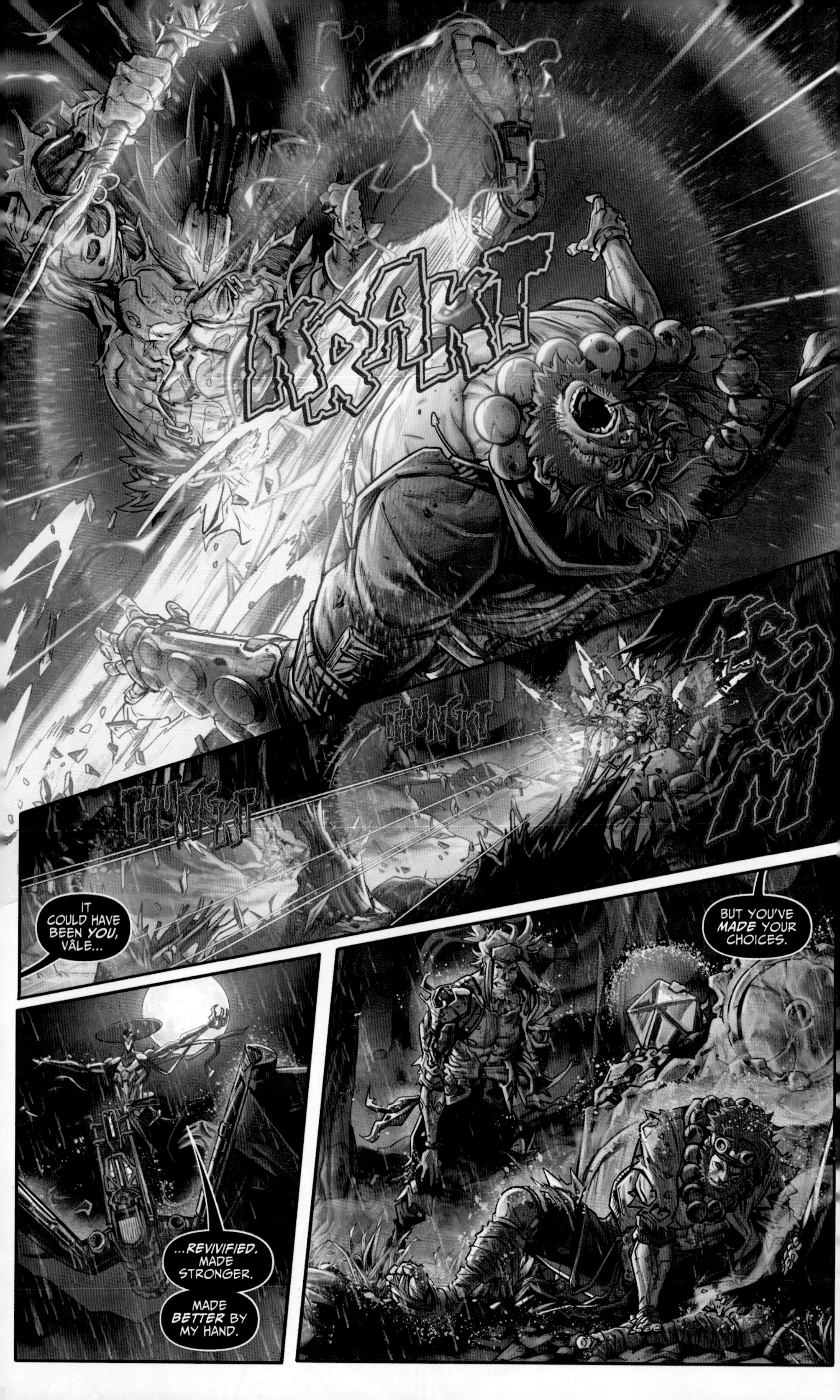

KRAKT
THUNGKT
THUNGKT
IT COULD HAVE BEEN *YOU*, VÅLE...
BUT YOU'VE *MADE* YOUR CHOICES.
...*REVIVIFIED.* MADE STRONGER.
MADE *BETTER* BY MY HAND.

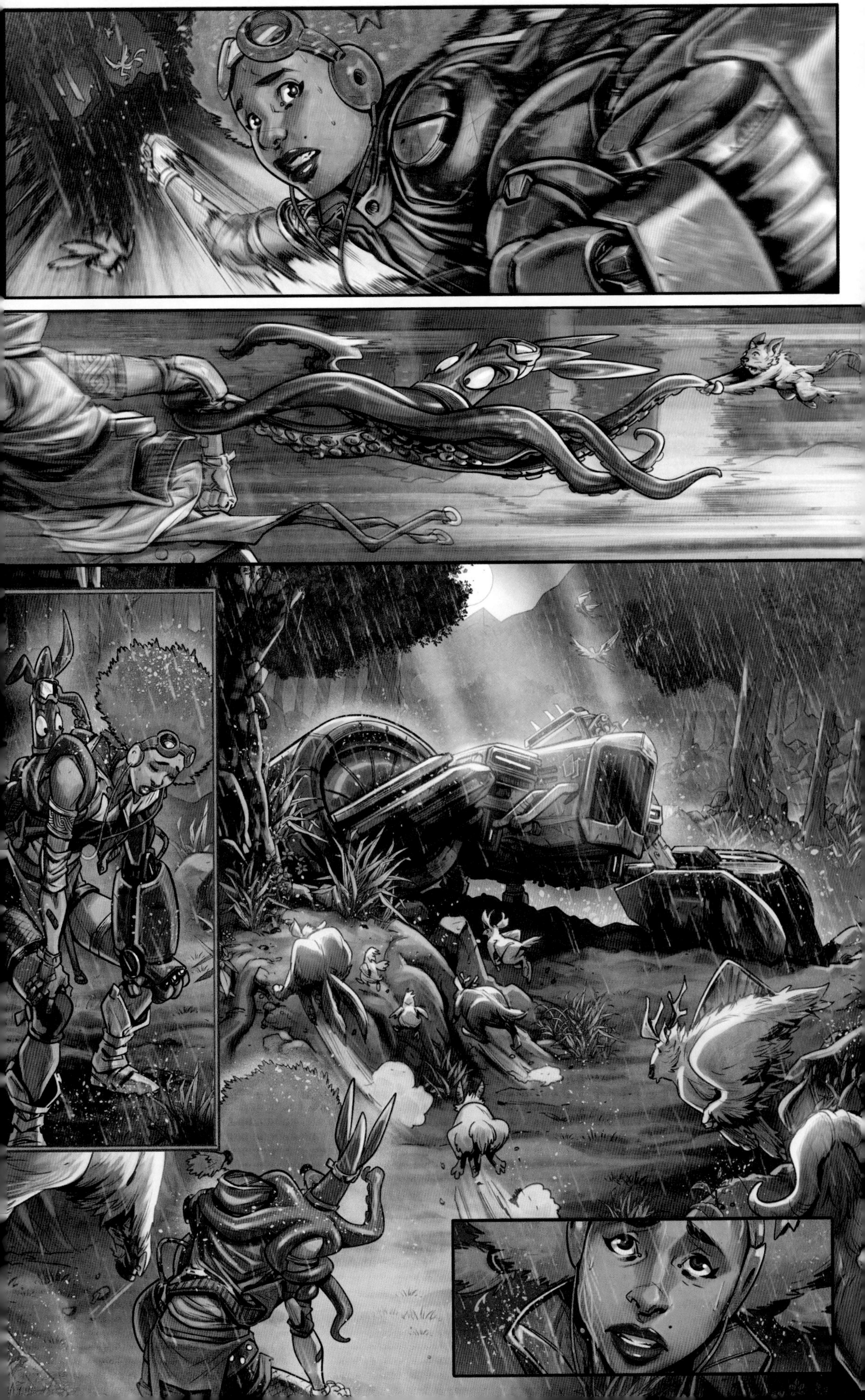

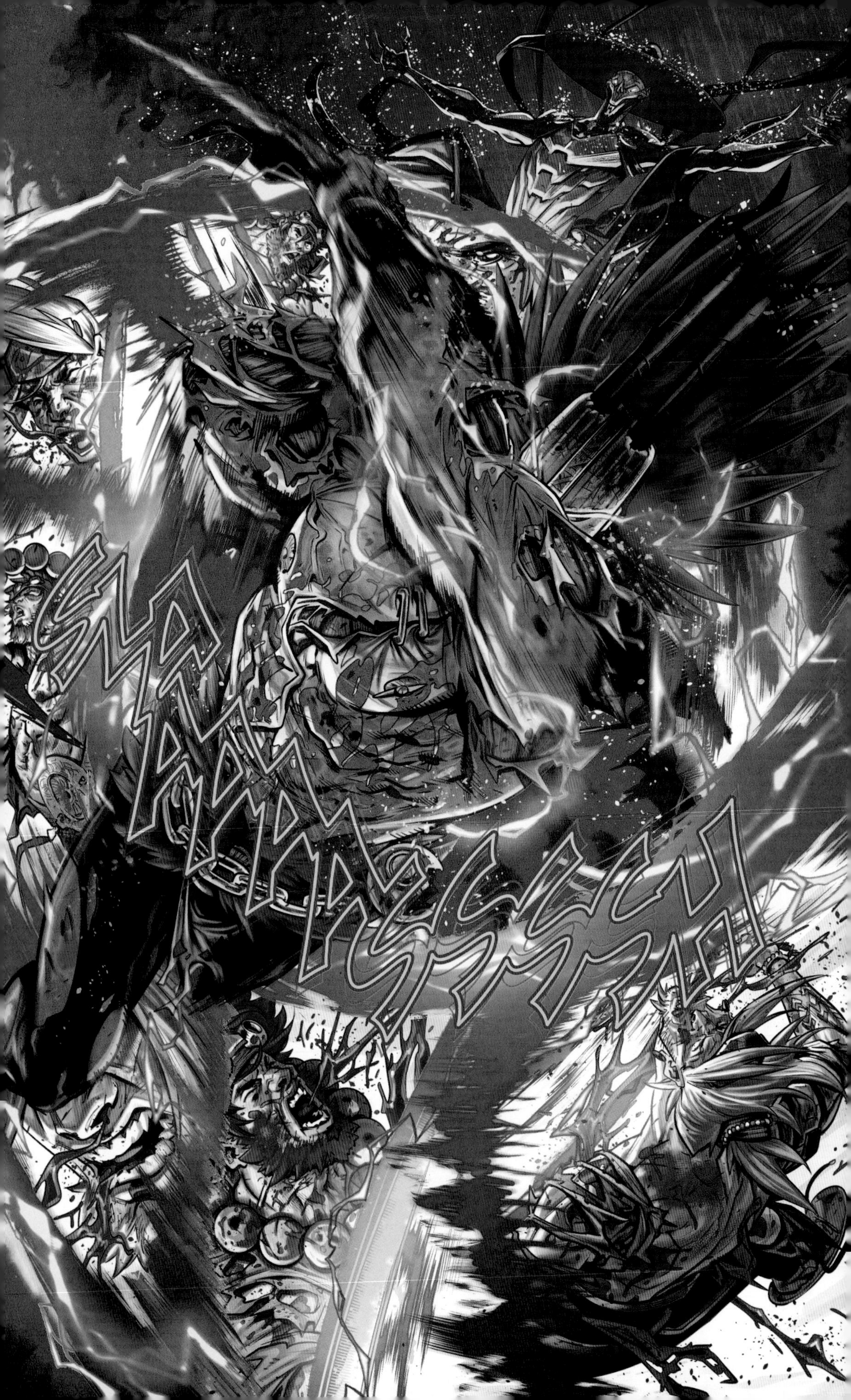

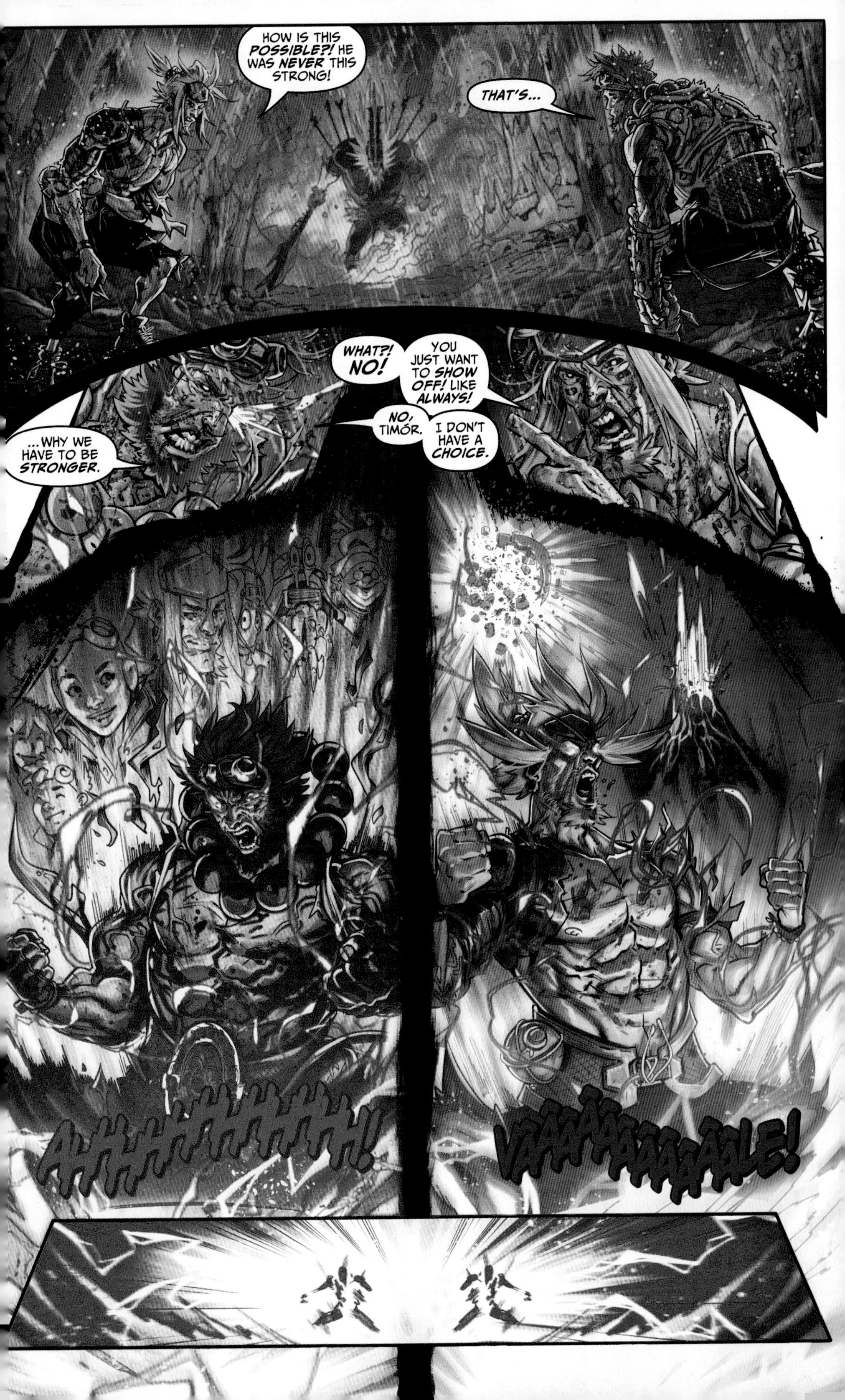
HOW IS THIS *POSSIBLE?!* HE WAS *NEVER* THIS STRONG!
THAT'S...
...WHY WE HAVE TO BE *STRONGER.*
WHAT?! NO!
YOU JUST WANT TO *SHOW OFF!* LIKE *ALWAYS!*
NO, TIMÓR.
I DON'T HAVE A *CHOICE.*
AHHHHHHHHHHH!
VÁÁÁÁÁÁÁÁÁLE!

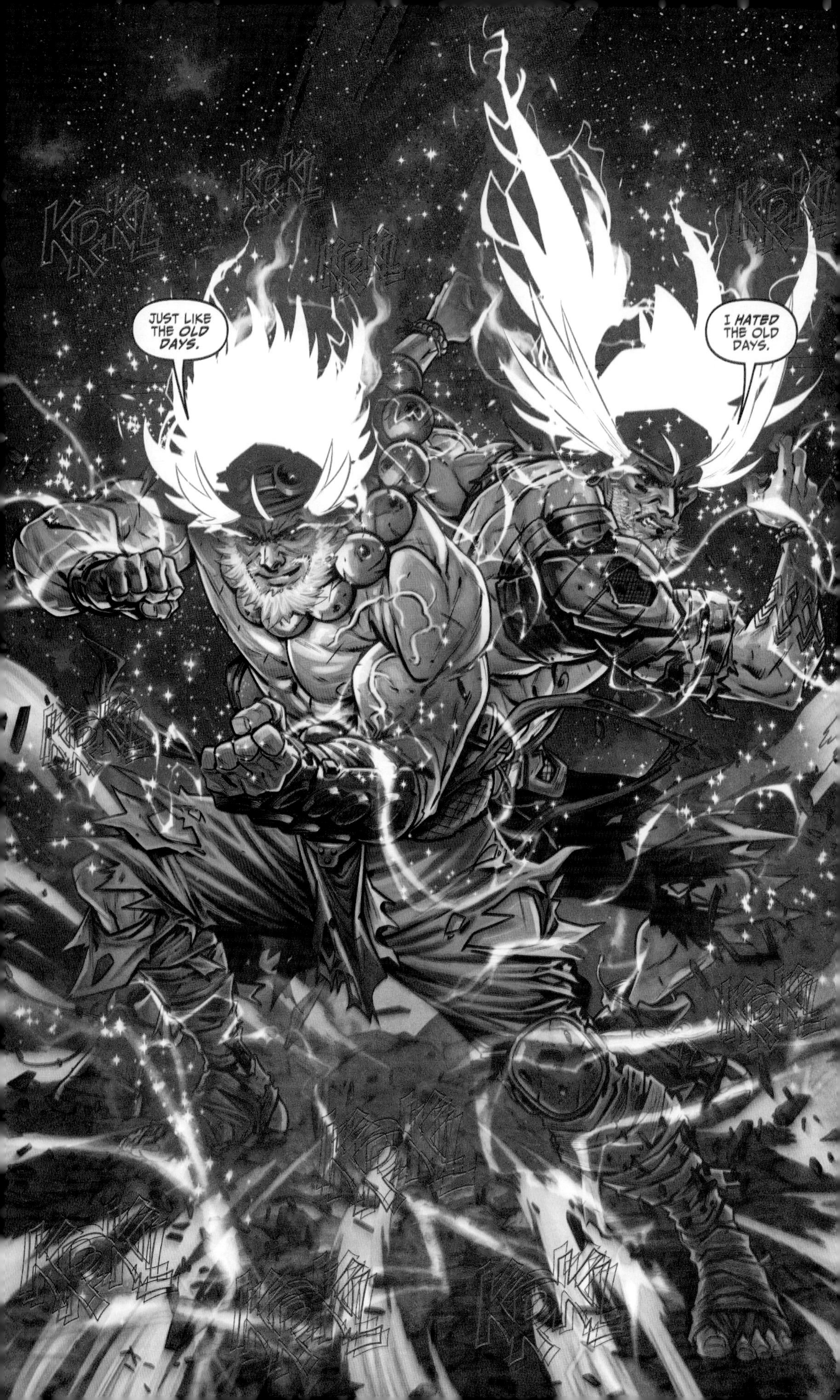
JUST LIKE THE OLD DAYS.
I HATED THE OLD DAYS.

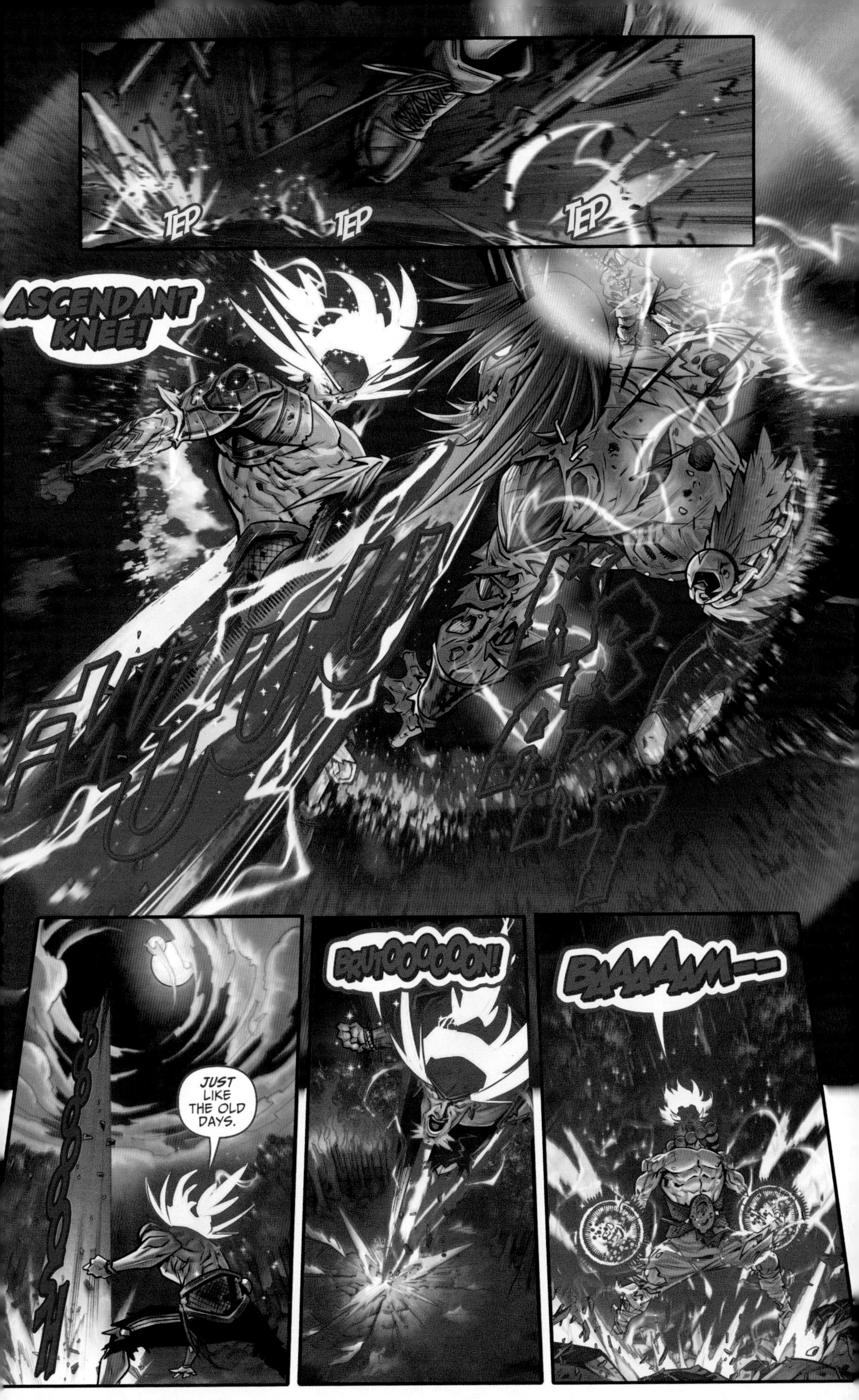

TEP
TEP
TEP
ASCENDANT KNEE!
JUST LIKE THE OLD DAYS.
BRUTOOOOOOON!
BAAAAM---

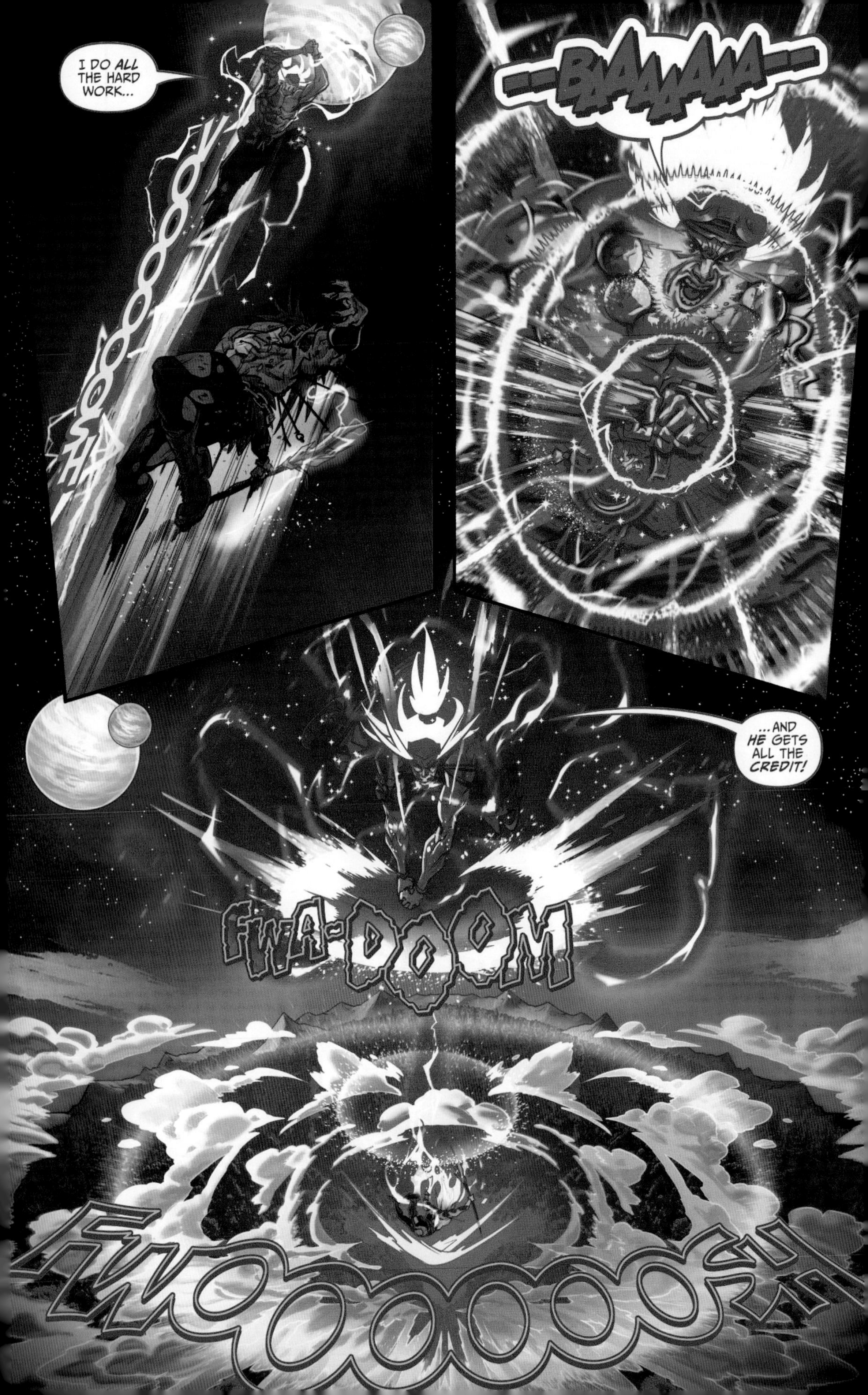

I DO ALL THE HARD WORK...
VOOOOOOOOM
--BWAAAAAA--
...AND HE GETS ALL THE CREDIT!
FWA-DOOM
FWOOOOOOOSH

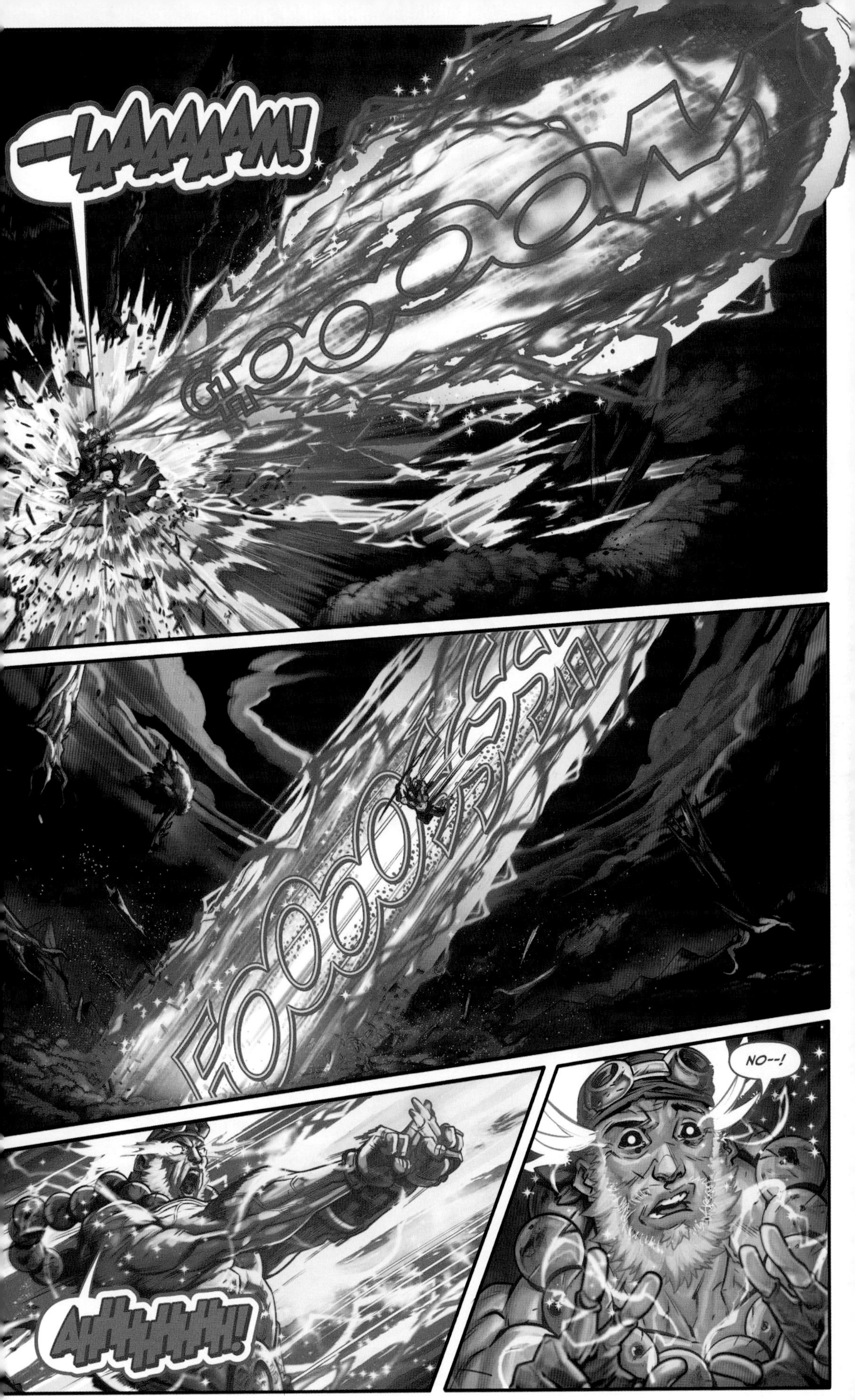
--LAAAAAM!
AHHHHHHH!
NO--!

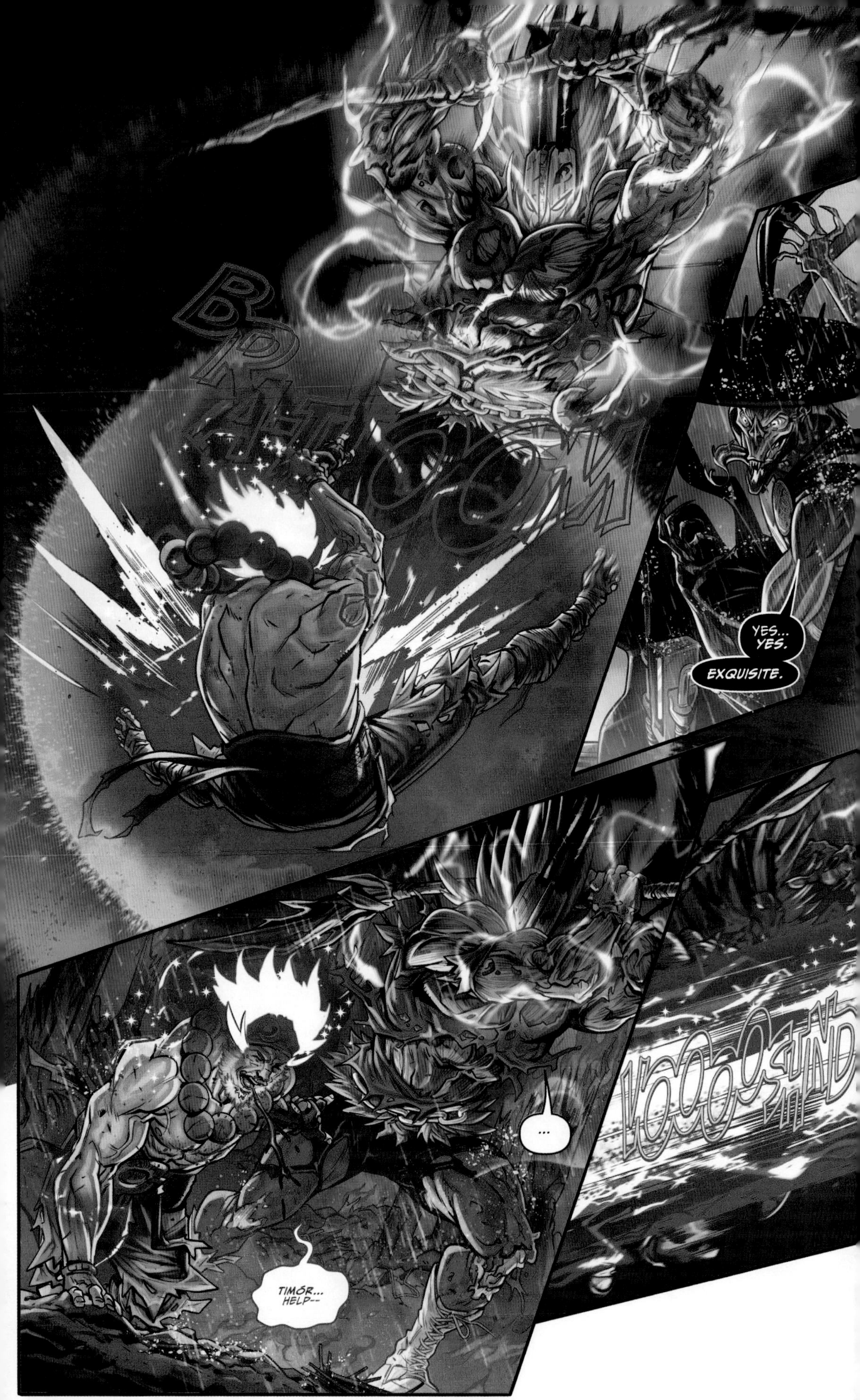

BRAHTOOOM
YES... YES.
EXQUISITE.
VOOOOSHHND
...
TIMÓR... HELP--

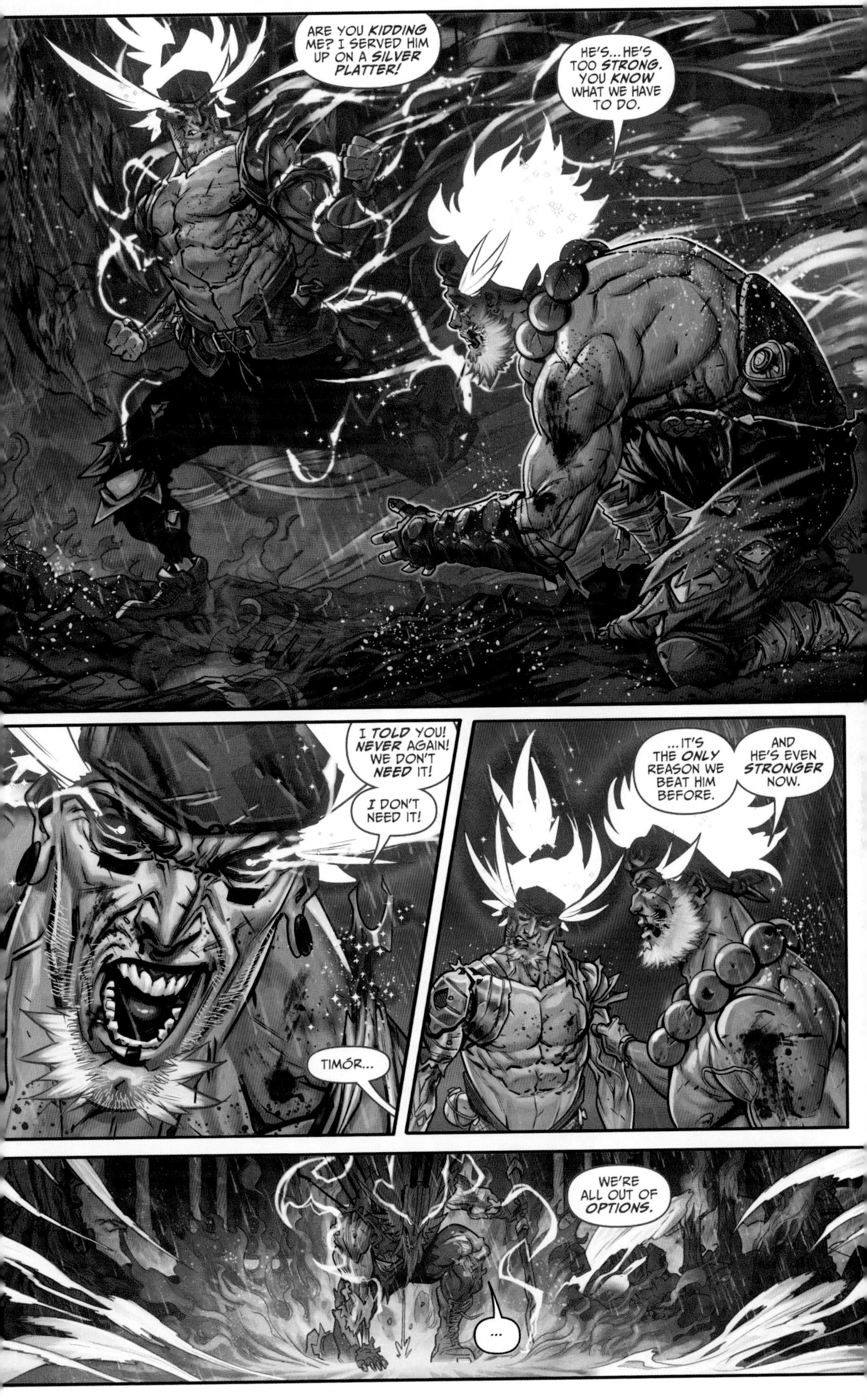

ARE YOU *KIDDING* ME? I SERVED HIM UP ON A *SILVER PLATTER!*
HE'S... HE'S TOO *STRONG*. YOU *KNOW* WHAT WE HAVE TO DO.
I *TOLD* YOU! *NEVER* AGAIN! WE DON'T *NEED* IT!
I DON'T NEED IT!
TIMÓR...
...IT'S THE *ONLY* REASON WE BEAT HIM BEFORE.
AND HE'S EVEN *STRONGER* NOW.
WE'RE ALL OUT OF *OPTIONS*.
...

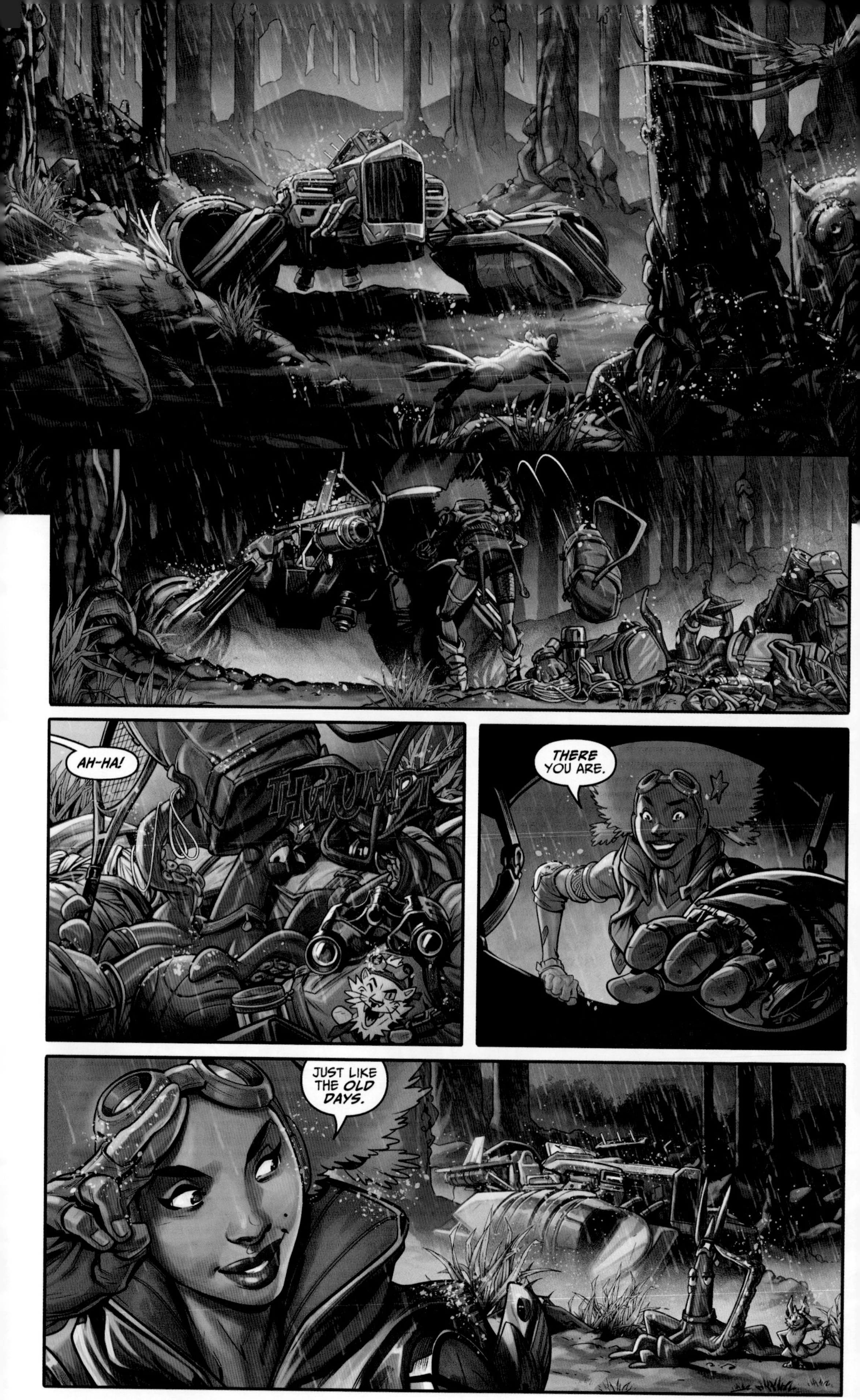
AH-HA!
THWUMP!
THERE YOU ARE.
JUST LIKE THE OLD DAYS.

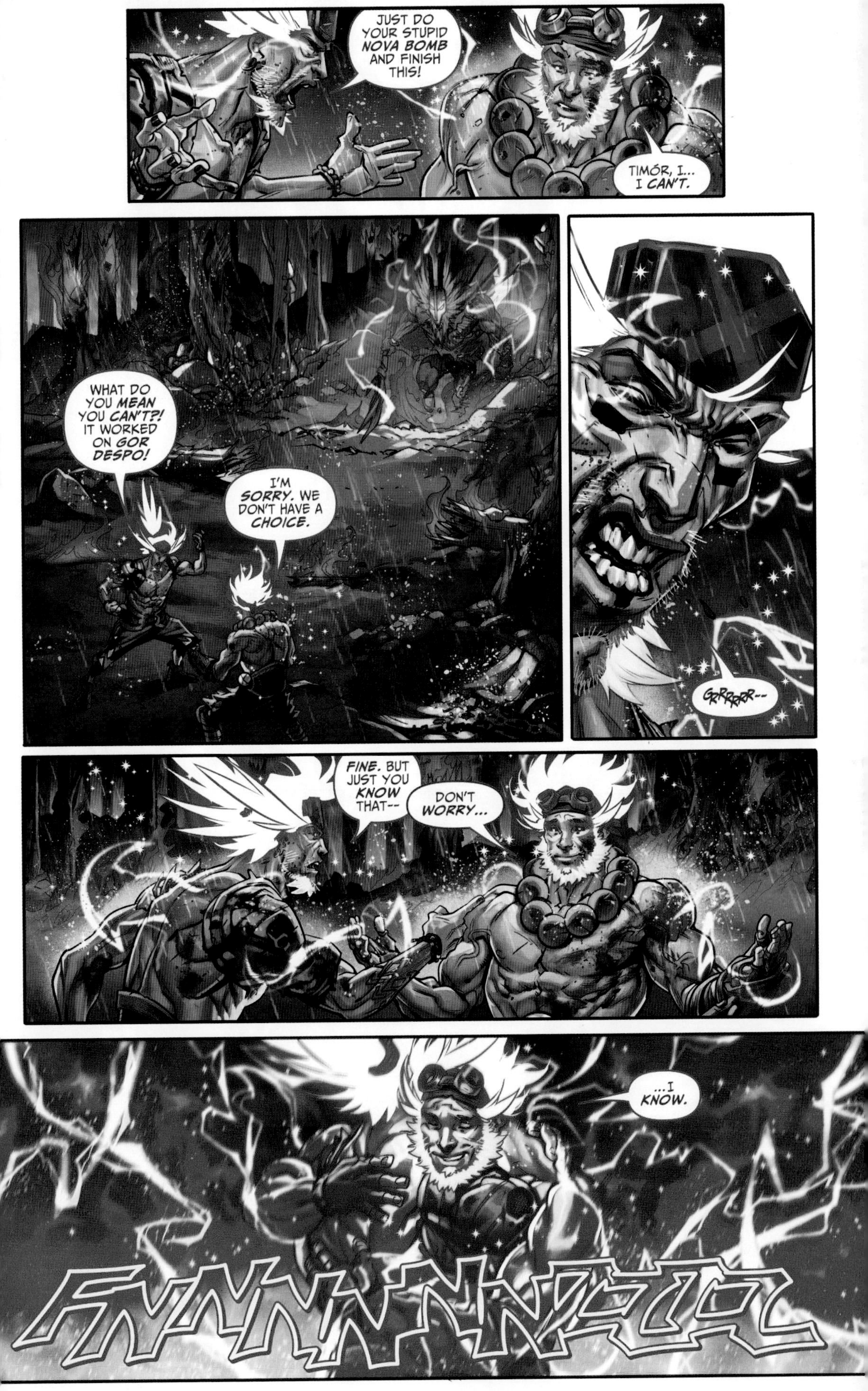
JUST DO YOUR STUPID NOVA BOMB AND FINISH THIS!
TIMÓR, I... I CAN'T.
WHAT DO YOU MEAN YOU CAN'T?! IT WORKED ON GOR DESPO!
I'M SORRY. WE DON'T HAVE A CHOICE.
GRRRRRR--
FINE. BUT JUST YOU KNOW THAT--
DON'T WORRY...
...I KNOW.

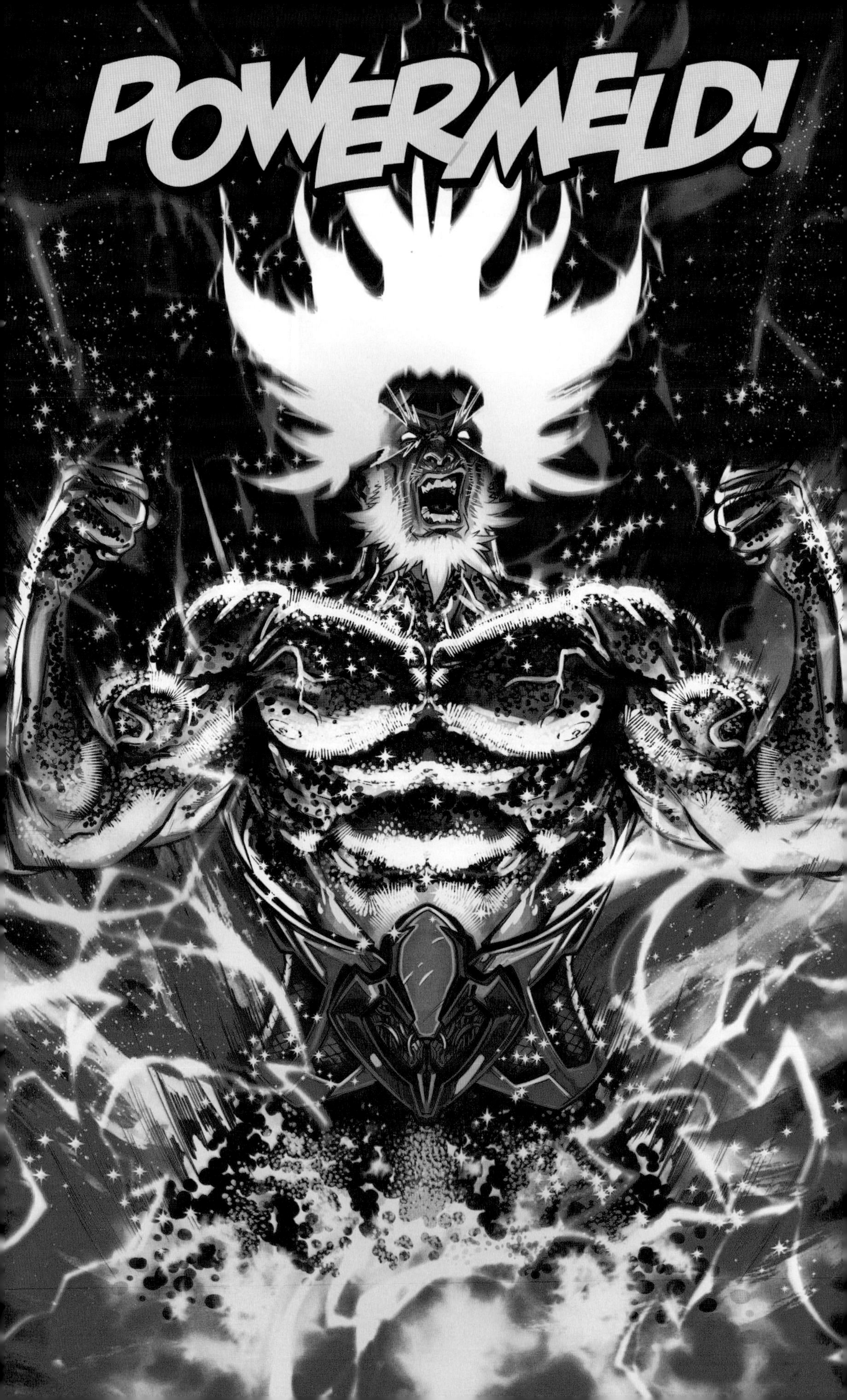
POWERMELD!

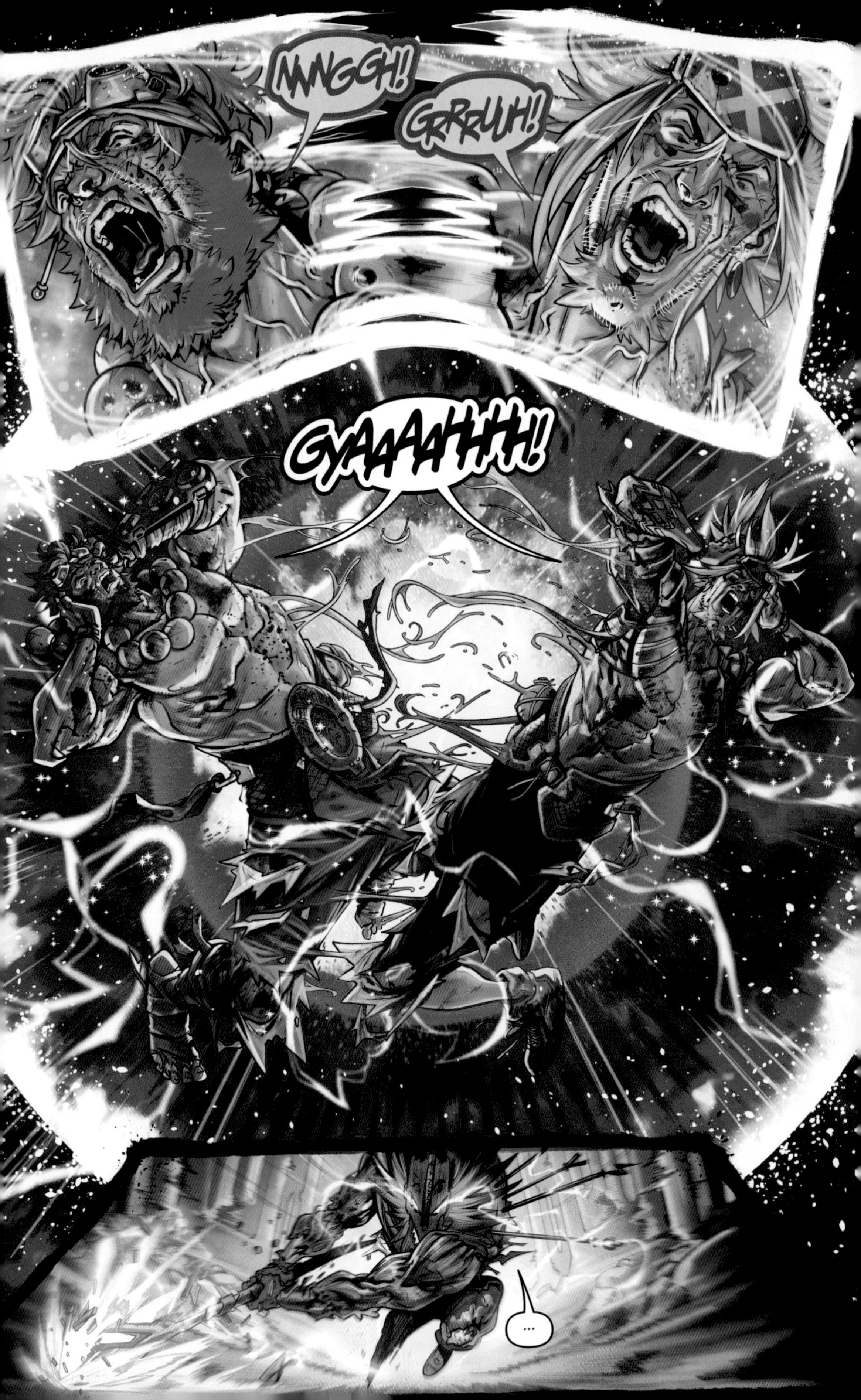
NNNGGH!
GRRRUUH!
GYAAAAHHH!
...

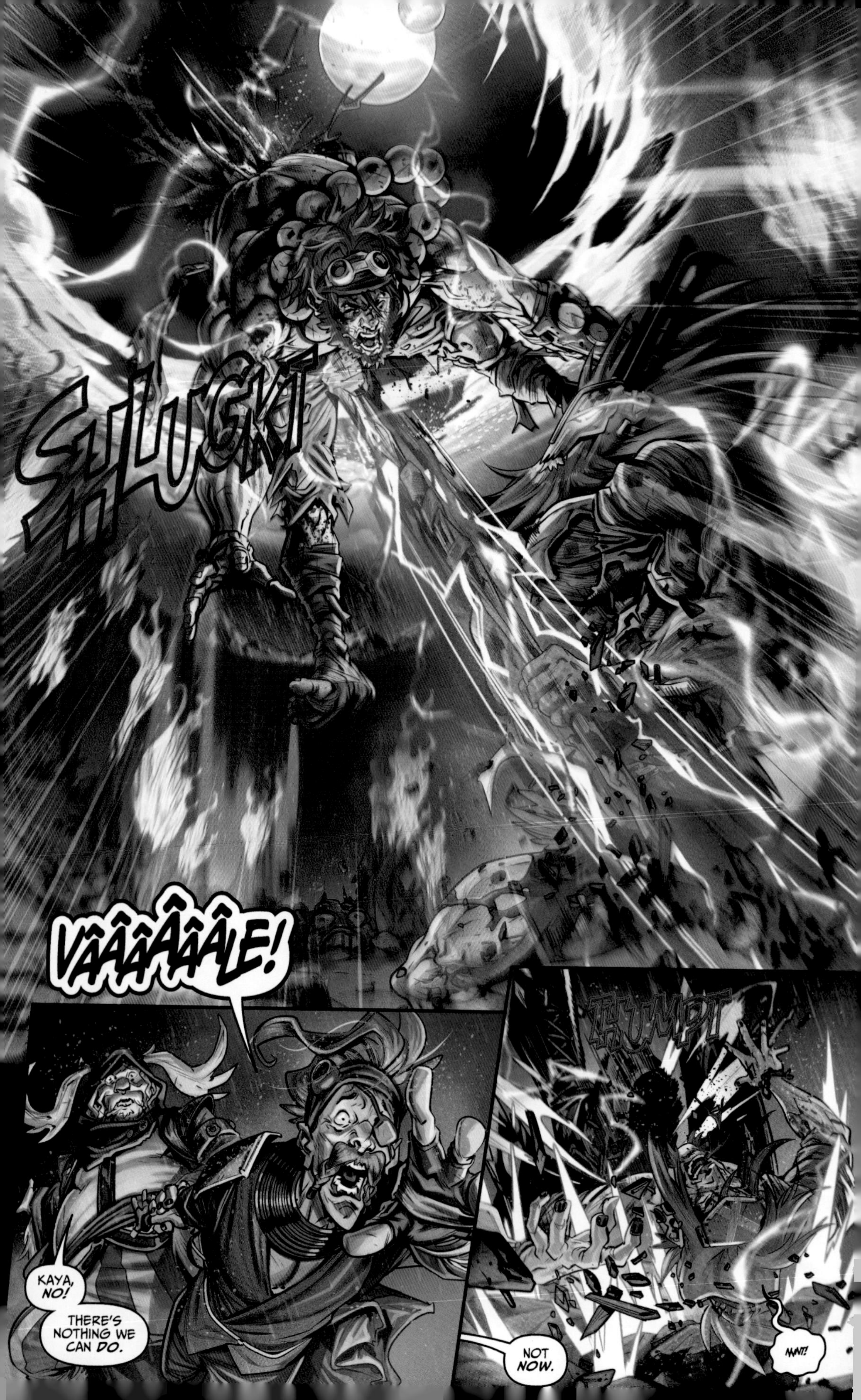
SHLUGK!
VÂÂÂÂÂÂLE!
KAYA, NO!
THERE'S NOTHING WE CAN DO.
THUMPT
NOT NOW.

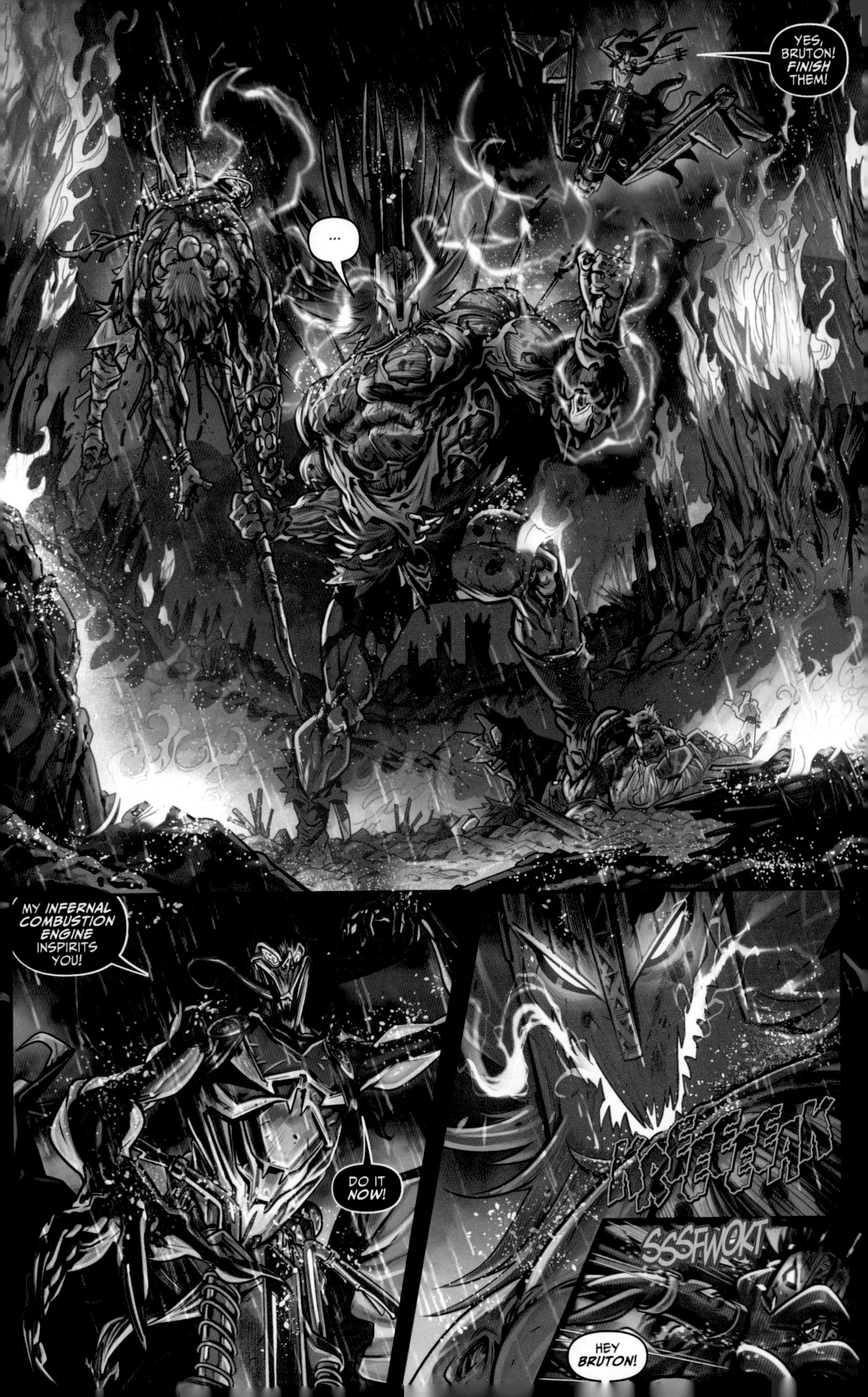

YES, BRUTON! FINISH THEM!
...
MY INFERNAL COMBUSTION ENGINE INSPIRITS YOU!
DO IT NOW!
KRREEEAK
SSSFWOKT
HEY BRUTON!

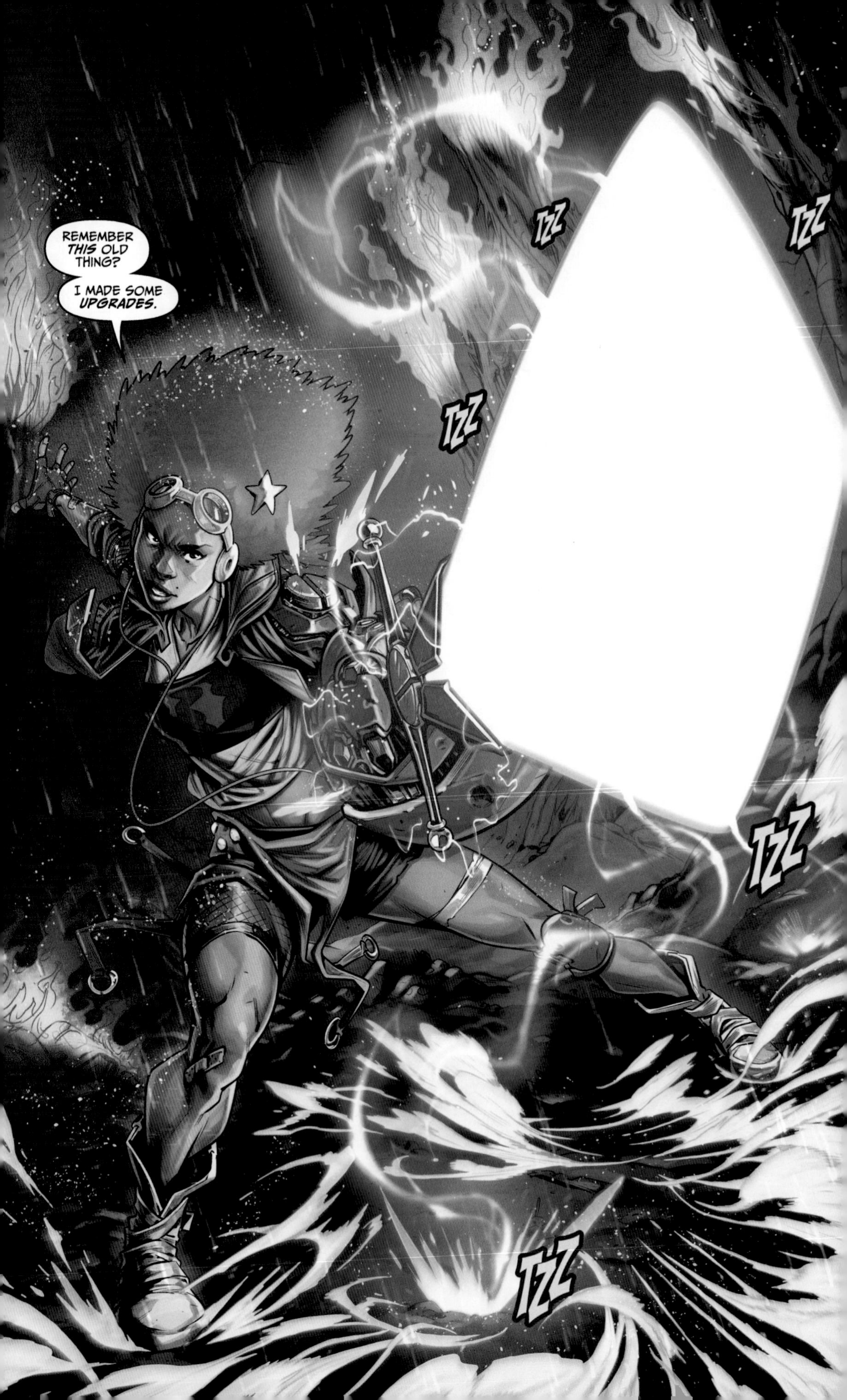
REMEMBER *THIS* OLD THING?
I MADE SOME *UPGRADES*.
TZZ
TZZ
TZZ
TZZ
TZZ

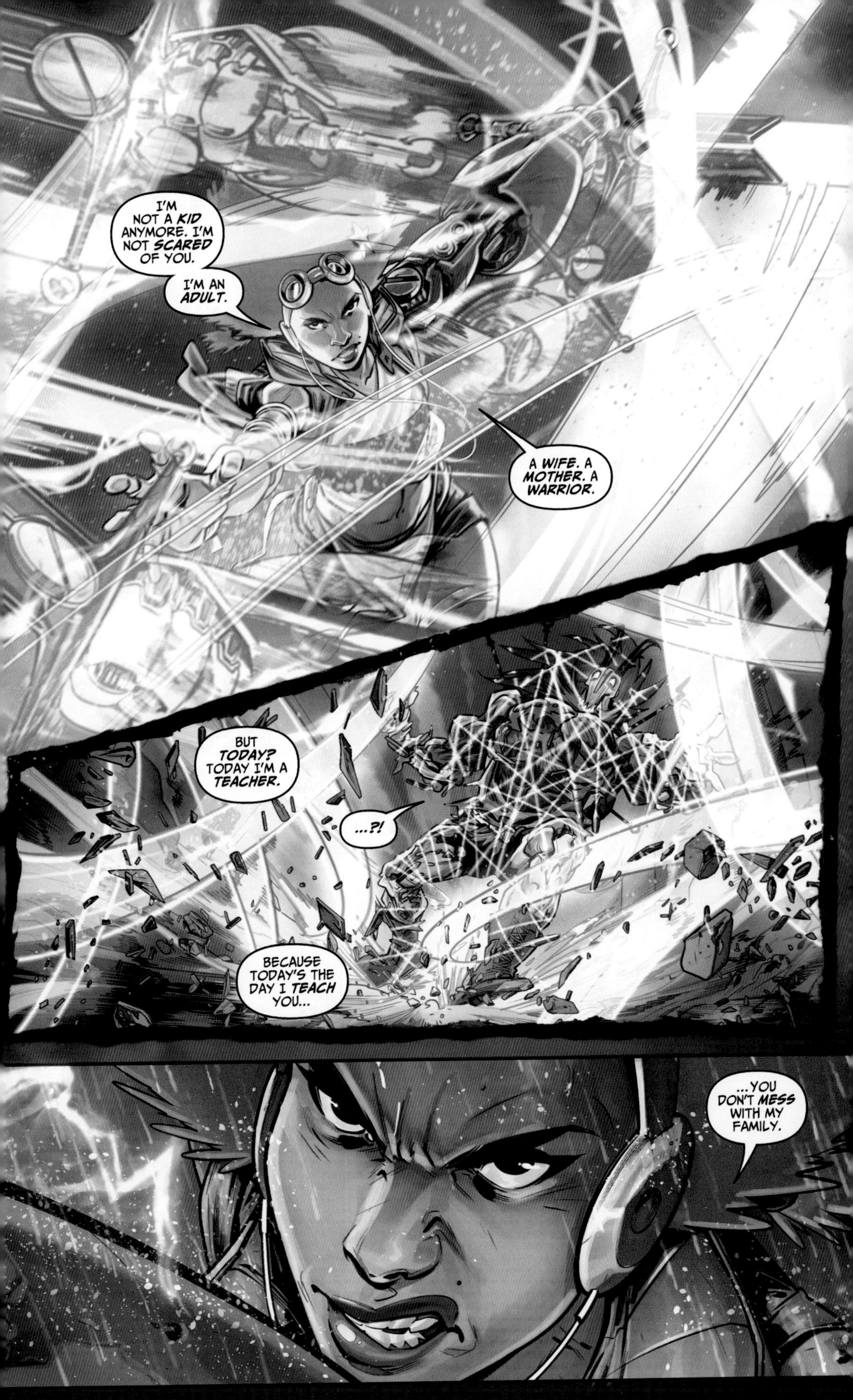
I'M NOT A KID ANYMORE. I'M NOT SCARED OF YOU.
I'M AN ADULT.
A WIFE. A MOTHER. A WARRIOR.
BUT TODAY? TODAY I'M A TEACHER.
...?!
BECAUSE TODAY'S THE DAY I TEACH YOU...
...YOU DON'T MESS WITH MY FAMILY.

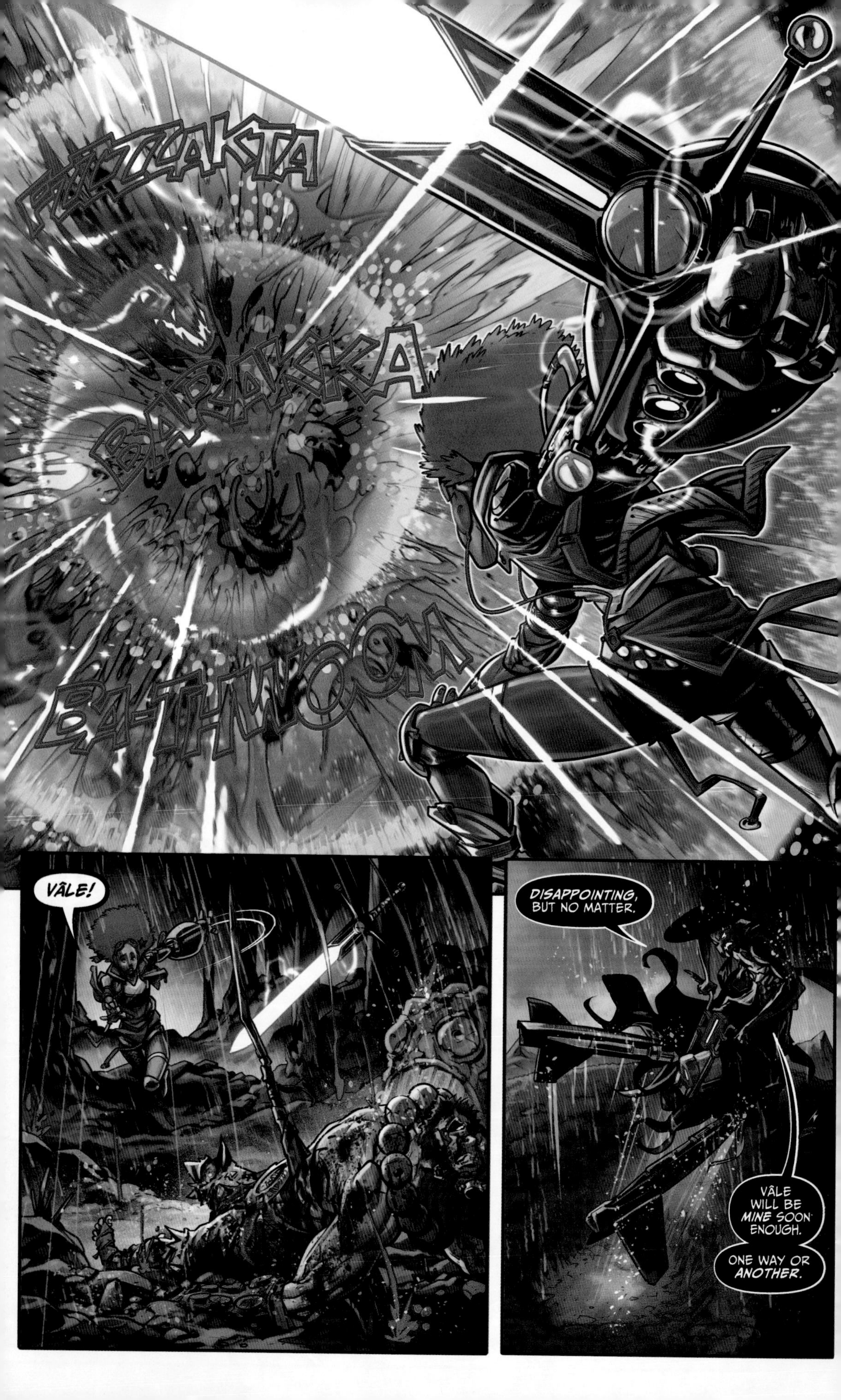

BA-THWOOM
VÂLE!
DISAPPOINTING, BUT NO MATTER.
VÂLE WILL BE MINE SOON ENOUGH.
ONE WAY OR ANOTHER.

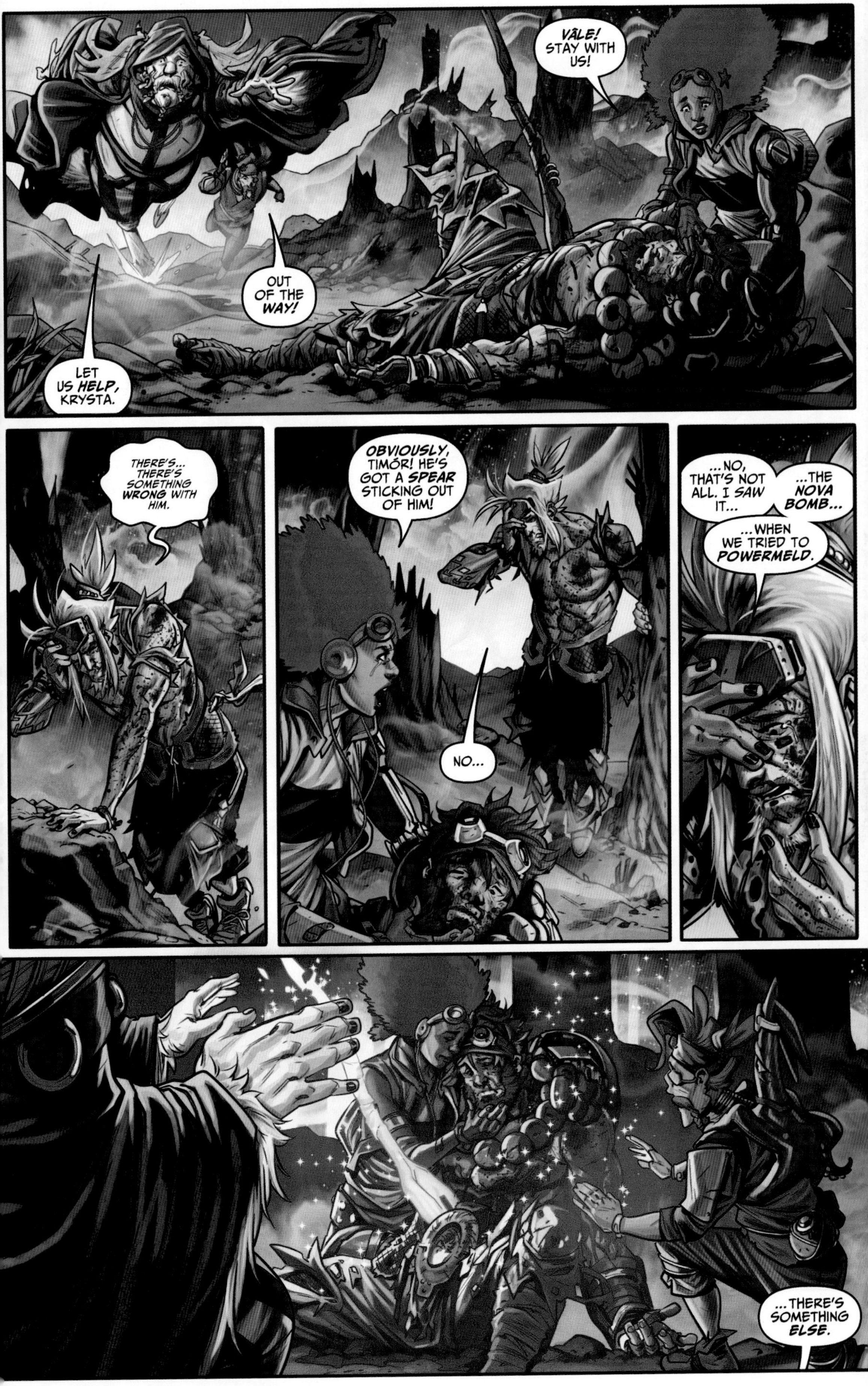
VĀLE! STAY WITH US!
OUT OF THE WAY!
LET US HELP, KRYSTA.
THERE'S... THERE'S SOMETHING WRONG WITH HIM.
OBVIOUSLY, TIMÓR! HE'S GOT A SPEAR STICKING OUT OF HIM!
NO...
...NO, THAT'S NOT ALL. I SAW IT...
...THE NOVA BOMB...
...WHEN WE TRIED TO POWERMELD.
...THERE'S SOMETHING ELSE.

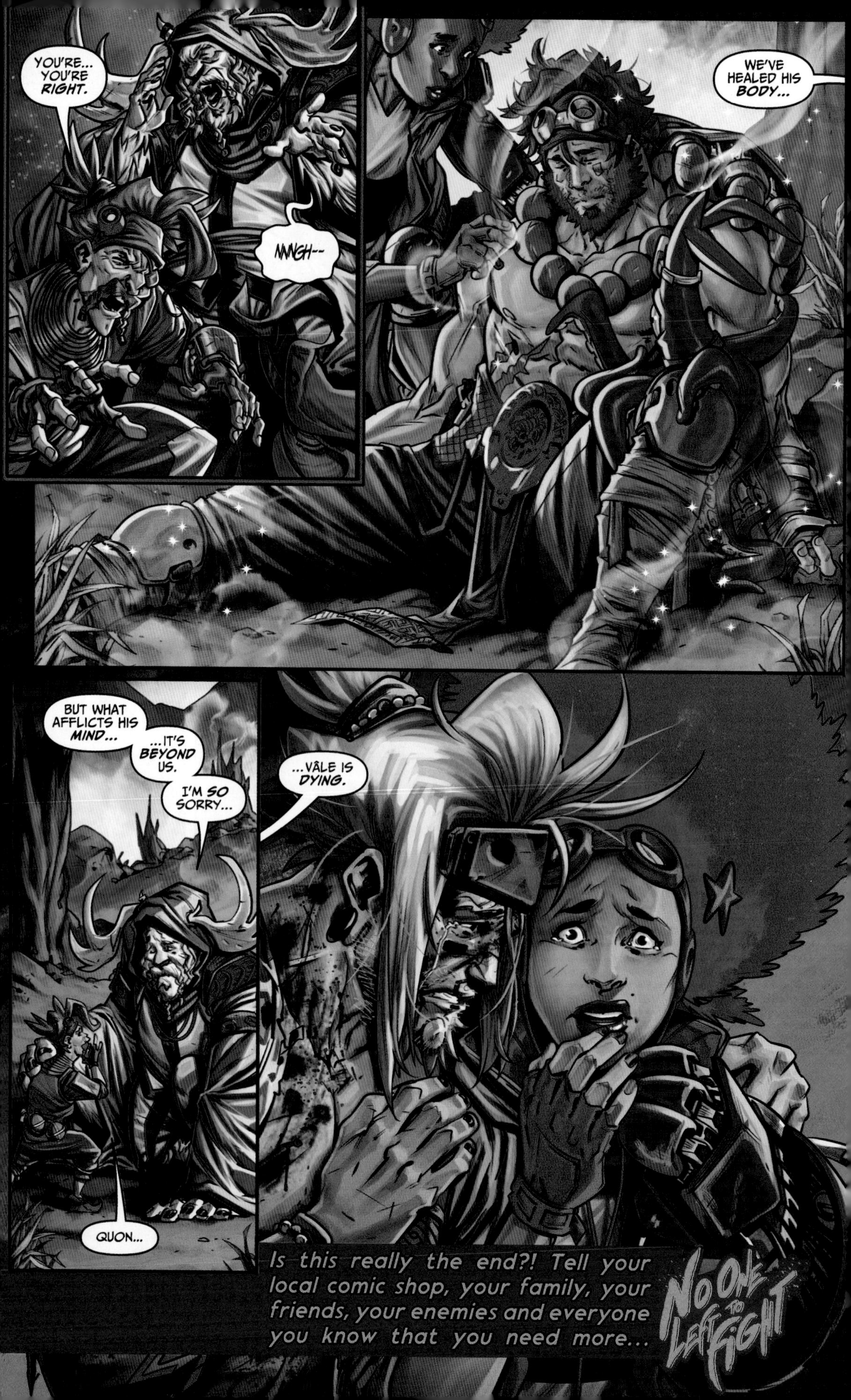

YOU'RE... YOU'RE RIGHT.
NNNGH--
WE'VE HEALED HIS BODY...
BUT WHAT AFFLICTS HIS MIND...
...IT'S BEYOND US.
I'M SO SORRY...
QUON...
...VÂLE IS DYING.
Is this really the end?! Tell your local comic shop, your family, your friends, your enemies and everyone you know that you need more...
NO ONE LEFT TO FIGHT

VOLUME 1
SKETCHBOOK
Commentary by FICO OSSIO

VALE   KRYSTA   TIMÓR

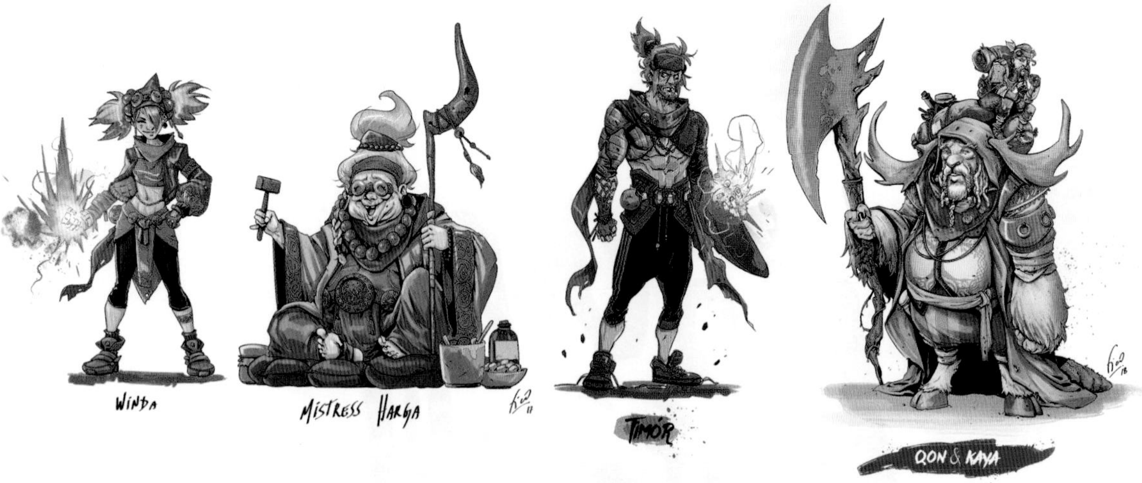

WINDA
MISTRESS HARGA
TIMOR
QON & KAYA

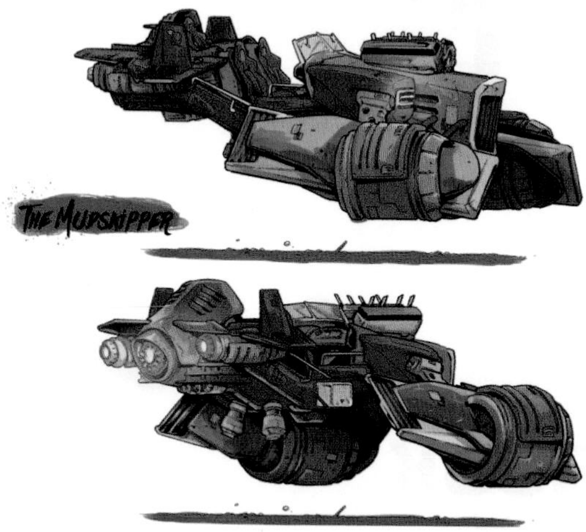

THE MUDSKIPPER

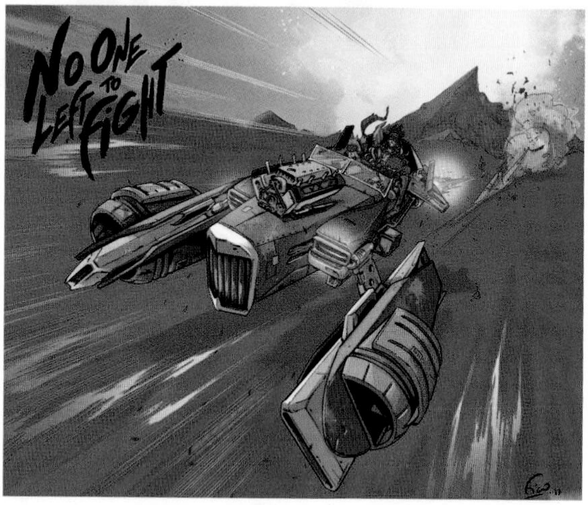

NO ONE LEFT TO FIGHT

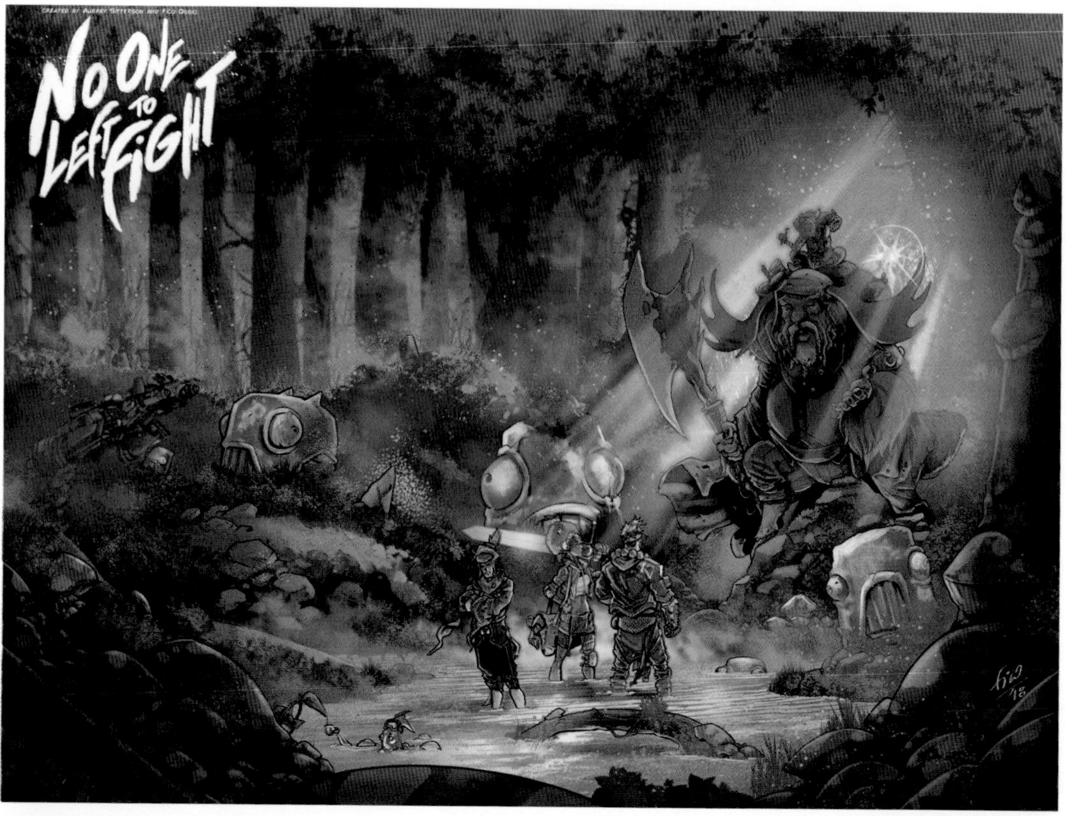

CREATED BY AUBREY SITTERSON AND FICO OSSIO
NO ONE LEFT TO FIGHT

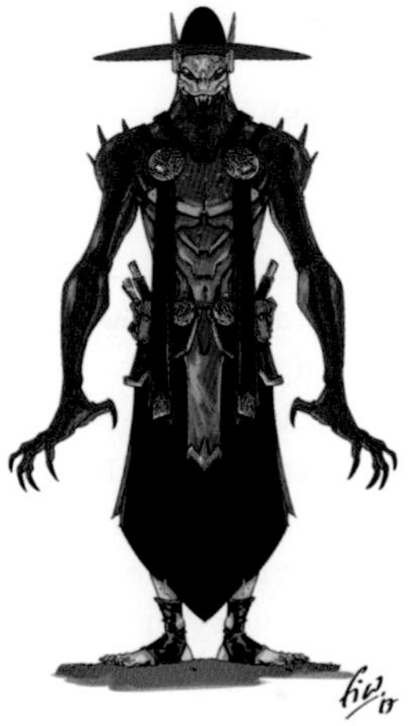

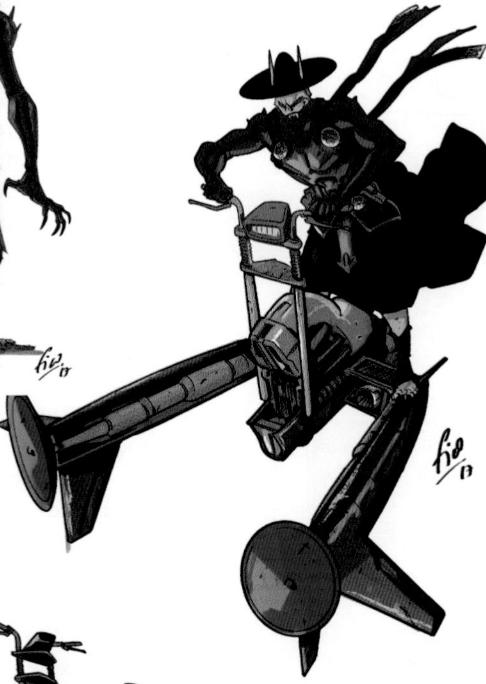

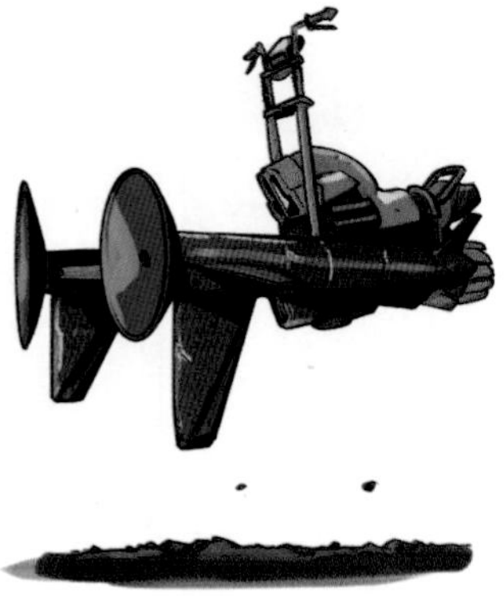

For the Hierophant´s vehicle I wanted it to have a retro sci fi motorcycle vibe. When designing this, the Storm Trooper bikes from *Return of the Jedi* were an influence, as well as other '80s sci fi movies. Initially, the bike had buffers at the front so that he could announce his arrival with heavy metal music! Too bad we scrapped that . . . We could´ve had a music battle between Billy Von Katz and the Hierophant!

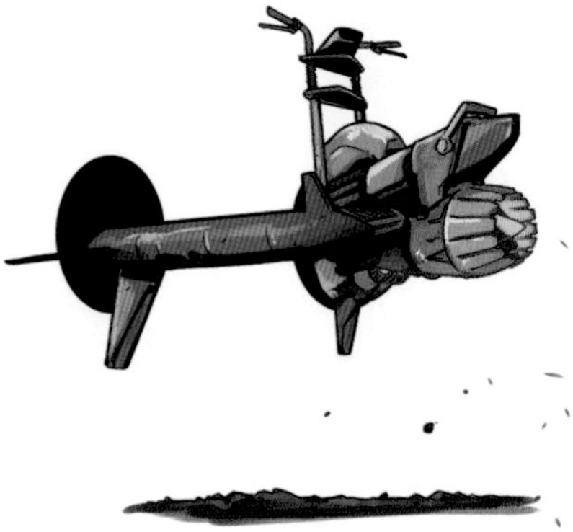

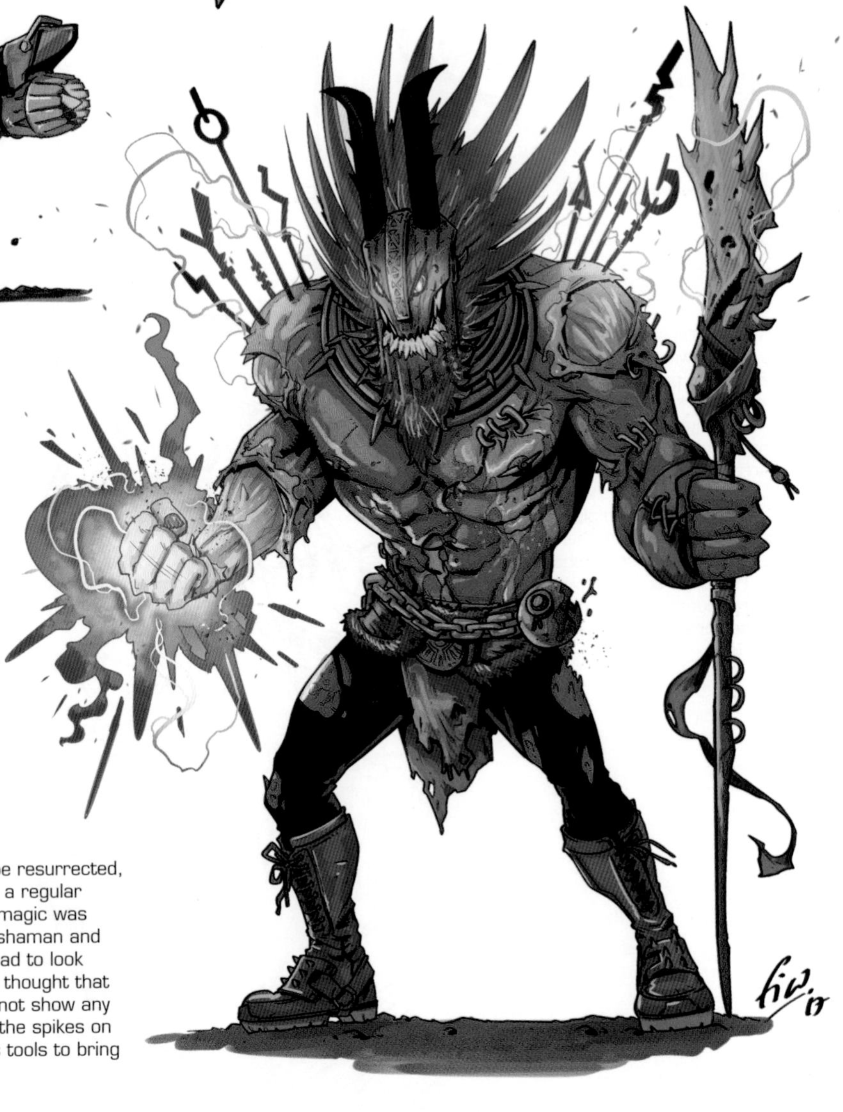

We knew Bruton was gonna be resurrected, but didn´t want him to just be a regular zombie. I thought some dark magic was at play here, so I used some shaman and tribal influences for him. He had to look relentless and menacing, so I thought that having him wear a mask and not show any emotion was a good idea. All the spikes on his back are the Hierophant´s tools to bring him back to ¨life.¨

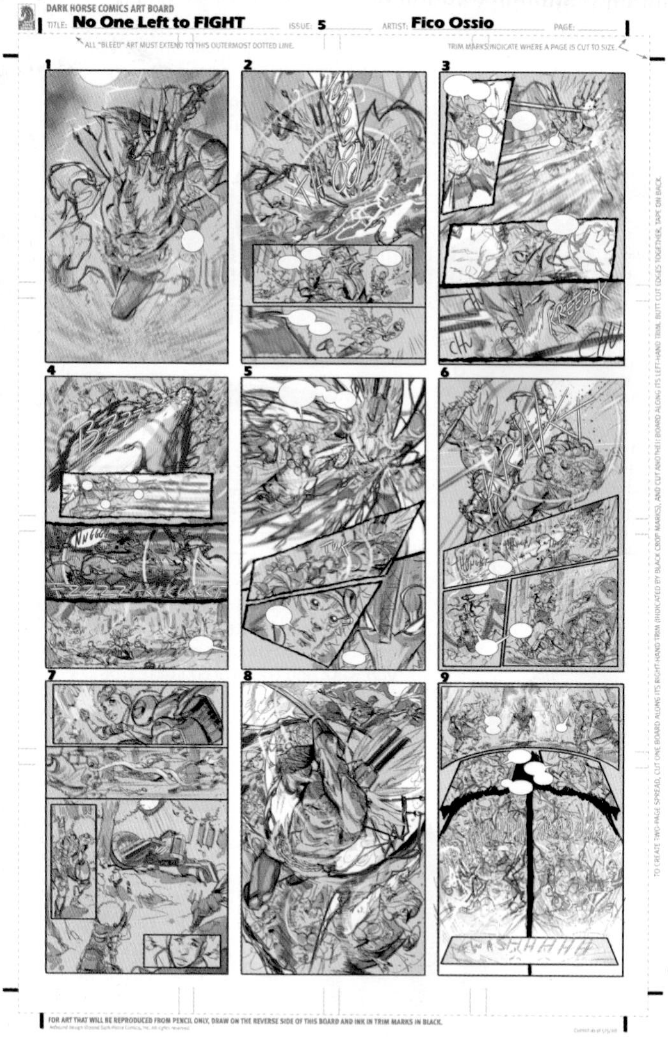

DARK HORSE COMICS ART BOARD
TITLE: No One Left to FIGHT
ISSUE: 5
ARTIST: Fico Ossio
PAGE:
ALL "BLEED" ART MUST EXTEND TO THIS OUTERMOST DOTTED LINE.
TRIM MARKS INDICATE WHERE A PAGE IS CUT TO SIZE.
FOR ART THAT WILL BE REPRODUCED FROM PENCIL ONLY, DRAW ON THE REVERSE SIDE OF THIS BOARD AND INK IN TRIM MARKS IN BLACK.

PAGE ONE: Splash page

PANEL ONE
Right where we left off last time. Bruton charges toward us, wicked grin on his face, his massive polearm raised above his head. I imagine he's charging out of the glowing green water, it's splashing everywhere, algae falling off him, etc. This should be a gnarly, bananas splash to start on, as evocative and stunning as your first page to issue #1, but instead of contemplative…VIOLENT AND ACTION-PACKED!

This is how I transform the script into pages. I start with small pencils; as you can see, 9 pages fit into a regular page size. Working this small gives me a better notion of composition and the values in the page, as well as the narrative rhythm. AND it´s super-fast! Lately, I jump from this layout directly to inks. Since I'm also doing the colors, I start placing them in the ink stage, as well as some shadows values. I do color brush strokes and all the energy bursts early to give me a better feel for what the finished pages will look like.

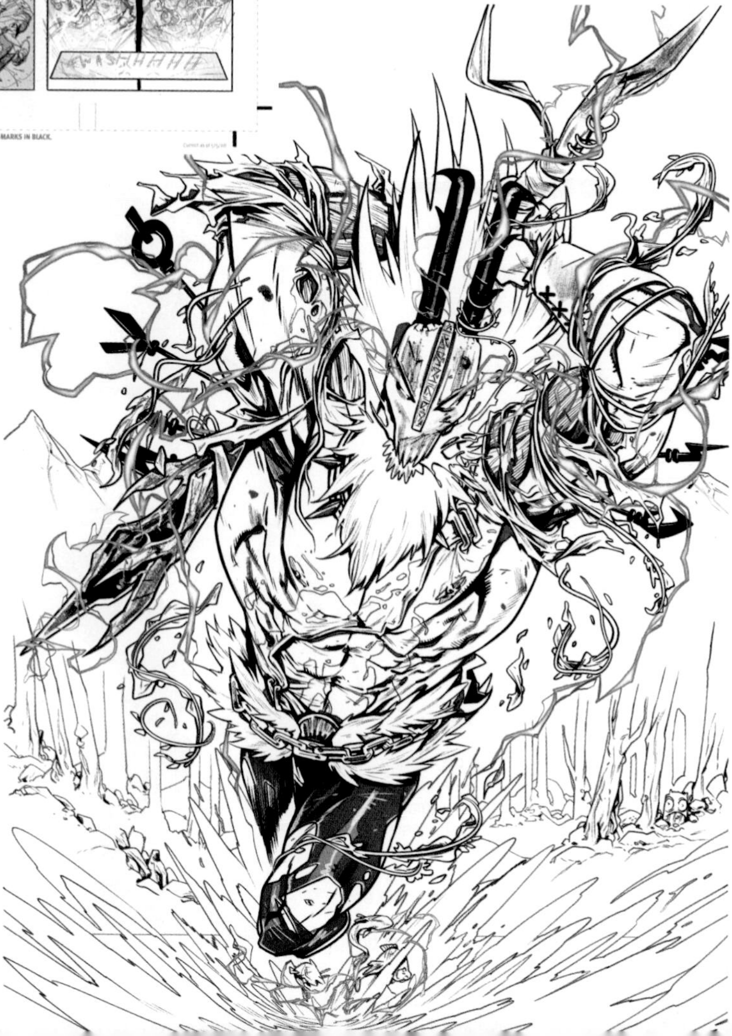

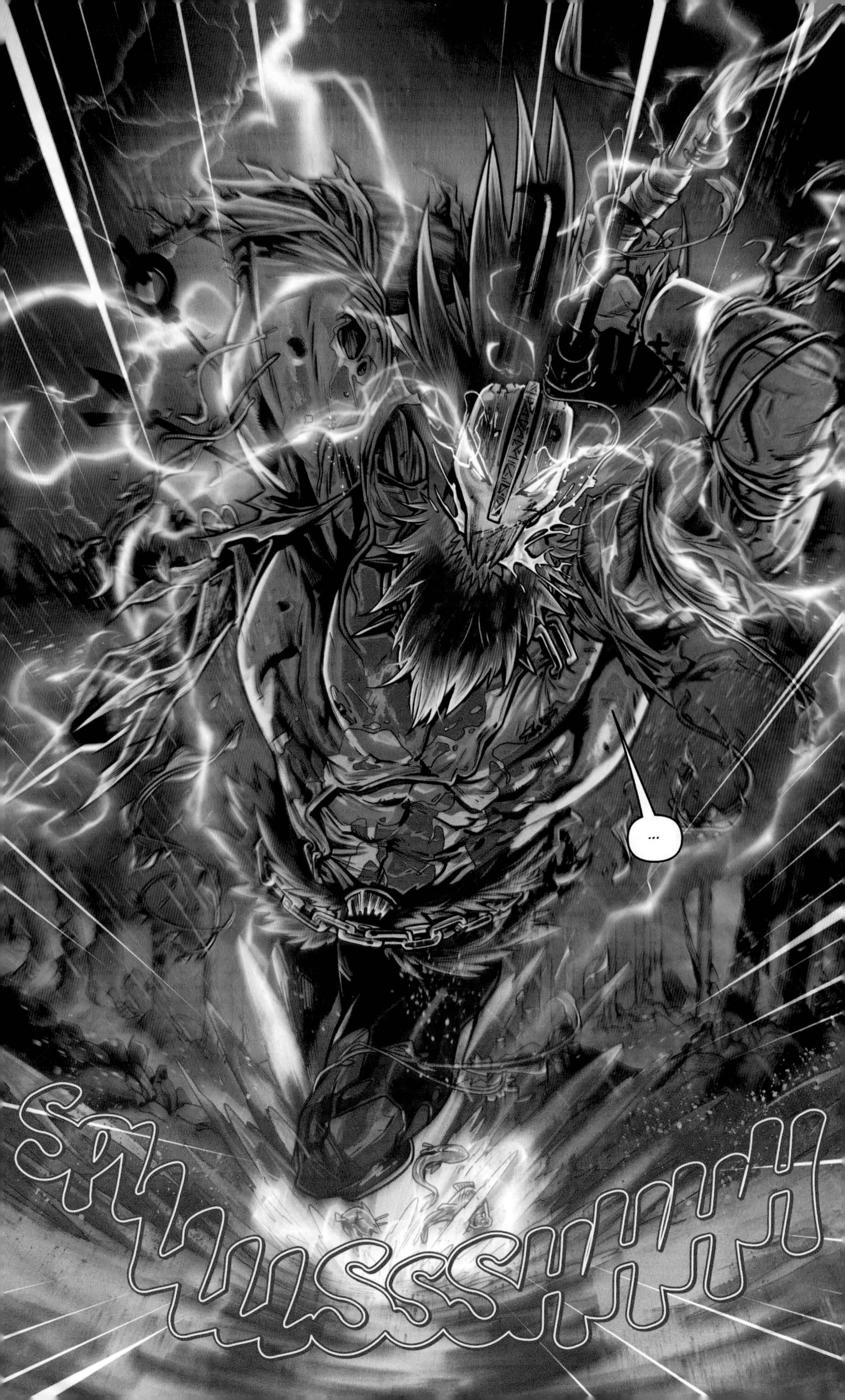
...

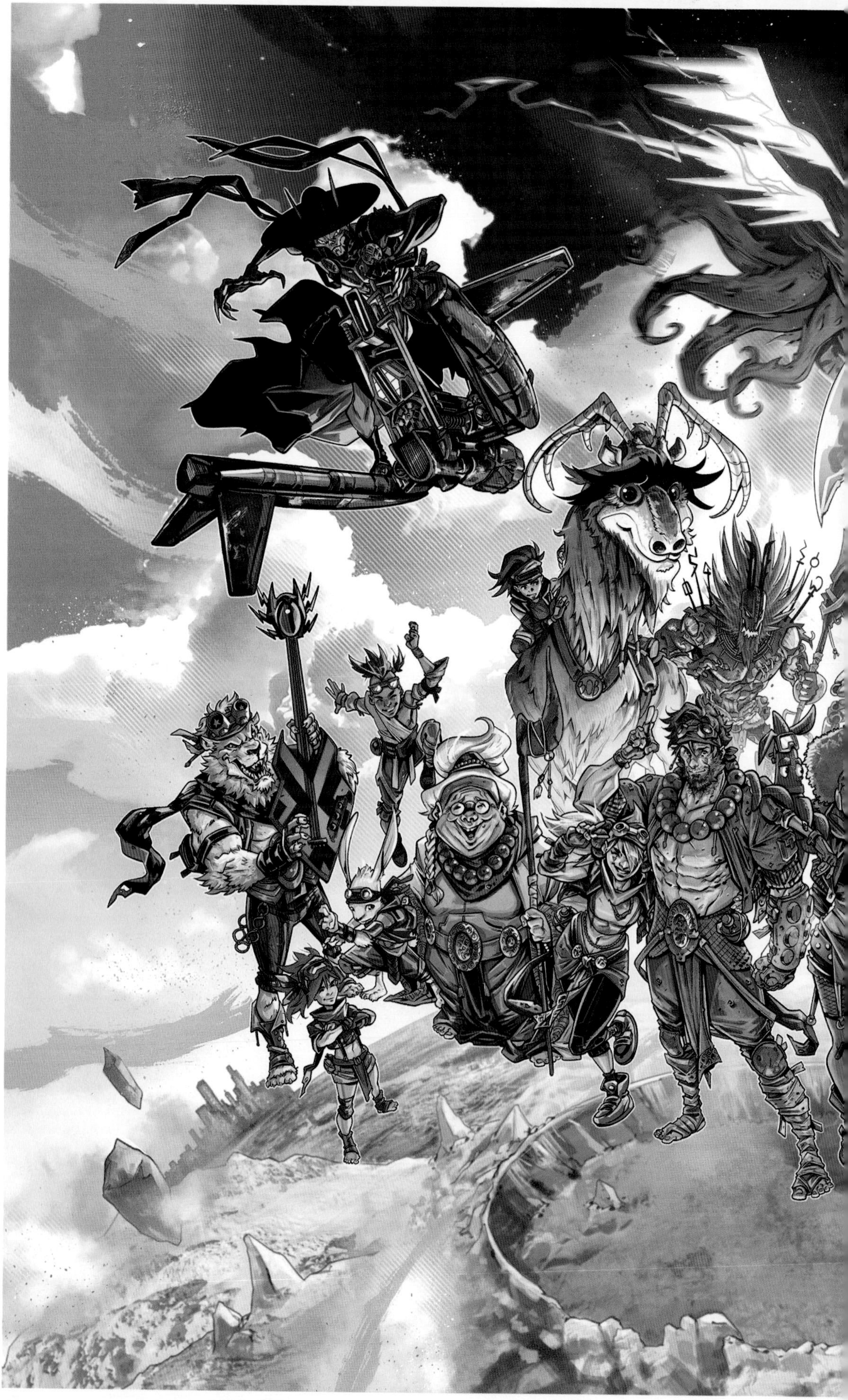
BOB

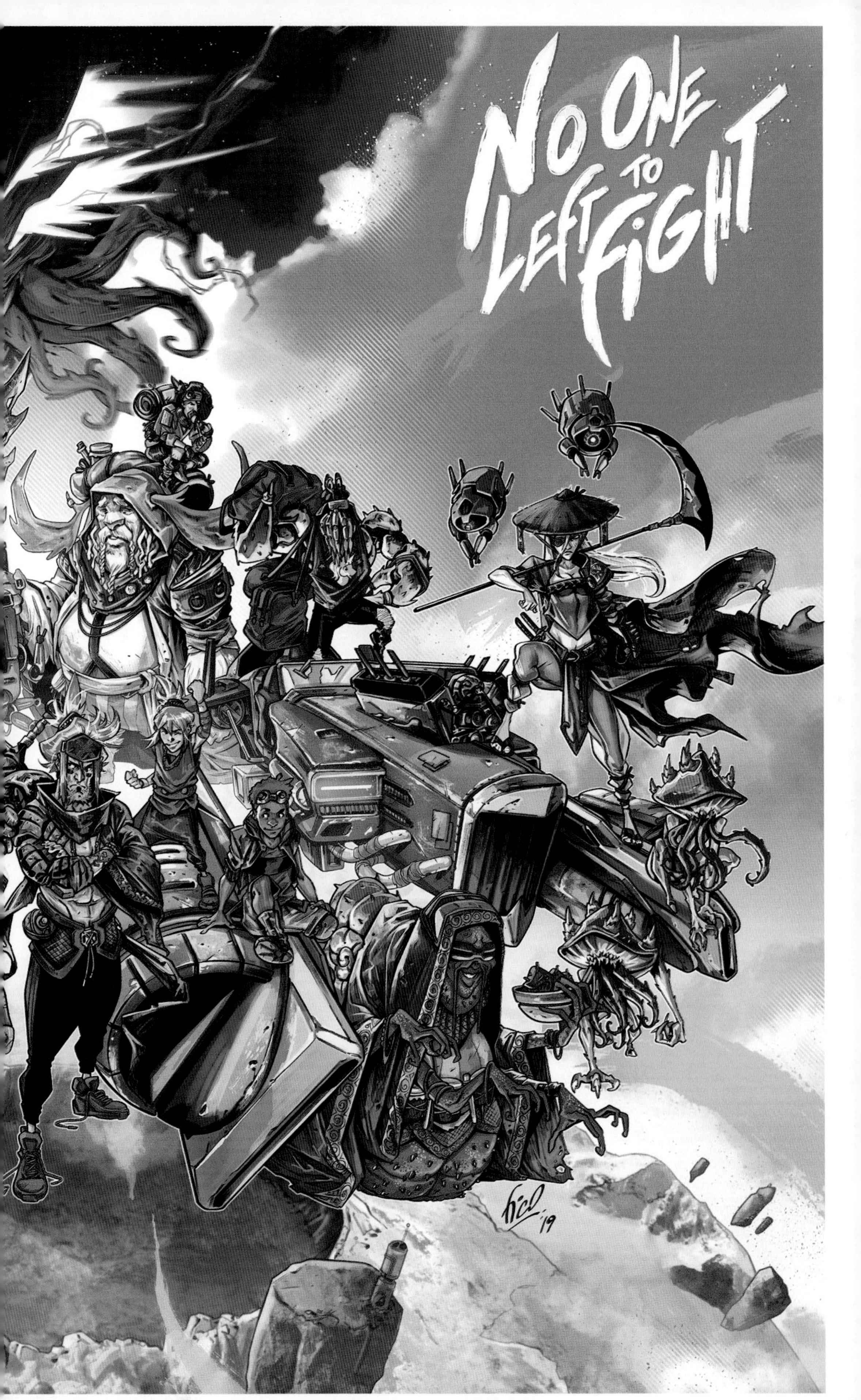
NO ONE LEFT TO FIGHT
'19

ALL HAIL, MY TOMCATS AND FINE FELINES!

I'm intergalactic rock star Billy Von Katz! You know and love me from "Grimalkin Boogie," "Night of the Werecat," and my dozens of other hit singles!

And that...can't be the ending, right? Not only have I, the star of The Comic You Always Wanted, not shown up yet, but Vâle is dying, that creepshow The Hierophant is still up to no good and, worst of all, I haven't even shown up yet!

It's like a Billy Von Katz concert without an encore, which is to say: A total bummer! We want to keep *No One Left to Fight* going forever, but we need your help. Talk up The Comic You Always Wanted to your friends and family, ask your local library to carry it, and buy it as gifts for everyone you know. The holidays are less than a year away!

It also wouldn't hurt to get a campaign going for the Billy Von Katz Galactic Jamboree spin-off.

Just putting it out there.

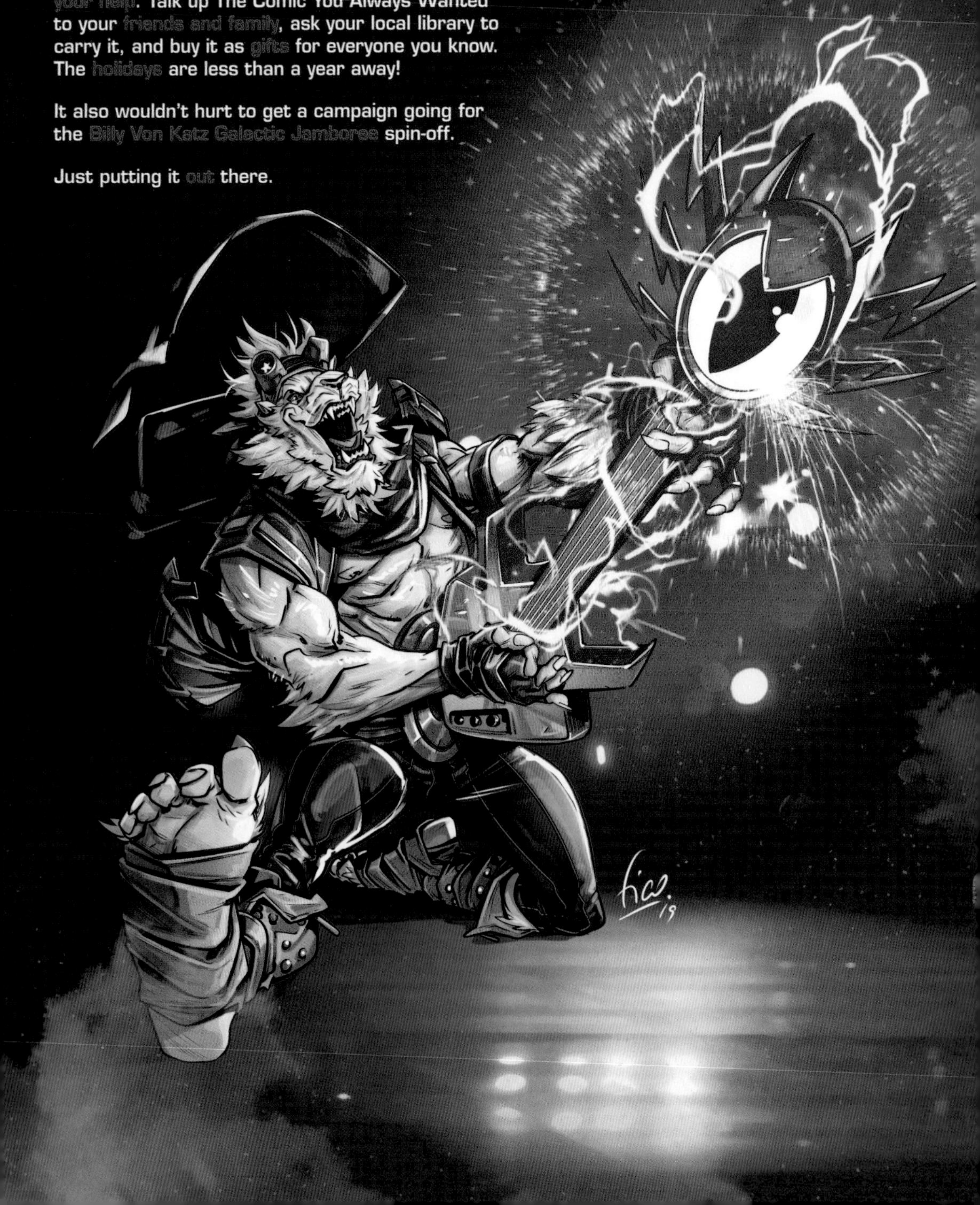